SITTINGBOURNE and MILTON

An Illustrated History

GW00361794

SITTINGBOURNE
and MILTON
An Illustrated History

Dr P BELLINGHAM

SAWD
BOOKS

Cover:

Map from 'Milton Hundred"
  Hasted, Edward,
  The History and Topographical Survey of the County of Kent,
  Volume 6, Wakefield, EP Publishers (Reprint), 1972

First published 1996 by SAWD Books, an imprint of SAWD Publications, Plackett's Hole, Bicknor, Sittingbourne, Kent ME9 8BA.

British Library Cataloguing-in-Publication Data
A catalogue record for this book is available from the British Library

ISBN: 1-872 489-16-8
Produced & Printed by SAWD PUBLICATIONS

CONTENTS

and FINALLY

LIST OF ILLUSTRATIONS

A note regarding the illustrations

The decision was made to use the sketches rather than photographs so that they could be placed with the text they illustrated rather than placing groups of photographs in a separate section.

The majority of the sketches are based on my own collection of photographs, however I am grateful to the following for allowing me to make use of theirs:

Mrs Dolding, Methodist Church (Pre-War).
Mrs Goodwin, Carnival Float.
Mr Grant, Duke of Kent in Milton High Street.
Mr M Peters, Plan of 93 High Street.
Mr E Rose, Schamel; Unity Street Bomb Damage, Bomb Damage Second World War, The West End of Sittingbourne High Street.
Sittingbourne Library, Whitehall Preserve Works (Dean's Jam Factory).

In addition the following were based on EKG photographs:
The Cement Works, Inside Lloyds Daily Chronicle Mill, Kemsley Mill, Milton Workhouse, Milton Congregational Church, Queens Picture Hall, Col Donald Dean VC at Sittingbourne Recreation Ground War Memorial (1982) and the Rose Hotel.

The following publications were used:
The New Vitruvius Britannicus Vol 1-2, 'Plan of Gore Court House' in Sittingbourne Library.
Drawing of 'Rose Hotel' in Sittingbourne Library, from Sittingbourne, by W.A. Scott Robinson
And finally 'Sittingbourne Tide Mill' was based on a painting in Milton Court Hall Museum.

Introduction

What's in a Name

Sittingbourne, at the end of the 20th century, includes what were until recent times, two towns, Sittingbourne and Milton. Of the two, Milton is the older and it was, until the early 19th century, the larger and more important of the two. (See Chapter Two) Milton was originally called Middleton, the middle ton or town of the King of Kent in the days before the Norman Conquest in 1066. There is evidence of early settlement in this area along the main London to Dover (and Canterbury) Road and Sittingbourne itself later developed as a resting place or overnight stop for pilgrims on their way to the shrine of Thomas à Becket at Canterbury. The name Sittingbourne may have originated, as local tradition has it, from pilgrims sitting by the bourne, or stream, to wash their weary feet. However there have been other spellings of the name, Sydyngborn and Sythingborn were both common in the late 15th and early 16th century. The name may have originated from it being the area of land owned by a tribe with a name such as Sything, or it may have derived from the Saxon word Saething meaning seething or babbling brook, the true origin is lost in the mists of time! (1)

Something about this book

Whenever possible original documents have been used to provide information for this history of Sittingbourne. This has affected what is included and much of the book is concerned with the 19th and 20th centuries as far more documents for that period survived, especially the local paper, the East Kent Gazette. Many aspects of the history of the town would justify a book to themselves, indeed there are already books on brickmaking and barges. As this is intended to be a general, comprehensive history it has not been possible for any aspect to be covered in great depth. However references to the source documents used throughout the book should enable anyone interested in any particular subject to find out more for themselves. (2)

After the first two chapters, which deal with local agriculture and the town in the period from the late 15th century to the early 19th century, the rest of the book is about the 19th and 20th centuries. Each chapter deals with different aspects of the life of the town. This should prove 'readable' for anyone interested in the town as a whole, as well as making it easier for those who want to find out about one aspect of the town's history, however it does mean that those interested in a particular historical period, such as the Victorians, will have to delve into different chapters. However in most cases each aspect is dealt with in chronological order and detailed subheadings throughout the book should make the task easier.

Although this history is concerned with Sittingbourne from the 15th century to the final decade of the 20th century, before it starts a brief look at the evidence of earlier times is relevant.

The Period up to the end of the Roman Occupation

The earliest remains found in the area are fossils of such things as 'sponges' from the time when the area was covered by water. Evidence of more 'recent' times include fossils of the woolly rhinoceros, wild horse, mammoth, cave lion and reindeer. There is evidence that the area was settled in the iron and bronze ages, an iron age cemetery has been found at Highsted and in 1928 a Bronze Age looped and socketed axe was found in the Ruins Barn Road. Between 1871 and 1878 circular pits, 10 feet in diameter and three to four feet deep, were excavated at Grovehurst. Flint weapons of the Celtic period were discovered and it is possible that the 'pits' may have been the remains of dwellings. The greatest evidence of settlement comes though from artefacts from the Romano-British period, many found as the result of excavations during the 19th century when brickearth was being removed from fields. (3)

Between 1876 and 1874 six lead coffins were found at Bex-hill in Milton. One of them had a lid ornamented with a lion's head, indicating the high rank and wealth of those interred. At that time only 36 lead coffins had been found in Britain and the find of six at Milton was more than on any other site. In 1889 there was another find, north of the cemetery site, which gives an idea of the wealth of local inhabitants in Roman times - a massive gold finger ring set with red cornelian and a winged cupid drawing a two-horse chariot. In 1874 several gold coins were found at Tunstall of the British King Cunobeline (who had ruled before the Romans invaded) and one of Claudius Caesar. Three years later, in 1877, a Roman interment green glass vessel, a copper goblet, a bronze lamp, a copper jug, a glass jug, a copper bowl and a set of bathing requisites of copper were all found east of Bayford Orchard. In 1879 a second grave was found containing a thick blue glass vessel, a greenish blue jug, a circular glass bottle, a bronze vase, an iron lampstand, a pottery cup, a red clay pitcher, samian ware and an urn shaped vase of Upchurch pottery. Excavations along the banks of Otterham Creek uncovered a great deal of pottery, showing that the Romans made pottery there, although no kilns were found. The style of pottery found there is known as Upchurch pottery. (4)

Further evidence of Roman burials in the area came in 1955 when excavations at Highsted Quarry unearthed 17 skeletons, dating from 75 BC to 20 AD, together with several pieces of remarkable pottery and a brooch. In addition to burial sites the area around Sittingbourne has also revealed buildings. The most important find was at Boxted Farm between Newington and Lower Halstow, where part of a Roman tessellated pavement was discovered in 1882. The walls of the building were nearly 200 feet long and 23 feet wide and frescos were found on them. It was clearly the home of a wealthy citizen. Other people lived to the east of Sittingbourne. In 1929, Roman graves, containing coins and potsherds, were found in Bapchild. Then in 1953 a site at Radfield close to the main road from Sittingbourne to Bapchild a circular

Romano-British refuse pit was found containing fragments of 1st and 2nd century pottery, oyster shells and pig and ox jaws. In 1972 further excavations in the area found a beaker, bowls, cooking pots, a flagon, a dish, pots, and bronze items including a straight pin, a brooch and a buckle. Evidence from the excavation showed that the site was used from immediately before the Roman occupation until at least the 3rd century. The archaeologists involved in the excavation concluded that during Roman times livestock raising, iron smelting and iron working on a small scale took place in the vicinity and the numerous fragments of Roman roof tiles indicated that there was at least one building on the site. The most important Roman legacy to the area is of course the old London to Dover Road, Watling Street, which forms Sittingbourne High Street. West of the town Key Street and Keycol Hill are thought to derive from the Latin 'Caius', the name of Julius Caesar. (5)

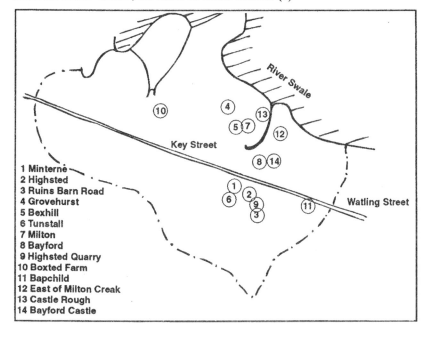

1 Minterne
2 Highsted
3 Ruins Barn Road
4 Grovehurst
5 Bexhill
6 Tunstall
7 Milton
8 Bayford
9 Highsted Quarry
10 Boxted Farm
11 Bapchild
12 East of Milton Creek
13 Castle Rough
14 Bayford Castle

The Location of Archaeological Sites

The 'Dark Ages'

Less evidence survives for the 'Dark Ages', the period from the departure of the Romans until the coming of the Normans in 1066. The area was though still occupied. St Augustine is reputed to have baptised 10,000 people in the river Swale near Sittingbourne after he arrived in Kent in 597. A less peaceful reminder of the period comes in the form of an Anglo-Saxon single edged sword, called a Scaramasax, which was found at Sittingbourne. Some late Anglo-Saxon, mainly 7th century, graves were found on land east of Milton Creek. They were the kind used by prosperous yeomen (small-scale farmers) and the first two contained a shield boss and a small dagger. In the third there was a female skeleton together with nine glass beads, red, blue and white, a silver ring, a necklace pendant, the remains of a bronze bracelet and the most important find of all, The Vallance Brooch. (6)

The Danes, according to the Anglo-Saxon Chronicle, came in 893 'with eighty ships into the Thames' mouth and wrought ... a work at Middleton'. This was Castle Rough, a fort constructed in the Swale Marshes near Milton. According to Hasted, the great 18th century Kent historian, who saw the remains when they were better preserved than they are now, 'it was of a square form, ... surrounded by a high bank thrown up, and a broad ditch. There (was) a raised causeway ... leading from it towards the foreshore. Hasted recorded that following the arrival of the Danes 'King Alfred ... marched his forces towards Kent, and in order to stop their incursions, sometime afterwards built on the opposite or eastern side of the Creek, about a mile from the Danish entrenchments, a fortification, ... at Bayford Castle.' At that time Milton was one of the six principal towns in Kent. Although it escaped attack by the Danes it was plundered and burnt by Earl Godwin in 1052 when he was in dispute with King Edward the Confessor, who owned Milton. However when William I became King and took ownership of Milton Hundred it was one of the wealthiest areas of Kent. (7)

The Locality at the time of the Norman Conquest

According to the Domesday Book the manor of Milton was one of the most valuable in the county, being worth £200 a year. It was included as part of the Terra Regis, the King's land. 'In the half lathe of Middletun, in Middletun Hundred', Middletun Manor had '309 villeins with 74 borders and 167 ploughs', there were '10 serfs', '6 mills', '27 salt pans' and '32 fisheries'. It had been an early minster, comprising, at the time of the Domesday book, of 12 parishes totalling 17,000 acres. Of these, Bapchild, to the east of Sittingbourne, was one of the oldest. It is recorded as Baccancelde on one of the oldest Kent charters, dating from the late seventh or early eighth century. Tonge was also well established, a mill there being mentioned in the Domesday Book. Sittingbourne itself, as a separate parish, did not exist at the time of the Norman conquest, like Murston it was still part of the parish of Milton. The name of Murston derives from its role as the 'mores tun' or moor farm of Milton. The names of Highsted, Woodstock and Tunstall also derive from their agricultural role in relation to the manor of Milton, Highsted being high pasture, Woodstock a dairy farm and Tunstall being an outlying stall or vaccary, (where cattle were kept). (8)

At the time of the Norman Conquest, the whole area known as Milton Hundred, centred on the royal town and manor of Milton, had been an administrative area within the Jutish Kingdom of Kent for centuries. The whole of Kent was divided into administrative areas known as Lathes, there were 5 full Lathes and 2 Half-Lathes, Milton being one of the latter. Within this system Milton was exceptional in that all the other Lathes were subdivided into Hundreds, smaller administrative areas, the other Half-Lathe,

Sutton, consisted of seven Hundreds, whereas the Lathe of Milton was also Milton Hundred. It may be that its unusual status related to its wealth. The area continued to be wealthy. According to a Lay Subsidy in 1334/5, north-east Kent, of which the Sittingbourne area was a part, was assessed at over twenty shillings a square mile. It was the largest area to be assessed at this level in south-east England and it was one of the highest levels in the country. (9)

The Medieval Period
Records surviving from the Medieval period show local involvement in national events. In the 14th century local residents became involved in Wat Tyler's insurrection against King Richard II. The revolt followed the introduction of a Poll Tax to raise money for a war against the French, however the men from East Anglia and the Home Counties who marched to London in June 1381 did so to demand changes in the agricultural system, which at that time included serfdom, by which the peasants were owned by the lords' of Manors and had to spend part of their time working without pay on their lord's land. The 'Presentment of Malefactors who have risen against our Lord King' included William Brown of Bixle and John Webbe of Maidstone who slew John Godwot of Borden, and also John Smyth of Tunstall, who, with others, slew John Tebbe at Canterbury. On the 10th June 1381 John Hales of Malling, Walter Teghelere of Essex and other malefactors made assault on William Septvantz, Sheriff of Kent, dragged him to prison and forced him to go to his manor at Milton and made him swear that he would deliver up all rolls and writs in his custody. (These would probably have been used for the collection of the Poll Tax.) He did so under fear of death and John Hales burnt them. (10)

Two events occurred in the 15th century which involved local inhabitants. The first was John Cade's Rebellion in 1450. According to the Patent Rolls of Henry VI a substantial number of the local townsfolk were involved, as well as those from the agricultural community. Three 'Gentlemen', John Goolde, Richard Grovehurst and John Buntyn of Milton were followers of Cade, as were the Tonges, who were yeomen (substantial farmers), and 6 husbandmen. Eleven members of the local fishing community took part, including Wills Maas and Will and John Colke, and also mentioned are a butcher, a smith, a fuller, a cordwainer, a tanner, a barbour, a bereman and a roper. (11)

It is not known whether or not local people were involved in Fauconberge's Kentish Rising in 1471, however it seems likely. The 15th century was the time when England was involved in the War of the Roses, between the Houses of York and Lancaster. In 1471 Fauconberge, a supporter of the House of Lancaster, landed in Kent with French mercenaries to rescue the former King, Henry VI, who was imprisoned in the Tower of London. He sent a letter to the "Commonalty of the City of London" asking them not to prevent him from entering London which was "written at Sittingbourne the eighth day of May". Fauconberge, together with his French mercenaries and supporters from Kent attacked London and set fire to London bridge, burning 60 houses on it. When King Edward IV approached with his army Fauconberge and his men retreated through Kent to Sandwich. King Edward IV marched as far as Canterbury but when, later in May, Henry VI died in the Tower, Fauconberge surrendered. It is possible that the troops of both Fauconberge and Edward IV may have passed through Sittingbourne, as had Henry V earlier in the century when he dined at Sittingbourne on his return from Agincourt in 1415. (12)

The town was to continue to receive royal visitors throughout the following centuries as this history will show.

Chapter One

Local Agriculture

Introduction

The modern-day town of Sittingbourne is surrounded by agricultural parishes and it provides services, shops, banking etc, for the residents of the local villages. However for most of the town's history the links between the urban and rural economies were much stronger. In order to understand the history of Sittingbourne it is important to see it in a wider context, as at the heart of the agricultural area known administratively as Milton Hundred. It is with the agriculture of the area around Sittingbourne then that this chapter is concerned.

In the north Milton Hundred is bounded by the Swale and Medway rivers. Running south from them is an area of marshland, both salt and fresh marsh, through which run a number of creeks. The most important of these were Milton Creek, which runs into the Swale, and two in the west of the Hundred, Otterham Creek and Halstow Creek, which flow into the Medway. The land rises gradually from the marshes and up to around 200 feet it is mainly clay. This is covered by a layer of loamy soil in the flat areas bordering the London to Dover road. South of this the land becomes increasingly hilly and changes to chalk with flinty deposits. These hills rise towards the 700 feet high ridge of the North Downs several miles to the south of the Hundred. Within the Hundred they reached around 400 feet with hills and valleys extending northwards across the area of clay. The springs which rose in the chalk hills run down to the creeks and marshes in the north of the Hundred. The Hundred is located at the western end of a fertile belt running for 35 miles from Rainham to the eastern extremities of Thanet, which averaged around eight miles in width, consisting of 'cornlands, hop gardens, woodlands, orchards, market gardens and pastures'. (1)

Throughout the timescale covered by this book the type of agriculture in Milton Hundred remained mixed. Although there were significant changes in agricultural practices during the 19th and 20th centuries, the type of agriculture found in the Hundred changed very little. As far more data is available for the earlier centuries extensive use is made of it to give a general picture of local agriculture, rather than a formal chronological agricultural history.

In order to give a geographical context to the chapter the 16 rural parishes, surrounding the urban parishes of Sittingbourne and Milton, will be grouped into four sections: those lying in the north-east, the south-east, the south-west and the north-west. Although different agricultural activities were spread over the area as a whole, in order to avoid repetition one particular activity will be dealt with in each of the four sections, corn in the north-east, trees in the south-east, hops in the south-west and livestock in the north-west. Wherever possible the quotations that are used will refer to the particular group of parishes being dealt with, although ones from Sittingbourne and Milton will be included where appropriate. The main exception will be references to the estate of Captain Osborne. He lived in Hartlip in the late 17th century and documents relating to his estate are one of the main sources for agricultural activity in the area at that time. As his farm included most of the main types of agriculture found in the Hundred, relevant quotations from these documents will be found in most of the sections. Also included will be quotations from Hasted's 'History and Topography of Kent' (1797-1801), which is one of the main sources of information for the early period of the agriculture in Milton Hundred. (2)

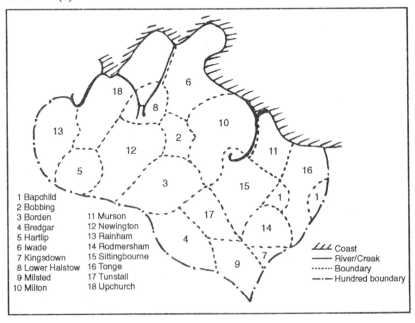

1 Bapchild
2 Bobbing
3 Borden
4 Bredgar
5 Hartlip
6 Iwade
7 Kingsdown
8 Lower Halstow
9 Milsted
10 Milton
11 Murson
12 Newington
13 Rainham
14 Rodmersham
15 Sittingbourne
16 Tonge
17 Tunstall
18 Upchurch

Coast
River/Creak
Boundary
Hundred boundary

The Parishes of Milton Hundred

The North-East of Milton Hundred: Before the 19th century
The four parishes lying in the north-east of the Hundred were Murston, Tonge, Bapchild and Rodmersham, which together covered an area of around 4,500 acres. All of them, according to Hasted, were blessed with land which was 'very rich and fertile for corn'. The size of the fields in this area were particularly large, farms often consisting of 'two or three or perhaps only one field'. A map of the Manor of Bayford and Godmanston on the boundary of Sittingbourne and Murston. shows that in 1590 there was one field of 49 acres. The average field size was 18.4 acres. This evidence supports a description, in 1549, of Kent as one of the counties 'where most enclosures be'. (3)

Kent was a county characterised by ancient enclosures. By the time of Hasted there were farms with fields of 60 or even 'one hundred acres or more'. Hasted related this to an important issue at that time, that of the replacement of a common field system with enclosure, and the consequent suffering of the rural population, by saying that in Milton Hundred the large fields were not the result, as elsewhere in the country, of enforced enclosure, rather they were large because the 'high rent' and the 'high rate of servants wages' which meant that a farmer had 'to make the most of his land, and not suffer it to be lessened by hedgerows'. According to Alan Everitt, in 'Landscape and Community in England', this area of Milton Hundred was part of an area which 'until recent generations has probably always been the wealthiest and most thickly populated part of Kent', being 'some of the most fertile land in England.' (4)

Tonge Mill

The use of the heavy Kent turn-wrest plough also maximised field use as it enabled the ploughman to work from one end of the field to the other without a break. The 'fine loamy soil', known locally as 'round tilt land' was 'continually tilled, without being made fallow (left without a crop), with ... barley, beans and wheat year after year'. Hasted provides evidence that by the second half of the 18th century the practice of using root crops, rather than leaving a field fallow, had been established in the Hundred. The quality of seed was important and farmers travelled far to get the best, Captain Osborne bought rye seed in Maidstone and wheat seed from Boxley. Some of the grain produced in these parishes in the north-east of the Hundred was processed locally. In Tonge, springs flowed into a pond which was 'sufficient to turn a corn mill'. (5)

However, the parishes and different areas of the Hundred were not isolated from each other, and much of the cereal produced in the agricultural parishes of the Hundred were taken to the quays found on the banks of its creeks, which together made up the Port of Milton. In particular, grain from the north-east of the Hundred was taken to the urban parishes of Sittingbourne and Milton, from where it was exported, usually to London. In 1649, of all the Kent ports, Milton was second only to Faversham in the quantity of cereal exported to London. It was one of the network of ports used by the fleet of coastal vessels to service the needs of London's growing population. As London grew both in status and size during the 17th century the economic links between the capital and Milton Hundred grew too, not only in terms of increased exports of cereals. These grew from 4,893 quarters in 1598-9 to 10,571 quarters in 1699-1700. On November 6th 1700, for example, 100 quarters of wheat were exported in the 'John and Johanna' of Milton. (6)

Exports were not popular with the local population when harvests were poor. In 1631 there was a report of the 'women of Sittingbourne and Milton band(ing) together by 50 or 60 in company', and Chalklin includes Milton among the places in north Kent where corn riots occurred in that year when grain was exported at a time when the poor were starving from lack of corn. It was clearly a bad year, E.P. Thompson in the book 'Customs in Common' quotes a magistrate in Suffolk in the same year as saying, after an export riot there, 'to see their bread thus taken from them and sent to strangers has turned the impatience of the poor into licentious fury and desperation.' Although the corn growing areas around Sittingbourne were relatively wealthy there is no doubt that the urban poor considered that their needs should take precedence over the demands of Londoners. (7)

The export of corn from the Hundred using its creeks and rivers had the advantage that water transport was relatively cheap compared to costs of land transport. Cheap transport was particularly important in an area where labour costs were high. Waggoners' wages in Kent at the end of the 18th century varied from £10 to £13 per annum with board, or from 10/- to 10/6 per week if they were married and lived in separate accommodation. This put them amongst the highest paid agricultural workers according to John Boys in his book 'General View of the Agriculture of the County of Kent', with only a bailiff earning more at £12 to £16 per annum. Ploughmen's wages were between £3/10/0 and £4 with board for five weeks work or £5/5/0 without board. Other areas in the Hundred not blessed with such good soil also had the cost of fertilising the land. In Halstow the 'clayey lands' were 'much improved by spreading them over with lime, bought at heavy expense ... a distance of between three and four miles'. In Newington, chalk was obtained 'by means of draw wells' and used 'for the manure of their land'. These were known as 'deneholes'. Usually they consisted of a shaft with three short chambers radiating from it. However one was found this century at Kingsdown where two shafts, one being nine metres deep, were linked by a common gallery. It seems likely that Chalkwell Road got its name from there having been a 'chalk well' there. The use of fertilisers is another example of the way in which new farming methods were developed in the Hundred during the 17th century. (8)

Although those working on the cereal growing land in the north-east of Milton Hundred were probably among the highest paid workers in Kent, as Hasted makes clear they earned it. The closeness of the farms to the marshes, particularly in Murston and Tonge, meant that the air was 'very gross, and much subject to fogs, which smell very offensive (and) ... which, with the badness of the water occasion fever agues, which the inhabitants are very rarely without'. The complexions of the local inhabitants were a 'dingy yellow colour' and Hasted described a whole family 'hovering over the fire in their hovel, shaking with an ague all at the same time'. They were, according to Dr Plot, likely to die young and Hasted remarks that if it were not for the 'high wages given for the hazard of life itself, these situations would probably be nearly deserted of inhabitants.' (9)

The South-East of Milton Hundred: Before the 19th century

The five parishes lying in the south-east of the Hundred, Kingsdown, Milsted, Tunstall, Bredgar and Borden, had a total acreage of around 5,000. They ranged in size from the 1,550 acres of Borden in the west to the 600 acres of Kingsdown in the east. Half of Kingsdown was covered with woods and it is the aspect of agriculture centred on trees which will be dealt with in this section. The southern parishes were situated on the range of chalky hills which rose to the escarpment of the North Downs. Hasted describes the soil of all of them as being 'very poor, chalky, and much covered with flints'. They were part of the old Forest of Blean and in 'Continuity and Colonization' Alan Everitt uses local place names to chart the gradual clearance of wood to form pastures - Highsted originated in 1197 and Woodstock in 1212. Highsted, or high pasture, lay between Rodmersham and Tunstall on the ancient droveway linking Kingsdown, or Kings pasture, with the royal Manor of Milton. In even earlier times than those with which the present study is concerned, agricultural links had been forged between different parishes of the Hundred. The names of woods give a clear idea of their use. In Bredgar there was Oak wood and Brodoak Forstall, a corruption of Broad Oak. In the west there were the chestnut woods of the Stockbury valley with the hamlet of Chestnut Street in the parish of Borden. (10)

Originally the woods stretched for five or six miles across the south of the Hundred to Milsted and Kingsdown in the east. Rents of chestnut woods in the 17th century were generally high and coppice wood was sold to a collier or dealer who was responsible for felling and carriage. In September 1684 Captain Osborne sold wood to Thomas Umfry for £8 an acre plus tithes and other charges. As was normal some trees were grown to their full height, the agreement stated that Umfry was to fell no oaks that 'stand single' and he was to leave 'twelve principles and eight score waverers of an acre'. Larger trees were sold individually or by the load. Wood from the oak trees grown in the Hundred may have been used in the developing boat building industry at Crown Quay in Sittingbourne, although the main bottom timbers would have come from men o' war broken up at Chatham and Sheerness. Bark from the trees may also have been used in the tan yard which was located at Chalkwell between Sittingbourne and Milton as bark provided the 'flaw' for tanners. There were also some exports of wood from the Hundred, Tappenden's hoy business at Crown Quay in the late 17th century was engaged in exporting brushwood from the Hundred to the Isle of Grain where it was used to reinforce the sea wall. Sometimes the wood was coaled on the site by colliers so that it would be lighter, and therefore easier and cheaper to transport. It is likely that charcoal was used locally as there are no references to any being exported. (11)

Chestnut wood was also used to manufacture Kent spike fencing and the fruit of the chestnut trees also played a part in the economy of the area. In 1575, for example, when Milton Manor was owned by Elizabeth I, one of her dues was 'nine bushels of chestnottes' or payment in lieu each year. Of far greater importance, however, was the fruit of other trees grown in these parishes. Hasted describes Borden village as being 'encircled by orchards of fruit trees', and elsewhere refers to 'orchards of apples, cherries and other kinds of fruit'. In 1623 the owner of a house in Borden had two orchards of three acres and a two acre cherry garden in Borden and another cherry garden in Tunstall. The value of orchard land was high compared to arable or pasture land and required less acreage than corn to make a living. The 17th century educational and agricultural reformer Samuel Hartlib refers to value increasing by 20 times if land was turned over to orchards, with £10 or £15 an acre being given for cherries and more for pears and apples. He describes orchards with trees planted 20 or 30 feet apart in rows. The land was ploughed and sown with corn until the trees began to bear fruit, then it was laid down for pasture. The grass in orchards grew two weeks earlier in spring than meadow grass and lasted better in hot dry summers. There was also the additional advantage that cattle or sheep kept in the orchards could shelter under the trees. (12)

Milton Hundred was the oldest of the five major fruit growing districts of Kent, and when the Fruiterers Company of London petitioned Parliament against importing Dutch cherries in 1624 they asked Kent M.P.'s to act for them, as they represented 'that county in which is the greatest plantation'. Another fruit grown in abundance in the Hundred was apples. These were used not only as fruit but for cider, especially windfalls and those which were bruised. When Captain Osborne of Hartlip had many of his apples blown down in August 1674 they were used to make a 'cider of reasonable quality'. No doubt much cider found its way to the inns in urban parishes as well as to the village inns of the Hundred. Much of the actual fruit was, though, taken to the urban quays to be exported. Packets of fruit are included among the exports in the 18th century port registers for Milton. It was the demand from the wealthy upper classes centred in London for such goods as fruit which, increasingly during the 18th century, encouraged the agricultural specialisation in counties like Kent. (13)

The South-West of Milton Hundred: Before the 19th century

The same ship which in 1700 carried wheat from Milton, also carried 'one packett of English hopps'. By the second half of the 18th century hop growing was on the increase as the 'high price of hops yielding a more advantageous return' meant that many orchards 'were displanted, and hops raised in their stead'. The soil of old orchards was particularly good for hops and lead to high yields. Hasted records one instance of 'an acre having grown after the rate of 34 hundred weight of hops'. This was in Newington, one of the four parishes lying along the London road in the south-west of the Hundred. The others were Bobbing, Hartlip and Rainham and together they covered an area of over 6,000 acres. In 1697 Celia Fiennes on her journey along the London to Dover road passed 'great hop yards on both sides of the road'. From the mid-17th century Kent had about a third of the hop acreage of the country as a whole, much of which would have found its way, in one form or another, to the growing population of London. In 1686 Captain Osborne agreed with Goodman Shrubsall that he should maintain his half acre of hop-ground for £2/5/0 the first year and £1/15/0 thereafter. This did not include poling which was one of the most costly elements of hop growing. The annual expense of an acre of hop ground ranged from £20 to £30, which meant that only the wealthier farmers could afford to plant, but for those who did high returns were possible. The fruits of their labours would have gone to the urban breweries or for export beyond the Hundred. (14)

Poles up which the hops were trained to grow, were obtained from the local coppice woods which were cropped every 13 years or so. In 1795 costs for poling were 10/- per hundred, sharpening old poles 2/- and sharpening new poles 6d. Hop garden labour was expensive, for rates for digging per acre were from 15/- to £1, and tying added a further 10/- per acre. The cost of hoeing at 5/- per acre was more expensive than for any other crop apart from turnips; hoeing barley for example cost less than 2/- per acre. Labour was mostly local, at times even the wife of a gentleman farmer might help with the hop picking, as on the farm of Richard Tylden, Esq, of Milsted in 1743. Chalklin in his work on 17th century Kent says that there is no evidence that hop growers relied for picking on other than local women and children. There is evidence that by the early 18th century the situation, in Milton Hundred at least, was changing. The Sittingbourne burial register for the autumn of 1719 included three poor hoppers, one of whom was from Birmingham. (15)

Hops, like fruit and corn, were grown on the fertile clay area that bounded the London road. To the south of this area the land was often poor and 'much covered with broom and furze'. In Hartlip there was a 'long tract of waste ground, called Queen-down, which was for many years a noted warren for rabbits'. In 1674 Captain Osborne hired William Hallom as his Warrener at

Queendown Park. Their agreement stated that each could give a quarter's notice except for the Christmas quarter when the warrener was not to leave until the 'slaughter of conies be taken off'. Coney is another name for the rabbits which were used both for their fur and their meat. Even up to the 1950s rabbit was often a traditional Christmas lunch amongst the working classes. (16)

The North-West of Milton Hundred: Before the 19th century
From rabbits, this study of the final rural area of the Hundred considers some of the other animals which were an important part of the agricultural economy. The parishes in the north-west of the Hundred, Upchurch, Lower Halstow and Iwade together covered an area of over 5,000 acres. They stretched from the northern edge of the belt of clay across the marshes to the Medway and Swale rivers. There, the steeple of the church at Upchurch was 'accounted as a sea mark'. (17)

The Church at Upchurch

Two main creeks flowed through this area into the Medway. On Otterham Creek lay a 'wharf for the landing and shipping of corn, and the produce of neighbouring woods'. Otterham quay formed part of the Port of Milton and, like the urban quays, would, as Hasted confirms, have been involved in the transit of wood as well as other goods along the established route between the Hundred and London. The other creek was Halstow Creek which had oyster grounds. In 1634 Sir Robert Darell leased them to John Pett for a rent of £10

14

and 'six bushells of the best oysters being sweete, new and good, and four barrells of ... well conditioned pickled oysters'. Running south from the Medway river was an area of salt marsh, separated from the fresh water marshes by sewers and a wall which protected the fresh water marshes from the sea. The local owners were responsible for keeping them in good order. The Milton will of Thomas Ayleff in 1529 refers to his heir receiving 'income from lease of Readom Marsh and Pykwynkell for life repairing the walls and dykes'. Maintaining the walls could be an expensive business. In 1606 Ralph Elmerston of Rainham agreed to inn and wall the saltmarsh. This work was to be done over a period of three years and the wall was to be 22 feet deep and seven to eight feet high. The cost was born jointly by tenant and landlord and was in excess of £300. Hasted described the results of not keeping walls in good repair. The 500 acre Slayhill marsh, part of the Manor of Gore in Upchurch parish was fresh water until 'the force of the tides, which from the walls of it being neglected, at length broke through them, and overflowed it, and it is now ... become a tract of salts'. (18)

This would have been a great loss, as the fresh marsh lands were important for the keeping of sheep and cattle. In 1610, Robert Sawyer of Detling had all his cattle in the marshes of Iwade. During the 17th century there was an increase in the keeping of cattle in the area with the introduction of new grasses, like clover, which were used as fodder. At a time when the average herd size in Kent was around 14, on the marshes it was about 22. Stephen Frood of Upchurch, for example, kept a herd of 23, in part using clover to feed them. Not only were cattle herds larger in marshland areas than elsewhere in the Hundred, so were flocks of sheep, particularly in summer when the marshes were used as pasture. By the end of the 17th century the average flock size in North Kent was 70, whereas on the marshes it was 376. The land in Iwade was particularly good for the keeping of sheep, being 'very even and flat, of a soft boggy nature'. Sometimes the wetness of the ground could cause problems for the sheep but not in Iwade. The 'great quantities of sheep' kept there did not 'rot in the marshes' as they did elsewhere, possibly, Hasted suggests, because they fed 'on the herb spearwort' which grew there 'plentifully among the grass'. (19)

Those keeping cattle and sheep in the rural parts of the Hundred had close links with the urban areas. There is no doubt that much of the mutton and beef found its way either directly to the inns in Sittingbourne, where many inn owners were also local land owners, to the market in Milton or to the quays within the Hundred. The wild fowl which were caught in the decoy situated in the marshes to the north of Milton were, according to Hasted, 'much esteemed for their size and flavour'; they were 'weekly taken and sent up to London'. Wool fleeces and hides were also exported directly to London, although the relationship between the rural and urban parishes was strengthened further as both wool and hides were used in the urban economy. (20)

The Rural Parishes of Milton Hundred Before the 19th century - Conclusion

One animal not mentioned in the agriculture of the north-west of the Hundred was the pig. They were, however, an important part of the agricultural economy, as is clear from the following comparison of two farms in different parts of the Hundred in the first half of the 18th century which brings out the mixed nature of the Hundred's agriculture. The farm of Valentine Ruck, yeoman, in Hartlip in 1729 had 50 acres of winter wheat, and wheat, barley and oats stored in the barn. In Murston, on the other side of the Hundred, in 1748, the farm of John Prall, yeoman, had 72 acres of wheat, 46 of barley and six of oats. The wheat and barley would have been cash crops whereas the oats would have been grown to feed his ten horses - at a time before mechanization horses were an important part of the workforce on any arable farm, (there were eight on the Hartlip farm). (21)

Prall's Murston farm was not, though, given over entirely to the production of cereals. There were also 46 acres of beans, too much for his own consumption. Beans were also grown on Ruck's farm in Hartlip, there were 30 quarters of garden beans, valued at £45, and 40 quarters of small beans worth £46, stored in the barn. On Prall's farm there were an additional 17 acres given over to peas which, together with the 'tail' barley, was used to fatten store pigs. There were two hog pounds, three in-pig sows and 27 stores at various stages of growth on the farm. The six brine tubs and 64 score pounds of pork, valued at £37, showed that Prall was involved in processing the pigs as well as fattening them. Ruck, in Hartlip, also kept pigs, the inventory of his farm included 'six hogs a fatting, 60 score at five shillings and six pence a score ... two sows and ten sheats'.

Both farms, then, reflect the importance to the agricultural economy of the Hundred of cereals and butcher's meat, even though they were in geographically different parts of the Hundred. Prall's farm was in the flat north-east of the Hundred whereas Ruck's farm was situated in the hillier south-west. The differences in the soil of the two is clear from the inventory of the Hartlip farm. Unlike the rich loamy soil of Murston in the north-east the soil in Hartlip needed fertilisation, there are references to 650 loads of dung and five carriages of lime having been used the previous year, with 800 loads of mixed chalk and dung being ready for use. Ruck's farm also reflects the mixed agriculture of the Hundred as a whole. Although the picture of the area's agriculture has concentrated on one main aspect in each of the four geographical areas, individual farms, like Ruck's, often included all aspects of agriculture. As well as growing cereals and fattening pigs on the farm there were two cows, no doubt for domestic use, and 24 sheep. These may have been kept on the grass of orchards as there are references to apples being stored and to cherry sives. Hops may have been grown as 'old hoppoles' are mentioned and the inclusion of 'two paire of tugs', which were carriages for timber, indicated its importance to the farm.

The Hartlip inventory of 1729 comes at a time when changes were occurring, gradually, in agriculture, with new root crops and methods of rotation, as well as an increase in demands for wheaten bread, instead of that made from poor mixed cereals such as rye and barley. There is a reference to 20 acres of winter wheat being sown on land that had been fallow, however the remaining 30 acres of wheat had been sown on bean stubble. There are also references to the growing of clover and turnips, the latter being a new crop for Kent at that time, indicating that one at least of the farmers in the Hundred was at the forefront of agricultural change. The previous two hundred years had been a time of stability, the agricultural mix of the Hundred having been well established by the time of Elizabeth I. Sittingbourne and Milton wills of the second half of the 15th century and the first half of the 16th century include references to woods, orchards, corn, wheat, barley, grain, barns, meadows, pasture, cattle, bullocks, sheep and pigs, all of which were still found in the 18th century. As was noted in the introduction to this chapter enclosures had taken place by the mid-16th century, the last reference to land in common fields in the wills is in that of John Burdon in 1536. He had nine and a half acres in Buggesfield. The same field was referred to in the 1495 will of Thomas Clenche, he had one acre and a virgate there. He also had the same amount of land in Shamelesfield, which was mentioned in the 1456 will of John Polyver, who had one acre and a yard there. The common open field system was then in operation in the Hundred and the move to the single ownership of land in the mid 16th century, like the 'farm in Borden called Cryals' of Richard Bukmer in 1545, must have meant considerable change occurring over a relatively short period of time, even though some parcels of land held in the late 15th century had been quite substantial. In 1497 John Bromfield, for example, had 16 acres of wheat in Bramblefield and the 12 acres of barley at Bremth, although it is of course possible that these acreages may have been made up of several strips in different parts of an 'open' field. (22)

In the late 15th century there was still an occasional reference to the medieval practice of labour service, such as the 16 days work of land in Akerman's field mentioned in the 1473 will of William Tonbregge. It may have been linked to the payment of church tithes as it seems likely that William Maas' 'five and a half acres and three days work of land behind Middleton vicarage' was in 1464. William Maas also had a hemp plot, the only crop mentioned in the wills which was not found in the Hundred the 18th century. It seems likely that it did not survive beyond the 16th century, perhaps it was replaced by the hop fields which were abundant by the mid-17th century. (23)

The rural parishes of Milton Hundred in the period prior to the 19th century had then, from the late 15th century, an established mix of agriculture. Apart from the change to the enclosed system of farming in the early 16th century, the development of hop growing from the 17th century, and the moves to root crops and increased fertilisation in the early 18th century, the period had been predominantly one of stability. It had also been a period which was dominated by the need to satisfy the increasing demands of London. As early as 1630 the

Warden of the Cinque Ports was referring to north Kent as 'the garner to replenishe the storehouse of the Cittie'. (24)

The Rural Parishes of Milton Hundred in the Early 19th century - (The 'Swing riots' and 'Courtnay')

In the early 19th century falling prices for corn led to unemployment in many areas, including Kent. It was in Kent that the Captain Swing riots against the introduction and use of new agricultural machinery, seen as bringing more unemployment, started in 1830. In October that year Westlands Farm at Borden, on the estate of Valentine Simpson and occupied by a newcomer, Mr Knight, was attacked and between £1,500 and £2,000 of damage was done. The 'Maidstone Journal' reported that 'many of the farmers (were) terrified at the appearance of the rioters ... breaking the machines in open day, many being armed with hatchets, hammers, saws and even guns which they discharge in the midst of cheering, when their work of destruction is accomplished'. There was so much terror 'in the neighbourhood of Sittingbourne that it was found necessary to station a military force there'. This was a troop of the 2nd Dragoon Guards who according to a Memorandum dated 13/11/1830 were to arrive on 15th to relieve a troop of the 5th Dragoon Guards who were to go to Chatham. At Newington rioters demanded wages of 2/6 a day and a reduction in rent, other non-agricultural workers in Sittingbourne also went on strike for an increase in wages. There had been two years of bad harvests and the price of bread, a large part of the diet in those days, would have been high. The unrest then was not just against new agricultural machinery, it was a symptom of what the Rev. Poore of Murston, a local magistrate, described as 'general prevailing distress' as well as the chance to get back at individuals who were less than popular. A letter from Thomas Goodman, alias Swing, in fact said 'I have a revenge against you and your family and so ... you and your house shall be burnt,' and in a letter to the Home Secretary the Rev. Poore said that 'the poor (were) ... much prejudiced against Mr Knight' - hence the attack on his farm. However, that so few incidents occurred, compared to other areas of Kent, is an indication of the relative wealth of the Hundred. No incidents in fact occurred in the most arable of the Hundred's parishes, Murston and Tonge, where most of the new machinery would be most likely to be located; they were, as was established in the section on the parishes of the north-east prior to the 19th century, areas of high wages. Mr Lushington, who lived in Rodmersham in the same area of the Hundred, said at the time of the Swing riots that 'distress amongst the agricultural labourers is not the cause. In fact it does not in our district exist.' (25)

Although there was a 'bread riot' against the Corn Laws in 1838, this was largely an urban affair, a march being led through Sittingbourne by 'Sir William Courtnay'. Courtnay and his followers foretold 'the day of destruction and bloodshed, when the fire of the Lord should be kindled, and the enemies of godliness and the oppressor should meet with the just reward of the wicked. The Union workhouses were to be opened and the inmates released, and the walls razed to the ground. ... Courtnay's men were armed with bludgeons; he himself being laden with pistols and a dirk. A white flag, bordered with blue, and bearing the device of a lion rampant, was borne in front of the procession.' They marched along Watling Street, through Bapchild to Sittingbourne where they had breakfast at the Wheat Sheaf. How many local people joined them is unknown, but the whole affair came to a bitter and bloody end in the Battle of Bosenden Wood. The parishes in which agriculture was the main economic activity remained unaffected by such unrest, although their involvement in protests against changes in the Poor Law indicates that they must have had their share of 'the poor' in the early 19th century. (26)

Although the main concern in this part of the chapter is with the second half of the 19th century, the tithe awards made between 1836 and 1846 (70% in 1839 and 1840) confirm the continued mixed nature of the agriculture within the Hundred in the 19th century. Of the 26,081 acres recorded in the 16 awards at the Canterbury Cathedral Archives, (Rainham was not held there as it was part of the Rochester diocese, and that for Murston did not exist), 52% were arable, 34% meadow/pasture/saltings, and $9^{1/2}$% was woodland. In spite of the comments of travellers noted earlier on the fruit orchards and hop gardens found in the Hundred, only $2^{1/2}$% of the land was given over to orchards and 1% to hops. (Even this may be an overestimation as four parishes did not record them separately.) A further 1% was used for houses and gardens. In terms of the amounts of grain produced, as recorded in the awards, a total of 48,472 bushels were produced of which 19% was wheat, 33% oats and 48% barley. (27)

The Rural Parishes of Milton Hundred During the Second Half of the 19th century

This section is concerned mainly with evidence of changes in agriculture which occurred in Milton Hundred during the second half of the 19th century. According to the census of 1851, in England and Wales as a whole, half of the population was urban. In Milton Hundred the balance was still on the side of the rural parishes, which contained over half of the population. In the country as a whole only one in six males over the age of ten were engaged in agriculture, whereas 39% of those living in Milton Hundred in that year were engaged directly in agriculture. Only four percent of the local workforce were engaged in brickmaking, the main local industry at that time. Within 20 years the nature of the Hundred and the experience of its population had changed with over 70% of the population (14,000 out of 20,000) in 1871 living in the urban centres of Sittingbourne (6,500), Milton (3,500), Rainham (2,000) and the brickmaking parishes of Murston, Lower Halstow and Upchurch. In spite of this, the numbers engaged in industrial occupations were still only around half those engaged in agriculture. It was not until 1881 that employment in the industries overtook that in agriculture. In fact, the numbers in agricultural employment stayed fairly stable, increasing by about two percent between 1851 and 1881. (28)

Industrial development, though, had not affected all of the parishes in the

Hundred to the same extent. The geological structure of the locality ensured that it was only in the parishes on the belt of clay in the north of the Hundred that brickmaking developed. The parishes on the chalky hills to the south did not have any industrial development and continued with their agricultural economies, even though some of them, like Bobbing and Borden were within reach of the brickfields and had their fair share of brickfield labourers. Not all of the land in the northern parishes was used for brickmaking at any one time, as the fields were returned to agricultural use as soon as the clay had been removed. Agriculture continued to have a significant role in the economy of the Hundred as a whole, and in spite of the development of industry the urban areas continued their role as centres for merchants and traders and also as market centres. The introduction to the entry in the 1895 directory for Sittingbourne and Milton, included after brickmaking, the fact that they were known for 'the market, the supply of the neighbouring district, (and) the shipping of corn', London still had its important role as the consumer of produce from the Hundred. Corn, in particular, was in great demand, for during the Victorian period it was the staple diet of the poor, with as much as 20% of family income going on bread. (29)

Although corn was featured in the introduction in the directory, the agricultural occupations given in the census books reveal that, within the Hundred as a whole, agriculture remained mixed. The second half of the 19th century did, however, bring change, not only in the move towards urbanization and industrialization in the north of the Hundred, but also in agricultural practices. This was a time of national change in agricultural methods, in particular with increased mechanization and the use of steam traction engines, and with the greater use of fertilisers. Such changes within Milton Hundred can be seen through a study of job titles given by agricultural workers in the 1851 and 1881 census books, and through differences between the 1862 and 1895 Kelly's Directories for Sittingbourne and Milton. (30)

In both 1851 and 1881 shepherds and men engaged in the keeping of cattle - cowkeeper/man, cattle dealer, drover and grazier (those who feed cattle for market) were recorded. Some areas specialized in growing fruit, the term fruiter being used for fruit growers, as opposed to the use of fruiterer for fruit dealer/seller in towns. Other parts were devoted to market gardening or to cereals; a hay dealer, hay cutter, waggoners, thresher and plough servants (the latter in 1851 only) were recorded. It was on the arable farms, however, that the greatest changes in terms of mechanization occurred. By 1881, as well as the earlier occupations, farm workers included a steam ploughman, several traction engine drivers (separate from drivers of road locomotives who were a different category), an agricultural engineer and a small-scale farmer who was primarily a threshing machine repairer. Changes in land use are shown by increased numbers of market gardeners and hop growers; some farmers, like Robert Mercer of Rodmersham, called themselves 'hop planters'. (31)

The urban parishes were still closely linked to agriculture through traders and

20

specialist dealers, as well as having their own 'cowkeepers' and a dairy in Sittingbourne's 'East End'. The entries in Kelly's Directories for Sittingbourne and Milton, in both 1862 and 1895, include those dealing in the full range of agricultural goods produced in the Hundred as well as those selling to the farmers, like Singler Shrubsole who in 1862 was a 'corn-factor and agent for the sale of agricultural implements'. Shrubsaole was not the only 'corn-factor', and other traders included 'dealers in hay and straw', 'wool merchants' and a 'potato merchant and wholesale fruiterer'. The reference to potatoes in the last entry reflects the move nationally during the 19th century towards the growing and eating of potatoes.

The same occupations, related directly and indirectly to agriculture, were found in the 1895 Directory, but changes had occurred. Sittingbourne had the offices not only of the Sittingbourne Agricultural Association (established 1836) but also of the Kent Fruit Growers Association. Fruit was processed locally; Goodhew and Son Ltd, who had premises in Milton and London, (to where the jam was sent), were 'jam preservers' as well as 'fruit growers'. Hops continued to be processed locally with breweries in Milton and in Sittingbourne High Street, where G Payne's brewery had been taken over by H and O Vallence. Other Kent brewery firms, Shepherd Neame and Company and Mackeson and Company, had agencies in Sittingbourne by 1895. The increased use of steam was clear from the entry for John Bates, miller and corn chandler, whose Milton mill processed the grain by using 'steam' as well as 'water and wind'. The use of steam in local agriculture, seen from the 1881 census, is confirmed by the entry for R. L. Knight and Company who were 'Agricultural engineers, steam ploughing, threshing and traction engine proprietors'. (32)

Entries in the 1895 Directory which illustrate changes in the use of agricultural land, are typified by that for R. G. Hodgkin, who was a 'gravel, flint and manure merchant' - that is an exporter of raw materials taken from the land and an importer of manure for use on it. Once again the close links between the Hundred and London played a part in its agricultural economy, for the straw muck-outs from London stables were brought into the Hundred for use on the hop fields and elsewhere. At Halstow Dock, Charles Murrell's fleet of barges brought manure from Deptford cattle market which was left in smouldering heaps until it was collected by the local farmers. (33)

Evidence of local agriculture and of the involvement of Sittingbourne in the rural economy also comes from the pages of the local newspaper, the 'East Kent Gazette'. The Sittingbourne Agricultural Association held annual matches at the meadow behind The Bull Hotel in Sittingbourne High Street. Sheep-shearing and mowing matches were held in June and a ploughing match took place in the autumn. Annual sales of fruit were held in the Bull Hotel itself. In 1870 Jackson and Bassett sold fruit on the trees by the acre, including cherries, apples, pears, plums, walnuts, gooseberries and currants. There was a huge crop of cherries in that year and in early July it was reported that 170 tons had been transported by train the previous week and that double that amount was expected during the current week. In 1886 45 to 50 tons of cherries were taken every night by train from Sittingbourne, with a further 20 tons from Newington and 15 to 18 tons from Rainham. In the same year the first consignments of fruit were taken to London by water by the Sittingbourne Fruit Water Carriage Association. Potatoes were also taken by boat, saving a substantial amount on rail costs. (34)

Trains were though used to transport certain agricultural workers, hoppickers. In 1876 the paper noted that more strangers were being employed each year. Within the Milton Union there were 25 farms growing hops of which six employed 'foreign' (that is, not local) pickers. Agricultural workers were affected in the 1870s by the rise of Trade Unionism and in 1873 hop-tiers in Newington combined for an increase in pay, they wanted £1/0/10 an acre. They also said that no women ought to go 'tatering' or do any other work under 1/6 per day and not to go 'cherrying' under 2/- a day. Although the study of the census and Directory data showed that mechanization increased during the second half of the 19th century other changes in ploughing occurred first. In 1869 Ransomes and Sims at Rodmersham were testing a new iron turn-wrest one-way Kent plough, which would use two horses and one man rather than the old four horses and two men system. (35)

The urban firm of Shrubsoles, at Chalkwell, were agents for Ramsome and Sims. Also within the urban area agriculture itself was carried on with the harvesting of watercress from the beds at the Meads in Milton. Of greater importance though was the urban involvement in the sale of stock from local farms. The Tithe records from the early years of Victoria's reign show that John Bonny occupied offices, a house, shop and the Stock Market Meadow. In 1858 a Cattle Market in Sittingbourne was held on a Tuesday. In the 1890s a fortnightly stock sale on a Monday was instituted by F Austen Bensted. He was already well established as an auctioneer, in one week in September 1889 he went to London (Monday), Ashford (Tuesday), Barnet Fair (Wednesday), Bristol (Thursday), Tenterden Fair (Friday) and Canterbury (Saturday). A not inconsiderable achievement considering the transport available in those days. Local sheep were also sold at the Spring Teg sales, a record of 3,400 animals were sold at one in 1902, and other stock at the annual Xmas Fat Stock Prize Show. The sale of stock, including sheep, could though be affected by outbreaks of disease on local farms. In 1892, for example, there was an outbreak of Foot and Mouth at Woodstock Park, Sittingbourne, and 200 ewes and 200 lambs belonging to Mr Twopenny died. (36)

Local farms in the second half of the 19th century were often, as they had been in previous centuries, mixed farms. An analysis of two farm ledgers, for which I am indebted to Mr Chapman, show this. Between 1867 and 1883 W Chapman farmed at Coleshall, partly in Iwade and partly in Milton parishes. Cattle, sheep, cereals, root crops and hops all figure in the accounts. His costs for hops in 1887 came to over £75. This included the purchase of 4,300 hop poles, the picking of 51 cwt of hops, pole pullers, tally man, drying, twine, beer and samples. These costs were low compared to those for the purchase of stock. In 1881 he bought 121 ewes, 151 lambs and 36 tegs by valuation at a cost of £370. The farm also had a heavy expenditure for dung and manure which came by boat from London, £172 was spent on 50 such purchases in 1882. The accounts also show that he paid for outside assistance for ploughing and threshing. In 1882 he paid Chittenden and Knight £2 a day for threshing and 16/- an acre for ploughing. Outside contractors were also employed at Ufton Farm at Borden in 1887 when men were paid 2/6 for threshing. (37)

Like Mr Chapman's farm, Ufton Farm also used dung, fetched 'from the Quay'. As well as outside contractors around twelve men were employed on the farm. At Michaelmas 1887, Alfred Winchester was hired as Waggoner at 15/- a week, with 10/- a week for board or mate and other items, such as one ton of coals and $2^1/2$ dozen lbs. candles. His mate, Frederick Crackneil, was paid £9 for the year, although this obviously included board, and in addition an allowance of furniture and fittings for his bedroom was specified. Evidence from the ledgers show that the farm produced grain (wheat, barley, oats, maize and beans) and also kept livestock (sheep, ewes, tegs, lambs, rams, hogs, hens) as well as growing apples and cherries.

Another payment made in the accounts of Ufton Farm was 6d a day for a boy to scare the birds. Birds were not only scared by local farmers. Farmer's Clubs paid for flocks of sparrows and starlings to be destroyed. These were not covered by the Wild Birds' Protection Act which came into force in 1873. Certain wild birds, namely game birds were also shot, legally or otherwise, in the marshes in the north of the Hundred. (38)

A final item of interest from the 19th century relates to the effects of industrialisation on the agriculture of the area. In 1884 the local paper had a report of an article in the national journal, 'Gardeners' Chronicle', about a pear wall in the Orchard Lane Nursery Gardens belonging to Mr A J Thomas. It said that the site was formerly a cherry orchard but that had ceased 20 years before when the soil was excavated for brickearth. Since then the ground had been cultivated with 165 pear trees against a brick wall 8 - 12 feet high, (presumably utilising the lower depth of the field after the brickearth was removed). There were a hundred varieties of pear trees and also peach, apple and cherry trees. Mr Thomas also had 100 acres of fruit orchards in Bapchild, Tonge and Rodmersham and supplied London and the Northern markets, including Scotland. (39)

The Rural Parishes of Milton Hundred in the 20th century
As well as supplying the markets in London and elsewhere local fruit sometimes went direct to the consumer. In 1913 there was a report that Sittingbourne cherries had been sent for three years to Buckingham Palace by J T Macey, wholesaler. In an interview in 1992, Mr Goodhew, of Silver Street Farm, Bredgar, spoke of one of the developments which occurred in the

Hundred during the first part of the 20th century, the increase in the production of soft fruits. He said that one of his relatives had started a 'same day' fresh strawberry service to London. His workers would pick the fruit at dawn, it would be boxed, taken to the nearest railway station and would reach Covent Garden in London later the same morning. Apart from the limited increase in the growing of soft fruits, the agricultural community within the Hundred before the Second World War seemed, though, to have changed little since the late 19th century, however changes were on their way. (40)

In 1991 John Jennings of Tonge, a newly-retired farmer, wrote a newspaper article which illustrates one of the major changes which has taken place in the agriculture of the Hundred during the second half of the 20th century. In it he said that during the early 1970s he farmed just over 700 acres and employed nine full time workers. All of the workers lived on, or near, the farm and together with their families amounted to 29 people. In 1945 the same land had supported over 100 people (including the families of workers), whereas in 1991 it provided a living for just one farm worker and his family. The reduction in the numbers of farm workers on this farm in the Hundred can be seen as 'a sign of the times' and as a reflection of increased mechanization, and possibly also of change in land use. (41)

In order to study any changes in land use between the 19th and pre-19th century periods and the late 20th century, a sample of farmers from different parts of the Hundred were interviewed in 1992. In all, the sample of farmers had a total of over 3,300 acres, there were only two farms for which the size was not available, and with them the sample represented around $17^{1/2}\%$ of the acreage of agricultural parishes in the Hundred, based on the figures for parish size obtained from Hasted given in the first part of this chapter.

An analysis of the land use on the various farms showed that it had, with one main exception, changed little since the 19th century, or even the earlier period. Cereals were still the main crop grown, with over 40% of land use devoted mainly to wheat, with some barley. There were differences between the parishes in the north and south of the Hundred, as those growing cereals on the clayey soils to the north of the London to Dover road (the A2), all used a four year rotation system, whereas those in the south did not. The rotation system meant that fields had two years of cereals followed by two years of two different crops (one year each) such as potatoes and beans, beans and rape, or rape and linseed. Although beans had been grown in the Hundred since the 18th century and potatoes since the 19th century, rape and linseed were both 'new' crops. Mr Jennings' article referred to the planting of 'trendy crops such as linseed', and it was in his part of the Hundred that linseed was used as a rotation crop. It was also found in Borden where it was grown on the land of the largest farm, or more correctly, group of farms. The survey showed that many of the farms were part of larger chains, some based outside the Hundred; in fact the two for which no acreage figures were available were part of such a group. (42)

Almost the same amount of land that was used for cereals was devoted to two of the other main aspects of the agriculture of the pre-20th century period, sheep and fruit. Most of the main areas of grassland for sheep were in the north-west of the Hundred, as they had been in the past. One farm in Newington also kept cattle on the grassland during the summer, the cattle were kept indoors during the winter on another farm. Some sheep were kept in the hilly southern parishes, such as Kingsdown, and from observation they were still being kept in orchards. Orchards of top fruit - cherries, apples, pears and plums, were found in most areas of the Hundred, the main exception being the north-east, which had been the main cereal producing area since the pre-19th century period. There were signs though of a decline in the fruit-growing aspect of the agricultural economy, and no mention at all of the soft-fruit grown in the early part of the 20th century. One farmer in Bredgar had only a few acres of cherries left, and they were due to be grubbed out to be replaced by rape and linseed - easier crops to grow for a new generation. He was retiring and passing the business on to his grandsons who had an agricultural machinery business. (43)

Arable crops like rape and linseed certainly require less labour per acre than fruit. One farming group employed three labourers for their 400 acres of cereals, beans and potatoes and yet needed four regular men for their 170 acres of fruit in another parish. This farm, in Rodmersham, had 1,000 tons of cold storage space and packing facilities. The firm employs casual labour, both to pick the fruit and to pack it, in times of recession they can get all the workers they need from Sittingbourne and Milton, but at other times bring in workers from the Medway towns. Gone are the days of workers living on the fields in wooden huts for the season although now some 'tax exiles' travel round in caravans doing a few hours casual work and using names such as Ronald Reagan or Donald Duck!

Gone too are the days of seasonal hop pickers from London. The annual influx of Londoners for the 'season' had continued until well after the Second World War, even in the late 1960s London children were still being sewn into their winter underwear after they had returned from hop-picking. In the 1950s about a third of the 150 adults and 200 children who were engaged in picking hops at Woodstock Farm, the Shell Agricultural Research Station, came from London and they were accommodated in huts on the farm. They were paid $\frac{1}{2}$d per bushel, the hops being tallied (measured out) into six bushel baskets and then packed into pokes (sacks) holding 12 bushels. Good workers who could work at the same pace all day could pick, if the hops were 'good' and not 'leafy', up to one poke (12 bushels) a day. The decline in hop growing in Milton Hundred was the greatest change in the agriculture of the area since the 19th century and none of the farms surveyed grew hops. A tour of the Hundred revealed only a few hop fields, in the area between Rainham and Newington. The tour also showed changes in the orchards in the Hundred, although some old ones with large trees where the fruit would be picked by hand remained, many of the fields had smaller trees more suited to mechanized picking. Apples still continue to be grown, in spite of fears in the 1980s that the import of French apples would threaten local orchards. The Hundred also has its share of the modern form of land use: nature reserves. In the south of the Hundred, Queensdown warren in Hartlip, noted for its rabbits in the 18th century, is now run by the Kent Trust for Nature Conservation and is noted for its orchids, whereas the Royal Society for the Protection of Birds manages conservation sites on the marshes in the north of the Hundred. (44)

A thing of the past, though, is the Sittingbourne Stock Market. A never to be forgotten experience for girls from the Grammar School in Highsted Road in the 1960s was to walk on Mondays past the weighing machine and the cattle in pens when on their way to the 'old' Swimming Baths at the Butts (St Michael's Road)! In 1969 Bensted's firm joined with G W Finn and Son and all that remains of the once weekly market are three sales a year, one for implements and two for sheep. The meadows and stockyards which once stretched from east to west from the Cattle Market, where Roman Road is now, to the junction of Albany Road with Remembrance Avenue at the rear of Bensted's High Street property next to the Baptist Church, are also a distant memory. The matches held by the Sittingbourne Agricultural Society ended during the first part of the century, the Association itself ceasing in 1933 after a 97 year history. (45)

Conclusion
Whatever the reasons for changes during the 20th century in local agriculture, and no doubt many farmers would include Government action, or inaction, in this - in 1970 militant farmers angry at a raw deal from the Government clogged Sittingbourne High Street on a Saturday with slow moving tractors, Milton Hundred reflects 20th century national changes in land use and agricultural trends. The changes in the late 20th century can perhaps only be matched by the change which occurred during the period of enclosures in the early 16th century. London no longer plays the dominant role that it had, even during the first half of the 20th century, and the close relationship between the urban and rural parishes in terms of agriculture has ended. However, the changes have been in production methods and the size of the workforce, not, to any great extent, in what is produced. Some crops have come, and gone, but the area around Sittingbourne is still noted for its production of corn, fruit and wool, as it was in days when Hasted was writing about it in the late 18th century, and as it had been in the late 15th century. (46)

It is with a study of the urban area in that period, and in particular the role of the town in relation to the rural area surrounding it, that the next chapter begins.

Chapter Two

The Urban Area in the Pre-Industrial Period

Introduction

The late 20th century urban area of 'Sittingbourne' was, until the 19th century, mainly farmland surrounding the two distinct, and very different, towns of Sittingbourne and Milton. This chapter will look at the economic history of the two towns in the period from the 15th century to the early 19th century. The emphasis will be on the occupations of the people, not on their way of life, and on the differences between the two urban areas. As this history relies on using original documents, and as the amount available varies from one time to another, it is not possible to consider all of the centuries in the same depth. After setting the scene, with a detailed look at the late 15th and early 16th century, (the early period) the emphasis will be on the changes which occurred in the economies of the two towns from the late 16th to the early 19th century (the later period).

The Early Period: Market and Agricultural Centres

A study of wills from Sittingbourne and Milton in the late 15th and early 16th century shows that both towns were market centres at that time. There are references to 'my tenements next the market place' in the Sittingbourne will of William Cayme in 1491, and to 'five shamels in Middleton market place' in John Colke's will of 1474. Shamel is a term used for a portable stall and in the will of William Maas, who like John Colke was a shipman, there are references to two fish shamels and two tanner shamels. (1)

As market centres the two urban parishes were at the economic heart of the Hundred as a whole with produce from the agricultural parishes coming into the markets. The parishes themselves were also to a large extent agricultural, nearly two-thirds of the occupations mentioned in the wills were related to agriculture. Urban houses, like that of Thomas Martin in 1493, might have a 'garden and orchard', or a 'hive of bees' might be kept. Other local inhabitants had a more direct involvement in agriculture. They included farmers like John Bromfield of Milton, who in 1497 left to his wife Joan 'six horses, nine kine, a bull, 180 ewes, all lambs, a cart and plough, 16 acres of wheat in Bramblefield, four acres of wheat in a little croft at Ore, 12 acres of barley at Bremth, (and) five acres of barley at the Thorn in Sayers field'. His land was in 'Bobbing and Middleton'. Other local farmers had land spread over even more parishes in the Hundred. In 1537 Thomas Wells of Sittingbourne, had 'cattle at Tonge parish and in Cytingborn both sheep and bullocks ... piece of pasture in Murston ... three acres in Baxchild ... (and) wood ground in Warmesell'. Sometimes land ownership extended further, most commonly, as in the case of of William Randolf, to the Isle of Sheppey. There were also the exceptional landowners who had property many miles away. Ralph Chiche, Gent of Milton, for instance, in 1500, not only held property in the town and agricultural land in the Hundred, but also had 'lands in Ivychurch and Brookland in Romney Marsh ... (and the) Manor or Thoreton ... with all woods, rents thereto in the Isle of Thanet. John Pett, in 1551, even had a 'house in Chelmysforth in Essex in Moussant Street'. John Pett also owned a boat; it is the role of the towns as a port and fishing centre that is considered next. (2)

The Early Period: Port and Fishing Centres
Milton Creek served both towns, and each had a role as a port. There are references in the wills to the 'wharf at Holeryche' in Sittingbourne and to the 'wharf called the Key', in Milton. Both these references are found in the wills of substantial landowners, so they may indicate that the wharves were used for the shipping of agricultural produce, almost certainly to London. One of the two references in Sittingbourne wills to ships - 'my part of a certain small navicule' - may support this suggestion. A register of 1566 compiled for the war with Scotland records 29 vessels at Sittingbourne and Milton, the largest being 26 tons. Although most were fishing boats, some were probably coastal trading vessels (navicules). (3)

Of the two towns, though, Milton was the centre of fishing. Of the Milton wills nine, (10%), refer to the ownership of ships or boats. Often they show substantial ownership; for example, in 1512 John Rykman owned 'a boat called "Gods Grace", (with) two dreges, two boats, two ankers ... (and) all nets ... a boat called "Gregorie" with all thereto and a boat called "Lytell Crussyen". The reference in this will, as in others, to 'dreges' together with John Pett's 'dredging boat', indicates that the fishing may have been for oysters which were known in the area in Roman times. This is confirmed by the will of Garrard Johnson, another boat owner, who in 1528 bequeathed 'A wasshe (40 bushels) of oisters at my burying day'. Oysters were found not only in Halstow Creek, as was noted in Chapter One, but also in the Swale estuary to the north of Milton Creek and possibly in Milton Creek itself. Fish caught by the boats which sailed from the Creek were not only sold in Milton market, on the fish shamels already mentioned, but were also taken directly to customers by men like 'Pelham the Ryper' a pedlar, who carried fish for sale in a rip or basket. Fish was also taken directly to London both by land and by water, and the sale of Milton oysters in particular was well established by the 19th century. (See Chapter Four) (4)

The Early Period: Trade and Manufacturing Centres
An important factor, with regard to the differences between Sittingbourne and Milton, was that Sittingbourne was actually on one of the major roads to London, Watling Street, whereas Milton was not. Sittingbourne's origins as a

settlement are directly related to the fording of the London to Dover (and Canterbury) road over the streams that fed Milton Creek - to the west at the junction of Ufton Lane and Cockleshell Walk, the start of the one-way system, and to the east at the Bell Road / Crown Quay Lane junction with the High Street and East Street. The main urban properties in Sittingbourne were located on the hill between the two main streams, and one of the main economic roles of Sittingbourne was to provide accommodation for travellers. These included, not only pilgrims on their way to St. Thomas a Becket's shrine at Canterbury, but also foreign dignitaries and even royalty travelling along the road. In 1518 Cardinal Campeggio stopped at Sittingbourne, 'attended by five hundred horse', and in 1532 Henry VIII paid 'to the wife of the Lyon 4/8'. (5)

Some inns were referred to throughout the period, like the 'George' which was mentioned in William Springett's will of 1478 and in Thomas Norden's will in 1545. There is no clear chain of inheritance between the two men, so it seems likely that the ownership of inns changed quite frequently. None of the owners appeared to be running the inns themselves, most were substantial landowners, like Thomas Garrard, who in 1486 as well as 'the Lion', visited by Henry VIII nearly 50 years later, also owned 'tenements, lands, rents, wood pasture etc in Sidingbourn, Borden, Wormesell, Newyntan, Middleton, Tenham, Doddington ... and all the woods in Tenham, Milsted (and) ... Highsted.' At least some of the agricultural produce from these lands would probably have gone directly to his inn, then one of the largest in the town, rather than to the local market or for export to London. Inns were also owned by people engaged in manufacture, such as Thomas Smithson, shoemaker, who in 1504 owned 'the Crown in Sidyngborne' and Richard Robyn, a smith, who in 1544 owned 'the Bull in Sydingborne'. (6)

There were other references to smiths and to mills in the wills. Milton had a 'wheelwrights shop ... (and) forge with tools', and a Sittingbourne will referred to 'all my tools of the smiths craft'. A Sittingbourne will of 1464 refers to 'Mille Hill beside the Townsend ... (and) the new Melle', and another of 1545 refers to 'Pyriwinkle Mill'. 'Piriwikill' was mentioned in another will in 1499, and in 1545 John Sheppard of Milton referred to 'the lease of my Mill'. Some may have been windmills, however most, like the Pyriwinkle Mill' would have been water mills; a will of 1513 refers to 'the Mill pond', and another of 1497 to the 'Water Mill of Thomas Iden'. It is likely that most of the mills were used to process the grain that was produced in the Hundred. (7)

This was a time when wool was fundamental to the economic wellbeing of England. The Hundred was an area in which sheep were kept; there are references in wills to 'shepherds', 'sheep', and 'ewes and lambs'. There is also a reference to a fulling mill in State Papers of the time, although there is no reference to this process in the wills. The wills do, though, include references to weavers. Some, however, used linen rather than wool. For example, in 1508 Margery Smythson requested that all her 'linen yarn be put to a weaving'. There are also several references to saffron gardens, like that of Thomas Berry, which may have been used as a dye in cloth manufacture as well as for culinary purposes. John Dyne in 1545 styled himself 'weaver', others like William Pykyll in 1530 referred to 'my loom with all thereto'. A closer study of the different manufacturing occupations though reveals differences between the two communities. In Sittingbourne wills there are references to John Shavelock a 'Draper', and to tailors like Thomas Hunte and William Mytar, whereas Milton wills refer to weavers only. Differences between Sittingbourne and Milton show up even more clearly when considering the other manufacturing processes which contributed to their economic life. Unlike Sittingbourne, Milton wills have references to brewing and tanning. Brewing at that time was usually home-based, with larger houses, as well as inns, having their own small brewhouse. However, in 1513 Adrian Martin referred to himself as 'brewer' and in Thomas Bladesmyth's will of 1541 there is a request that 'four brewers' carry him to church, so it seems likely from this that he was himself engaged in brewing. (8)

The references to tanning in Milton wills show that owners of a business were also the operators. In Joane Colyng's will of 1505, she refers to 'the tan house' and to '20 tan tuns with 13 loads of tan'. Her bequests also included 'a dekyr (ten skins) of leather half sole, and one dekyr and half of other leather ready to be sold'. Her son, who inherited the business, said in his will of 1508 that 'the profits of the 13 loads of bark and 20 tuns with all belonging to the craft' should be used to pay his debts. Although in this area tanning was an urban-based manufacturing process it was, as in cities like Lincoln, located apart from the main centres of housing. It was at Chalkwell near the junction of the road from Milton and Watling Street, about a mile from each town centre. There are also references to 'taynters' and to 'the taynter lands' in Milton. Taynters, according to the 'Archaeologia Cantiana', were tenter hooks on which skin or cloth were stretched. There is no evidence for either brewing or tanning in Sittingbourne although the products would have been used there. The inns would no doubt have been the major customers of the brewers, and may also have been the homes of the brewers. There are also several references in the wills to shoemakers such as John Deanes, who would have used the leather produced by the tanners, as would glovers like John West and Edmonde Haywood. (9)

One of the other differences between the two towns was that Sittingbourne seemed to be more concerned with manufacturing the final product, as bought by the consumer, than Milton. In 1538 a candlemaker, Henry Amys, left 'all stuff in my working house ... three pans with chopping knives and other tools to the occupation of my candlemaking'. In 1552 a bow and arrow maker, Lawrence Benett, bequeathed half of his 'tools, timber, feathers and other things of (his) craft called Bowyers craft and fletchers craft' to his brother and the other half to his servant. At that time it was still the law of the land to practice archery each week, and there are references to 'the Butts in Sidyngborn', the butts being the targets used in archery. It is probable that a second bow and arrow maker operated in Sittingbourne, for also in 1552 Richard Cranwell left 'half my tools, half my arrow heads (and) ... all other bows and timber' to his son-in-law as well as making individual bequests of 'half a dozen of my sharfts' to each of three others. In contrast, during this early period, Milton was the main commercial centre of the two. Wills refer to 'shops' as well as houses around the market place, and as early as 1490 'William Mason of Middleton' was described as a merchant. (10)

Milton Court Hall

In this look at the urban area in the 15th and 16th centuries both Sittingbourne and Milton have been seen to be market and manufacturing centres. However there were differences between the two, in particular, the fishing industry was important to Milton whereas inns were important to Sittingbourne's economy. Although much of the land in the parishes of Sittingbourne and Milton was still used for agriculture, the two settlements differed from those in the surrounding rural parishes in having specialist non-agricultural economic functions, and in having areas of concentrated housing. These features are considered fundamental to the existence of any town. Although small in terms of population - according to a survey in the eighth year of Elizabeth I

Sittingbourne had 93 houses and Milton 136 - both Sittingbourne and Milton were thought of as towns by those who made wills in the pre-Elizabethan period. William Pykyll, for example, left to John Row in 1530 his 'house and garden in the town of Syttyngbourne'. Another characteristic of a town of that period can be seen in the political organisation of Milton, where the 15th century Court Hall is still standing. Much more information about the political organisation of Milton and Sittingbourne can be found in the period from 1550 to the early 1800s and it is to a study of the urban parishes during that period that this chapter now turns. (11)

The Later Period: Administrative Centres

It is in terms of the status which comes from fulfilling the role of an administrative centre that Sittingbourne and Milton were very different in the 16th century. This was a period during which many towns, including Sittingbourne, received charters of incorporation. Milton remained though the more important of the two. As the paramount manor of the Hundred, Milton was the judicial and administrative centre of the whole area, including Sittingbourne. Manorial rents were collected on property and land throughout the 18 parishes of the Hundred at the Court Baron held at the Court Hall. At the Court Leet two high constables were appointed annually to administer justice at courts being held every third Thursday. The cells were in the Court Hall; the building also housed a school in the 17th century and marriages were solemnised there during the Commonwealth (the period in the mid-17th century following the Civil War). The administration of the Hundred was organised carefully. Those holding the higher offices were clearly in positions of power and influence and were able to affect the appointment of junior office holders. In 1654-5 Richard Tilden, constable of the West Division of Milton Hundred appeared at the Quarter Sessions held at Maidstone regarding the officers in his Hundred. He requested especially that Thomas Ellis should be chosen for the borough of 'Lucyes' and there was the Court records noted that 'Ellis (was) to be Borsholder'. (12)

As well as being the administrative centre for the Hundred, Milton had its own town administration system, headed by the Portreeve. Elections for this post took place annually on St James' day the electorate being 'the inhabitants of the parish paying church and poors rate'. This office was a very important one as the Portreeve was responsible not only for upholding the law but also 'set the price of all things which came to the quays, or any other creek within the Hundred'. Sittingbourne had no administrative function, and, even after it was incorporated in 1574, Milton remained the more important town. (13)

However, by the 18th century there is evidence from the burial registers of a change in the relative status of the two towns. Milton still had a Portreeve, but otherwise had only clergymen and a clerk, whereas Sittingbourne had a

'Chyrgeon (Surgeon), an Apothecary, two Excise Officers, a Lawyer and an Attorney.' An early 19th century directory confirms this trend, Sittingbourne had 16 'Clergy and Gentlemen' whereas Milton had only four. Two of the three attorneys' firms, three of the four chemists and two of the three surgeons, were in Sittingbourne. In 1763 it was to Sittingbourne that Milton parish officials turned when appointing Edward Shore, Apothecary and Surgeon, to attend poor persons in the workhouse and those poor persons receiving alms in Milton parish. (14)

The Later Period: Market Centres

The charter given to Sittingbourne in 1574, following a visit by Queen Elizabeth I to Grove End Farm, Tunstall, the home of the Cromer family, confirmed its right to hold a market. As has already been shown, both towns had markets during the 15th and early 16th centuries. Apart from Sandwich, Canterbury and Faversham, Sittingbourne and Milton were the only market towns in the rich agricultural area of north-east Kent. Market activity in Sittingbourne seems likely to have increased significantly following the granting of the charter, for within a few years Sir William Cromer, who received part of the tolls from Milton market, objected to the market at Sittingbourne. In 1579 his objections were upheld and a State 'decree of court' revoked the 'grant of a market and fair for the town of Sittingbourne being prejudicial to' that of Milton. The right to hold fairs and a market was reinstated in the town's second charter of 1599 but only the fairs continued. (15)

There were signs, then, that even by the end of the 16th century the economic relationship between Sittingbourne and Milton was beginning to undergo change, with Milton developing its market role and Sittingbourne abandoning its. A number of factors influenced this change. First there was the close proximity of the two centres, at less than a mile apart they were much closer than the normal distance between market centres, the average area around market towns in England and Wales was seven miles, and even in a county like Kent where market towns were numerous they are more commonly ten or more miles apart. The closeness of the centres of Sittingbourne and Milton meant that Sittingbourne residents could easily run stalls in Milton market. This practice continued through to the late 18th century. For example, when the decision was taken in 1800 to move the market stalls from Milton market place to the Clock House it was agreed that 'Mr John Barnes of Sittingbourne, Butcher, (was) to have the use of two stalls in the said Clock House free and clear of any expense other than fitting up the same'. (16)

Another factor which would have played a part in the shift of Sittingbourne's marketing function to Milton was the importance of inns in the economy of Sittingbourne. Their requirements would have been for produce, from grain to meat, in 'bulk', in contrast to the more common small scale needs of households which would be satisfied by a local market. It seems probable that the inns were supplied either directly by local farmers, who might also own the inn, or through a wholesale system. One of the town's jurants (leaders) mentioned in the town's second Charter was an authorised 'badger', a wholesale dealer in farm and dairy produce and other 'dead victuals'. That Sittingbourne was dealing in commodities on a large scale in the 18th century is also clear from the change of use of a property from a small inn to a bakehouse. Given the special requirements of the inns, and the accessibility of Milton's market for the rest of the population, it would seem that Sittingbourne did not 'need' a market as much as other towns of similar size. (17)

The final factor influencing this change in the function of the two towns, was that not only was there no great advantage in holding a market in Sittingbourne, there was also a positive disadvantage. The inns which dominated the town's economy were sited along the High Street which was part of the London to Dover road. It was literally a one-street town, running from West Street along the High Street to East Street. This was ideal for the growth of inns as it allowed for the development of stables and coach houses to the rear. However the width of the road was fairly uniform with only one place where it widened slightly, near the top of the hill between the George and the Bull inns. It is possible that this is where the market would have been located, however, there would only have been room for only a few stalls on this site. Any increase in the size of the market, such as may have occurred following the grant of the first Charter, would have restricted the free movement of traffic along the road. The close proximity to the probable market site of some of the town's main inns would have also meant that increased market activity would have reduced access to the inns themselves. Clearly this would have been a disadvantage for the town's main economic activity. (18)

Meanwhile, Milton continued to grow as a market centre. By the end of the 18th century the market was described as 'a very plentiful one for all sorts of butchers meat, poultry etc'. Sittingbourne abandoned its role as a market town but developed that of 'resting place'. Whatever the reasons for the end of Sittingbourne's market the least important was the legal action of William Cromer, as will be seen, the townsmen of Sittingbourne were more than willing and able to fight for what was important to them. (19)

The Later Period: Sittingbourne, A Coaching Centre
In 1675 Ogilby, in his 'Britannia', described the Dover Road as 'in general a very good and well beaten way chiefly chalky and gravelly and none better provided for conveniency of entertainment, being the most frequented road in England'. The residents of Sittingbourne had throughout the 15th and 16th centuries ensured that the road was maintained in good condition; many of the

wills included bequests for the 'repair of the road'. The town's second Charter of 1599 refers to it as 'receiving and lodging ... (and) providing horses and other necessary things for many right honourable and worthy men, Ambassadors, couriers and their mounted attendants ... (for which it) is most suited ... by its situation, being at a convenient distance from other places'. The Sittingbourne Charter, of 1599, followed action taken by townsmen in 1591 to protect their trade of supplying the needs of travellers. In that year on 'the aucthoritie' of their first Charter given in the 16th year of Elizabeth's reign, they did 'refuze that the victuallers of that town should enter into bond for not killing, eating and uttering of flesh' during Lent. The success of their action in defending the town's economy is clear in that Robert Netter, a butcher, who was one of those 'sent for by warrant to aunswer' objections to their actions, far from being penalized was in fact named as a jurant of the town in the second Charter. (20)

In the 16th century the 71 mile journey from London to the Kent coast took five days. Overnight stops were made at Dartford, 16 miles from London, Rochester after 30 miles, Sittingbourne at 41 miles and Canterbury after 57

The Rose Hotel

miles. The 1599 Charter referred to Sittingbourne as 'a convenient distance from other places'; at this time many small towns were overnight resting places. However by the 18th century it was specifically Sittingbourne's

35

geographical position in relation to London which affected the economy of the town, as a national change in transport to faster stage coaches took place. By then 'the Rochester, Sittingbourne, Ospringe, Canterbury, Dover and Deal Flying Stage Coach', which left London three times a week, did the journey in one and a half days with only one overnight stop. Because of its position, 40 miles from London and 30 from Dover, Sittingbourne was that one overnight stopping place. In 1726 George II travelled directly to Sittingbourne from Hythe 'without making any stay at Canterbury'. Royal patronage of the town was to continue through until the 19th century when the young Princess Victoria stayed at the Rose, described by Hasted as 'perhaps the most supurb of any throughout the kingdom'. (21)

Inns made changes to cope with the growth in coach transport during the 18th century. Whereas in a will of 1707 the Red Lyon had 'stables', by 1780 it also had 'coach houses'. At that time it was both owned and run by James Fordred. This was uncommon, as inns were usually run by tenants; the same inn had been owned earlier in the 18th century by the Barling family but was in the 'tenure or occupation of Thomas Banghurst'. Evidence from the record of licensed victuallers in Sittingbourne during the 18th century shows that there was a high percentage of medium and long term licence holders indicating that the economy of the town supported a fairly large and stable innkeeping fraternity. The licensed innkeepers do not present a full picture of the trade within the town's economy, however. Many others no doubt operated without licences. In the 17th century Widow Sparrow was prosecuted for 'keeping a common tipling house', and in 1610 Roger Tillyarde, a tailor, was brought to court for taking in lodgers who were 'people that work in the same town and sometimes travellers'. (22)

Owners of inns were often, as they had been in the earlier period, local gentry or businessmen. One family, who illustrate the importance of individuals within the economic life of the Hundred, is the Lushingtons who, in the late 17th and early 18th centuries, owned a house in Sittingbourne, together with three manors, three farms, orchards, woods and land in the parishes of Sittingbourne, Milton, Rodmersham, Minster and Thurnham, as well as the Horn Inn and the George in Sittingbourne. The importance of innkeeping to the economy of Sittingbourne continued until the 19th century. A study of the occupations given in the 1650 - 1659 burial register for Sittingbourne shows that the town had much in common with industrial centres as around 40% of the workforce was engaged in occupations which supplied the needs of travellers. One occupation closely linked with innkeeping was, as was the case in the pre-Elizabethan period, that of brewing. Here again another local family rose to prominence. (23)

A plan of a house in 1733 shows it as being between the Lushingtons' George

Inn and and the 'White Hart Inn belonging to Mr Tong' a local brewer. In the 18th century the Tong family owned the White Hart Inn, the Horne, the Ship and the Bull alehouse, but was better known for its role in the town's brewing industry. In 1736 John Tong, who styled himself 'Brewer', built a brewhouse which survived into the 20th century with the family initials and the date 1753 in the brickwork, and in 1768 James Tong the younger, Chandler and Maltster, inherited a malthouse from his father. Although inns and private homes at that time often had their own small malthouse the plan of 'Ye Malthouse at Sittingbourne', shows the large-scale malting and brewing that had developed in Sittingbourne. It was 149 feet long and the estimate in 1753 for taking 'down the working flour end of ye malthouse and new frameing it againe' came to £95/15/0, a substantial sum which indicated the financial commitment of families like the Tongs to the local economy. (24)

Innkeepers themselves also played a significant role in the economic wellbeing of the Hundred. Thus, in 1670 when coins were in short supply Mr Webb, of the George Inn issued halfpenny tokens. Mr Webb was the local postmaster and the position of Sittingbourne on the London to Dover road had led to the town's early involvement with the development of the postal service. Innkeepers who were postmasters dealt with more than just mail. They provided a horse and a guide for the next stage, as well as food and accommodation. The financial rewards of the job were shown by John Peirce who, in 1666, admitted that he had 'sent away a horse and guide' and 'several times had stopped foreigners and strangers who would have otherwise have gone to the posthouse'. Being on the main road to the continent, Sittingbourne may well have been the first overnight stop for foreigners on their way to the capital. Sittingbourne was not though just a stopping place for travellers as collarmakers were included amongst the town's craftsmen, they would have been supplying the carriers who brought in produce to the towns, much of which, as was established in the study of agriculture in Chapter One, would have been shipped to London. It is to a study of the importance of Milton Creek to the town that this chapter now turns. (25)

The Later Period: Milton, A Fishing Port

The growth of Sittingbourne, during the 17th and 18th centuries, into a coaching centre, increased the differences between the two towns. Just as the importance of the position of Sittingbourne on Watling Street, and its location in relation to London, had affected that town's development, so the position of Milton on Milton Creek affected its economic growth. A breakdown into occupation groups based on occupations given in the 18th century burial registers of Sittingbourne and Milton shows that fishing continued to dominate the economy of Milton. Hasted, writing at the end of the 18th century, described Milton as 'for the most part inhabited by sea faring persons, fishermen and oyster dredgers'. Almost all of the fishing-related occupations recorded in the Milton burial registers from 1752 to 1757 were 'dredgermen.' (26)

Oysters known as Milton Natives were, according to Hasted, 'esteemed (the) finest and richest flavoured of any in Europe.' The fishermen or dredgers held the fishery by lease from the owners. The Crown took over ownership from the Abbey of Faversham during the reign of Henry VIII. In the 17th century ownership passed first to Sir Edward Browne and Christopher Favel, then to James Herbert, and by the end of the 19th century to Mrs Ann Herbert and Philip Viscount Wenman. The company of dredgermen, which by 1800 numbered around 140 freemen, was well organised. They appointed their own officers and operated under rules or bye-laws made by ancient custom at the Court Baron of the manor. Like the townsmen of Sittingbourne the Milton oyster dredgermen also had to fight for their trade. During the reign of Queen Anne the fishermen of Rochester and Strood objected to being prevented 'from fishing and dredging for oysters within the Hundred and Manor of Milton'. The rights of the Milton dredgermen were upheld and, as will be seen in the Chapter Four, fishing continued to play a very important part in the economy of the town. (27)

The quays at the head of Milton Creek above Crown Quay were all referred to as 'Milton' quays, even though they were closer to the centre of Sittingbourne than to Milton. A survey in the eighth year of Elizabeth I mentioned 'Holdredge' and 'Crown Key' in Sittingbourne and 'Reynolds', 'Hammond', 'Fluddmill' and 'Whitlocks' quays in Milton, the latter was known as 'Town Quay' by Hasted's time. Milton being the 'head' port meant that all of the records of imports and exports for the Hundred were grouped together under 'Milton', so it is impossible to establish the relative importance to each town of the waterborne trade. However evidence from the 19th century strongly indicates that Milton rather than Sittingbourne was the centre of the shipping trade. (28)

Destinations were mainly to London, the furthest in 1599 being Woodbridge in Suffolk. By the mid-17th century Milton was handling over 10% of the grain shipment from Kent to London. During a six month period in 1700 there were 78 outgoing cargoes, which included 'oats, wheat, malt, hops, wool and copperas.' It was at this time that another influential family was involved in the economy of the area. The Tappendens had a well established hoy business on Milton Creek by 1680. As well as carrying goods they also, as was becoming increasingly common amongst merchants, transmitted cash for well-to-do clients, by the 1700s a credit policy operated and loans-at-interest were made. The family's hoy business was taken over in 1733 and they started the Faversham Bank. Exports of wool from the Hundred increased during the 18th century with 275 tons of wool being exported in 1709 to London, Southampton and Exeter and 490 tons being exported by 1744. Imports were largely of coal from north-east England, such as that on September 20th 'Out of the 'Lily' of Bridlington ... from Sunderland with 15 chaldn's of coalls'.

Hasted also refers to imports of 'iron and consumer goods' as well as pearl-barley which came from Holland. The wood which was to be used in the malthouse in Sittingbourne, according to the contract, was to 'come in a Sittingbourne or Milton Hoy to the Town Quay'. It is not clear whether or not the 'hoy' would have been built locally but ship building was established on the Creek and it is to a study of the other industries found in the two towns from 1550 to the early 1800s that this chapter now turns. (29)

The Later Period: Urban Manufacturing Centres

In spite of the widening gap between the two towns in terms of economic specialisation, both continued as manufacturing centres. According to a report in the 'Kentish Post' in 1729, a coastal hoy, with a capacity of 400 quarter of

Milton Windmill

corn under deck', was built at Milton in that year. Shipbuilding was an industry that developed on both the Milton and Sittingbourne sides of Milton Creek. In the Milton burial register of the 1750s there was a reference to 'a boat builder from Sittingbourne' and in 1799 Sittingbourne fulfilled an order for a ship from Suffolk. Shipbuilding was a new development in the economy of the towns since the pre-Elizabethan period. There were other changes. Weavers survived through the 17th century, but by the 1700s locally-produced

39

wool was being exported to cloth manufacturing areas in other parts of the country. Much of it was stored in Sir John Hale's wool warehouse in Sittingbourne. In 1774 a gang of 30 armed smugglers broke into the warehouse and stole much of the wool which found its way to France. (30) Sittingbourne continued to provide greater numbers of people involved in a wider range of service manufacturers than did Milton. Although there are no references in the burial registers to tanners, some were recorded in the 19th century directories. One entry notes 'Alston David Thomas, Tanner' of Milton; another directory refers to 'an extensive tan yard' at Chalkwell, the same site as that mentioned in the pre-Elizabethan wills. The burial registers include a reference to a miller. According to 'Watermills and Windmills', by W C Finch, there were a number of windmills in the town, including a tarred smock and stage mill half a mile west of St. Michael's Church at the junction of the road to Milton, as well as others at Chalkwell and Milton. (31)

Writing at the end of the 18th century, Hasted described the continuing importance of mills to the economy of the two towns: 'several mills here do not contribute a little to the benefit of this place, four of these are employed in the grinding of corn, and dressing it into flour; and the fifth, called Perrywinckle mill, was some few years ago applied to the manufacturing of pearl barley'. No doubt this mill was on the same site, if not the same building, as the 'Perriwincle' mill mentioned in the earlier period. Periwinkle Mill was a water mill and a 19th century directory refers to 'several large pieces of water used for mill ponds, upon these are mills for grinding corn'. It also says that there was one water mill 'for the making of paper'. There are references in the 18th century Sittingbourne burial registers to a 'widow from the papermill' and to a 'paperman'. This mill would have made use of a fast-running stream which flowed into Milton Creek to the west of Sittingbourne on the boundary with Milton. A paper mill was shown on that site on a map of 1769. (32)

This mill may have been an adaptation of the 16th century fulling mill. Hammers which had been used originally for pounding cloth could be adapted for paper and boardmaking and the papermill may have employed up to 15 men. As with papermaking there were early indications of the development of brickmaking; a brickmaker was recorded in the registers in 1668 and the 18th century customs registers record the importation from London of 'ashes', which were needed to make Kentish stock bricks, used to build or refront 18th century houses and inns like the George. Both papermaking and brickmaking were to become major local industries during the 19th century. (33)

The Pre-Industrial Urban Economy: Conclusion
The period up to the early 19th century had been a time of change for the economies of Sittingbourne and Milton, but that change had come through the

growth of existing sectors of the economy, rather than the introduction of any radically new ones. At the start of the period Sittingbourne and Milton were at the heart of the agricultural economy of the Hundred as a whole, both as a port and as market centres. These functions continued, although they became increasingly centred on Milton. The basis for the development of Sittingbourne as a coaching centre, and Milton as a fishing centre, was in place at the start of the period. For both settlements their geographical location particularly in relation to London, was of prime importance. Although the economic differences between Sittingbourne and Milton had become more apparent, the greatest change in their relationship was social rather than economic. Although in the early 19th century Milton was still the administrative centre and was the larger of the two settlements, Sittingbourne was attracting more of the better class of resident. This trend was to continue. The geology, as well as the geographical position, of the area was beginning to affect the economy, with the beginnings of paper and brick making industries in the urban area and the use of Milton Creek for shipbuilding. These aspects of the urban economy were to transform the two towns from the second half of the 19th century onwards. It is with that later period, and with the dramatic changes which occurred, that the following two chapters are concerned.

Important Events
Finally it is worth mentioning some of the national events which involved Sittingbourne during the period covered by this chapter.

During the reign of Catholic Queen Mary in the 1550s Sir Thomas Wyatt led a Protestant rebellion. Locally he was supported by Sir William Cromer of Tunstall who was attainted and his estates forfeited to the Crown. These were restored by an Act of Parliament during the early years of Elizabeth's reign and he became Sheriff of Kent. Another local man was involved in Wyatts rebellion, Hornden of Sittingbourne assisted the Sheriff in executing prisoners after the rebellion. (34)

In the 17th century the area suffered little during the Civil War, the main battles occurring further north. However shortly before the execution of Charles I in January 1649 there was a Royalist uprising in Kent. In May 1848 Sir Edward and Sir James Hales, from Tunstall, signed a petition which was presented to Parliament. Sir Edward was then chosen as General to lead a Royalist force of 5-6,000 foot soldiers and 1,000 horsemen. They seized magazines and arms and the castles of Dover and Queenborough before marching to Blackheath outside of London. Ten men presented the petition whilst the rest of the force retired to Rochester. After this Sir Edward Hales was replaced as General by the Earl of Norfolk, and he took no further part in the war. (35)

During the period of the Commonwealth when the country was ruled by

Cromwell there were a number of 'suspected persons' living locally, that is Royalists or Catholics. Sir Edward Hales was one of these, as were John Throwling, a Maltster, of Milton and both Robert Barham, Webster, and Paul Graunt, Yeoman, of Sittingbourne. Sir Edward clearly had close links with the Royal family as in 1688 he was the only man to attend King James II when he left London and took the Great Seal of England and threw it into the Thames before staying at Hales House, Tunstall, on his way to Elmley, where he was caught. (36)

Chapter Three

Brickmaking and Allied Industries

Introduction

This chapter is the first of two on the economy of the area from the mid-19th century to the last decade of the 20th century. It concentrates on brickmaking and the allied industries of cement manufacture and boat building. A number of books have been written which deal, in far more detail than is possible here, with the local brick industry and barge building. These include memories of life in the industries and as it has not been possible to talk to any others who worked in the industry no such memories are included here. As far as is possible, this account of the industries seeks to complement the existing works by making use of information from the local newspapers and the 19th century census data not included in them. The first part of this chapter looks at the three industries in the 19th century. This is followed by a description of the strike which happened in the 1890s, then the final part of the chapter charts the changes and gradual decline of each industry during the 20th century. (1)

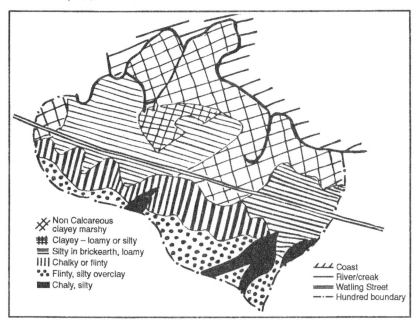

The Geology of the Area

The 19th century: Bricks and Smeed Dean

Traditional Kent bricks dating back to Roman times were red in colour. It was not until the 1740's that 'yellow' stock bricks were made in Kent, using brickearth mixed with ashes and chalk, and buildings in Sittingbourne High Street used locally-made stock bricks in the 18th century. The best brickearths, windblown clays with appreciable amounts of sand and silt, were found in the area around Sittingbourne. The addition of chalk gave the bricks their yellow colour. As the following map shows, there was a belt of clay running east-west through the area, rising from the marshes in the north to a height of around 200 feet just south of Watling Street; south of that the land was chalky. Two of the main raw materials needed to make stock bricks were therefore found in abundance locally. The third ingredient in the brickmaking process was ash, which was ignited during the firing process to 'cook' the brick. This had to be brought into the area and the 18th century customs books of Milton recorded the import of ashes from London. The enormous growth of London in the late 18th and early 19th centuries not only provided a profitable market for local bricks but also produced large quantities of the ashes needed in the brickmaking process. (2)

By 1825 the 'Kentish Gazette' was reporting that 'the speculative rage for the manufacture of bricks occasions considerable bustle where new brickfields are established'. The newspaper report estimated that at any one time 173,000 bricks were being fired in Kent, and that in Faversham a clamp of nearly two million bricks was being built. At Milton, according to the same paper, there was 'a little town of cottages' which had been erected for the workers of the new brickfields, and a quarter mile long rail road had been built from the brickyard to the loading wharf. No evidence of this brickfield is found in the 1841 or 1851 census books for Milton, which contain only a few brickmakers. It is possible that the paper attributed a development to Milton which was, in fact, in Sittingbourne. In 1851 brickmakers and brick labourers were living in Sittingbourne, in the area referred to as the Crown Quay Brickfield. There was also an unnamed brickfield between The Wall, which ran to Milton, and The Butts which was on the south side of the head of the Creek. By 1871 when Henry Packham, of the firm Wills and Packham, was living in West Street as a 'brick manufacturer', the area south of the Creek head was known as the 'Old Brickfield'. (3)

Brickmaking was not only an urban development; brickfields also changed the face of villages like Rainham, Upchurch and Lower Halstow during the second half of the 19th century. The greatest development, however, was in the area stretching from Murston Parish, to the north-east of Sittingbourne, along the eastern banks of the Creek, to the eastern parts of Sittingbourne itself. This was where Smeed Dean, the firm at the heart of the industrial development, was centred.

At the Murston works of Smeed Dean the bricks were stamped, by the end of the 19th century, with the letters S D, standing not only for the firm's name but also, according to a brochure produced for the visit in 1921 of the then Duke of York, for Strength and Durability. The same brochure cited some of the famous London buildings that had used Smeed Dean bricks. These included "The Law Courts, Tower Bridge, King's Cross Station, Westminster Cathedral and Buckingham Palace." By 1921 the firm had an average annual output of around 52 million bricks, and had made over 2,000 million bricks during the 40 years from 1881. That was the year in which the firm's founder George Smeed had died leaving a personal fortune assessed at £160,000. His obituary claimed that 'he made more bricks than any man in the kingdom' and that 'Sittingbourne would not have been anything like its present dimensions and importance ... but for (his) efforts.' Smeed certainly typifies the importance individuals could have for the growth of a local economy. By buying out the leases of small brickmakers in the area to the east of Milton Creek, his firm of Smeed Dean became not only the largest individual manufacturers of bricks in the kingdom, but also, reputedly, the largest in the world. (4)

Smeed employed a large labour force and he also built accommodation for some of them. He built over 200 cottages in the Murston Road area of Sittingbourne, as well as purchasing the freeholds of many houses and shops in Sittingbourne. In the tradition of agricultural workers, those engaged in brick and cement making often lived in tied cottages, this meant that if they left their job they lost their home. Smeed's ownership of land was also extensive and included much of the land to the east of Sittingbourne, from the Manor of Chilton in the south to the Manor of Bayford and the lands extending to the marshes in the north. The farming land was managed by his son-in-law, George H Dean, who was a substantial landowner in his own right. That the modern-day resident or visitor to Sittingbourne is so little aware of the largescale industry that covered a large part of the area during the second half of the 19th century results from the nature of the brickmaking industry. When the brickearth had been removed from Smeed's land the fields were returned to agricultural use as soon as possible so that the land could continue to make a profit. So, unlike many other industries engaged in extracting raw materials from the earth such as coal mining and gravel works, the landscape was not dramatically or permanently affected. The 'scenery' and more importantly the original land use of farming was restored within a few years, the only lasting difference being that the fields were lower. The sides of the road towards Rainham drop six to ten feet in places where the clay was cut out. More recently of course much of the land once used for brickmaking has been built upon.

The 19th century: Brickmaking
Brickmaking in the second half of the 19th century was labour intensive. The occupations of men and boys living in the Murston Road area, according to the 1871 census, give some indication of the nature of the industry. Although many are just noted as brickmakers or brick labourers, some of the specialist jobs are referred to. Brickearth was dug during the winter months. This could be a dangerous job as the ground was undermined - that is, after digging down

men then dug into the side leaving a layer at the surface jutting over them. In February 1859 a man was crushed when engaged in doing this at Mr Huggens' brickfield. The brickearth was then left for 18 months in washbacks, where it was layered with ash and chalk. The census book records one 'temperer', the man who cut and dug the clay from the washback, putting it into a 'pug-mill', where it was mixed. In the early years these were horse driven, but evidence that the pug-mills were driven by steam by 1871 comes from a report in that year, in the 'East Kent Gazette', about an injury to a man who got his foot caught between the frame and the wheels of a steam engine driving pug-mills. (5)

From the pug-mill a piece of mixed clay, the right size for making a brick, was taken to the 'moulder', the most important, and highest paid, of the members of a brickmaking gang. In 1877 when bricks were in high demand Moulders, Setters and Temperers earned an average of 50/- to 60/- a week. The 1871 census book for the Murston Road area recorded 19 moulders, together with three off-bearers, the men who worked with the moulder. Both took it in turns to mould the bricks, while the other loaded the new 'green' bricks onto a wooden pallet. These were pushed by barrow to the drying sheds, known as 'hacking grounds'. Payment was on the basis of the number of bricks made, and there was fierce competition between the five to six member strong brickmaking gangs. Careful records were kept of the numbers made, and the time taken to make them. Records included 40 to 50,000 bricks made in one week in the 1860s, and later, over a million in a season of 25 weeks. Evidence from the Lower Halstow census book of 1881, in which members of the same family, including children as young as 11, are recorded as brickmakers, indicates that this term may have been used by any members of a brickmaking team. In Lower Halstow that year the numbers of 'brickmakers' and 'brick labourers' was similar, (66/75). There are known to have been 12 handberths, where the gangs worked, there at that time, which fits with there being that number of gangs of five or six 'brickmakers' giving the total of 66 brickmakers. This means that on any brickfield the number of 'brick labourers', doing jobs other than making bricks, was likely to the the same or more than the brick makers. (6)

There were, though, other specialist occupations involved in the full brickmaking process. Once they had been dried the 'white' bricks were built by 'crowders', two of whom were noted in the 1871 census, into 'clamps' of up to a million bricks. These were then fired using burning faggots; probably wood from the Hundred. Because the clamps burn unevenly a firing could result in different grades of bricks from the top quality 'Yellow Facings' down to Chuffs, which were useless. Sorting them into the different grades was an important job, and four 'sorters' were recorded in the census. Most of the bricks made in the Sittingbourne were shipped by barge from wharfs and docks, along the estuaries, like Otterham Quay and Halstow dock in the west, and those along Milton Creek, where Smeed's wharfage extended over a mile along the eastern banks. The brick burning clamps were often sited near the barge berths, if they were further away then inclined tramways were used to transport the bricks to the barges, two engine drivers who may have worked on the tramway were included in the census. Gangs of four men loaded the bricks taking a day to load 40,000, there were two 'barge loaders' mentioned living in the Murston Road area in 1871.

The position of Sittingbourne in relation to London, played a fundamental role in the industrial developments which took place during the 19th century. In London and other cities, especially after the repeal of the Brick Tax in 1850, properties of greater height than before were being built. The taller buildings required stronger bricks, a demand that was satisfied by the Kentish stock brick. As London continued to grow, both upwards and outwards, the new houses not only consumed millions of bricks but, with their many fireplaces, also added to the city's already huge problem of refuse disposal. It was the refuse of London which provided the third of the three raw materials needed for the brickmaking process - ash. An advertisement in a local paper of 1889 invited tenders for barges to carry away 'dust, ashes, garbage, refuse and street sweepings' from the parish of Bermondsey for a period of twelve months, the estimated amount 'being 10,000 loads of dust and ashes and 9,000 loads of street sweepings.' An added benefit of these imports from London was that it provided a return cargo for the brick barges, so helping to keep down transportation costs. (7)

It was, however, a dangerous cargo to carry as there was the danger of spontaneous combustion and carbon dioxide fumes were given off by the coke. When it arrived in the Sittingbourne area the refuse was carted to a site and left to smoulder in huge mounds for a year. This gave time for the vegetable matter to rot away before the rest was sorted, usually by women, pensioners and children too young for other work. Of the 145 men living in the Murston Road area of Sittingbourne in 1871, who were recorded as brick labourers, 11 were aged 60 or more, the eldest being 73, they may well have been refuse sorters. The fine ash from the refuse was taken to be mixed with the brickearth and the coke was used to fire the clamps. Anything of value like jewellery went to the moulders as their 'perks', broken glass and china were dumped in areas like Glass Bottle Beach at Lower Halstow and anything that was usable was taken by the poorer brickfield workers who often lived in makeshift huts on the brickfields.

The 19th century: Cement Manufacture

Just as Smeed played a central role in the brickmaking industry, especially in the Sittingbourne and Murston area, so he did in the other two industries which developed there and in Milton. The first of these to be studied is cement manufacture. There is evidence from the Murston and Shortlands Road areas of Sittingbourne, and Murston parish, in 1871 of a number of different occupations associated with this industry. In these areas two cement manufacturers, one cement work's manager, one foreman, a cement miller, two cement burners, one close cell burner, two stokers, one engine driver and 35 cement labourers were recorded.

There were two stages in the development of the cement making industry in Milton Hundred. The first occurred during the first half of the 19th century following the expiration of Joseph Parker's 'Roman' cement patent (taken out in 1796). His method of making cement used septaria stone which was found in clay on the foreshore of the Swale. It was either dug out by hand or dredged out using fishing smacks. It was then burnt, in alternate layers with coal, in a bottle kiln, and after cooling it was crushed into powder in horse mills.

In the 1820s a cement mill was opened at Bayford by Samuel and Charles Cleaver. In 1860, during a thunderstorm, lightning hit the chimney of Cleavers' Cement Works and stripped 30 feet off the top of the chimney. Then in 1866 there was a fatal explosion there when the engine house at the centre of the works, with the Roman cement kilns on one side of it and the grinding mills at the back, was destroyed. In the 1830s John Huggens also owned a cement works at Crown Quay. He was recorded there in 1851 as a merchant, aged 74, living with two servants. There were several cement labourers living in the same area as Huggens, as well as near the Bayford Cement Mill managed by William Johnson. In the 1850s Smeed opened a Roman Cement Mill and then introduced the second stage in the development of the cement making industry by opening a Portland Cement mill near Adelaide Dock. (8)

Although this new cement-making process used the same method as before, the ingredients were different. Coal was eventually replaced by gas coke, a cheaper alternative, following the development of the Sittingbourne Gas Works by Smeed. The gasometer was erected in November 1863 and it provided gas for street lighting and homes. A gas works manager and two gas stokers lived in Murston parish in 1871. The main difference in the ingredients used to make cement was the change from using septaria stone to having a mixture of chalk and mud. The main raw material still came from the local area. Chalk was extracted from pits on Smeed's land, first at East Hall in Murston, and then further south at Highsted. From Highsted, situated on the northern edge of the chalky hills of the North Downs the chalk was dug by hand and was then washed and pumped through pipes to the Murston cement works. This was an environmentally friendly approach according to the 1921 brochure, as it meant the chalk was transported "noiselessly day and night ... without the slightest interference with traffic or damage to roads, which would have been the case had the chalk been surface-borne." However, after the initial outlay on laying the pipe the method would no doubt have been cheaper! (9)

The mud used in the process came from the group of marshy islands known as the Lillies at the mouth of Milton Creek or from the south shore of Elmley Island. Although no mudworkers are included amongst the residents of that part of the Hundred there were a number of mud labourers living in Upchurch in 1881 as well as Henry Waghorn from Dartford who was Manager of the Mudworks. The blue river mud used for cement manufacture was also found around nearby Lower Halstow and they may have been working there and supplying the cement works in Rainham rather than Murston, as there were no cement works in Upchurch itself. The mud and the chalk slurry was mixed in wash mills at the cement works together with water, which was later drained off by sluices in the decanting washbacks. The slurry was dried before being layered with the coal or coke in brick built kilns, possibly by the 'stokers' mentioned in census books. Under the chamber floor was a firing tunnel filled with faggots, (wood from the local area), which were lit to fire the contents of the kiln. After it had been burnt in the kiln the cement clinker that was formed by the firing process was allowed to cool before being raked out and taken to the cement mill where it was ground into powder. Once it had been sieved and graded it was packed into casks, if going to London, or into water- and airtight barrels if going further afield.

Self-sufficiency was an important part of the cement making industry and the 1871 census book for the Murston Road area of Sittingbourne included two coopers and a hoopmaker who may have been employed by the firm to make casks and barrels. Although Smeed had played a key part in the development of cement making in the Hundred, the Murston Cement works did not retain his name for long as by 1869 he had leased it to the firm of Webster and Company, of which he was a partner. Two years later Webster and Company formed a £200,000 capital limited liability company, the Burham Brick, Lime and Cement Company Ltd, of which Smeed was a director until his death. The changes which took place in the ownership of these works, and in the cement industry within the Hundred, will be dealt with later in this chapter.

The 19th century: Boat Building
Smeed's concern with self-sufficiency played a part in his involvement with the third of the industries which developed in Sittingbourne, boat building, particularly barges. In 1857 when the 'Eliza' was launched from his yard the workers there had a day's holiday with a cricket match and supper for 30. It is not known how much it cost to build the barges at that time, but in 1869 when he bought eight of the barges sold after the death of John Huggens they cost a total of £1,340. They were between 25 and 80 years old and only three of them had been built in Sittingbourne. At that time Smeed owned, according to the newspaper report of the auction, 58 vessels. The 1871 census books for the Sittingbourne areas of Murston Road and Shakespeare Street and for Murston parish recorded 14 shipwrights (including apprentices), a blockmaker and a sailmaker as well as many mariners and bargemen. (10)

Smeed was certainly not the only barge owner or builder in the area of Milton Creek. According to the East Kent Gazette of 1857 he owned only around half of the spritsail barge fleet of Milton Creek, which at that time was upwards of a hundred. The dramatic growth of the industry is apparent from the fact that 30 years before there had only been nine barges there. The paper stated that there was probably 'no other creek in the kingdom which (could) boast of a similar amount of traffic.' The size of the Milton Creek fleet continued to grow and Mercantile Navy lists record 190 Milton built vessels in 1872, 343 in 1886 and 410 in 1900. Another firm of shipbuilders was the Taylor family. In 1861 they are recorded in the census books at Crown Quay, the area where Huggens had been in 1851. Stephen Taylor was a barge builder and ropemaker employing 12 men and seven boys, and one of the barges Smeed bought from the Huggen's estate had been built by Taylor in 1846. In the same area lived his son Stephen Jnr, a barge builder and another son John, a ship and boat builder. By 1871 Stephen Jnr and John were still living there, Stephen being a shipwright with 14 employees and John, employing the same number, as a shipbuilder. Stephen's son George was an engine fitter and John's son, Alfred, was a boat builder. Another shipwright, John Gordling, was boarding with Stephen Snr's widow, Charlotte. In 1881 John Taylor and his family were the only surviving branch of the family still there, he was recorded as a shipbuilder employing 12 men and four boys. (11)

Garfield House in Park Road

In 1862 Taylors were building barges for London owners, as was another of the main boat building firms, Shrubsalls. In 1871 Shrubsall was recorded as a shipholder living in Charlotte Street, Milton. Sittingbourne and Milton built barges took part in the annual sailing barge matches on both the Medway and the Thames. In 1864 of the 15 boats in the topsail race from Erith seven were built in Sittingbourne, the highest placed coming second, and the one

Sittingbourne boat entered in the stumpy barge race came first. The brickmaking firm of Wills and Packham had their barges, known as 'Teetotal' barges as they were named after Temperance reformers, built at local yards. Mr Wills had a house built in Park Road with a turret room from which he could watch their barges sailing up the Creek. (12)

The size of boats built on Milton Creek gradually increased during the second half of the 19th century. In 1858 'the well-known ship-yard of Mr Taylor, Crown Quay' launched a cutter of 50 tons. In 1863 the same firm launched a 150 ton barge built for Burleys and in 1871 they launched a 200 ton schooner barge for a London owner. Although barges were the main type of boats built on Milton Creek other, more unusual, craft were sometimes made. In 1881 Taylors built a floating bath surrounded by a deck for changing rooms which was to be stationed near Southend. (13)

The Day Books from the Smeed Dean Barge Yard in the 1890s give an indication of the type of work done in the Milton Creek shipyards. In one year, 1898, agreements were made for two new barges to be built, one for Mr Burley, costing £900, and one costing £850 for Mr Wood. Other barges came in for repairs, some of them like Wakeley's 'Ada' and Mr Knight's 'Our Boy' coming in on more than one occasion. Some repairs were major ones such as those on the 'Dick Turpin' which cost over £300 including £60 for new timber and whale and £25 for deepening the barge. The busiest months were June, July and August with an average of 23 barges being repaired, the winter months of December to February were the slackest time with an average of under ten. Some barges would be in for several weeks with a number of different jobs being done on them whereas others would come in for a single job to be done. Not all jobs were done at the yard though, 3/- was charged for fitting a tiller to the barge 'Conservation' when it was at Halstow. The average charged for repairs was £20 and the total income of the yard for the year including the money for one new barge (the other was to be built the following year) was around £2,300. (14)

The 19th century: Industrial Unrest
By the final decade of the 19th century the three major industries in Sittingbourne, and the local area as a whole at that time, were firmly established. There were a number of medium sized firms, particularly in brickmaking and barge building, but these were dominated by the huge firm of Smeed Dean, with its interconnected business empire of cement manufacture and agriculture, in addition to brickmaking and the operation, as well as the building, of barges. It was in the most important link in the chain of interrelated occupations that industrial trouble occurred.

Apart from an isolated incident in the 1860s, when some of his shipwrights went on strike, Smeed had no trouble with his workforce. Shipwrights were one of the sections of industrial workers, nationally, who were at the forefront in the trade union movement in the second half of the 19th century. The dispute was soon settled by Smeed and there is no evidence of trade union membership amongst his workers, not until 1890. Events in London, in the previous year, had a dramatic effect on many of the area's industrial workers, and their families. Following a strike in the autumn of 1889 the London dockers obtained a pay increase from 5d to 6d an hour. Their success was instrumental in the formation of the 'Society for the protection of Bargemen and Watermen', whose motto was 'Defence, not Defiance'. The shipowners, however, were not to be fooled and quickly formed an association to protect themselves against any possible action. They did not have to wait long, as by the spring of 1890 the bargemen had come out on strike when the owner's association refused to consider their demands for increased freight rates. (15)

The bargemen of Milton Hundred were among the first members of the new union with Unity Lodge Number 2 quickly having between 400 and 500 members, in spite of the 2d a week membership fee. Their grievances are clear from the pages of the local paper, the 'East Kent Gazette', during March of that year. The owners, in the guise of Wills and Packham Ltd, produced figures to show that over a three year period bargemasters were paid an average £1/17/6 per week and mates 18/9. A reply from the bargemen refuted the figures and pointed out that from their gross wages the crews had to pay the hufflers (the extra hand that had to be taken on to negotiate the open span of the Kings Ferry Bridge, linking Sheppey to the mainland, and London bridges), towing and Sunday mooring fees. They also pointed out that tides and poor weather often meant that there were times between freights when no money was earned. (16)

The effect on the local community of the strike by the bargemen was dramatic. The owners of the main brickfields, Smeed Dean and Company Ltd and Wills and Packham Ltd, locked out the brick workers, even though according to a letter to the newspaper 'the brickmasters fully and painfully recognise(d) the ill feeling, suffering and distress which must come through the stoppage of the fields'. The brick workers were locked out because the the owners could not afford to stockpile bricks when no transport was available and the letter blamed the lock-out on the 'high handed and tyrannical action of an unknown power' which had brought the bargemen out on strike. The language of the letter made it clear that officially the owners did not recognise the existence of the barge workers' union - an attitude not conducive to a speedy settlement of the strike. By the end of the second week the strike and lock-out, as the paper of 22nd March reported, had extended 'all down the Kent coast'. Sittingbourne was at the centre of the dispute and on 15th March brickies from Faversham walked in procession to Sittingbourne, being joined on the way by workers from Conyer and then by Murston and Sittingbourne men. A brass band led the 5,000 brickies as they marched along Sittingbourne High Street to attend a meeting addressed by union officials from London. Three days later another local march, 3,000 strong, took place with men carrying banners with slogans such as 'Stick like Bricks'. Solidarity was important as the strike and lock out was certainly causing the 'suffering and distress' predicted by the earlier letter to the paper.

In Sittingbourne a relief committee was organised and soup kitchens were set up by the end of March, although it seems that there was a reluctance amongst the workers to accept poor law relief; the stigma attached to it by decent working people was widespread in the country at that time. During April, although the two sides were as far apart as ever, economic developments in another part of the country started to affect the dispute. The development of brick manufacture in the Peterborough area, using rail transport to London, gave very real cause to fear that important markets for Kent stock bricks would be lost to the Peterborough competition.

The brickfield owners drew up a new list of payments to be made for carrying freight, claiming that it represented a ten percent increase on the old rates, but this was rejected by the bargemen, who said that rather than being an increase it was instead two and a half percent less than they had received before. By the end of April the solidarity of the strikers was in doubt. There was an attempt to break the strike by sailing the Wills and Packham's barges 'Teetotaller' and 'Flora' down the Creek, but they, and Smeed Dean barges, were prevented from leaving by other crews forming a barrier of barges across the Creek. On land the men were less well organised, there were reports of isolated outbreaks of lawlessness and Mr Wragge, for the employers, claimed that bargemen who had not joined the union were being intimidated. Some bargemen did appear in court on charges of intimidation but all were reinstated after the strike was called off on April 28th. The bargemen gave in and accepted the new freight lists drawn up by the owners, and the brickmakers were allowed back into the fields to work. The decision by the bargemen may well have been influenced by fears of job losses, not only amongst local brick workers, but also amongst their own union members, if the brick industry in Milton Hundred were to suffer permanently because of sales lost to brick manufacturers elsewhere in the country. Having started because of events in London the strike ended because of developments further afield.

Brickmaking did, though, continue to dominate the economy of the area during the final decade of the 19th century. 'Kelly's Directory' of 1895 for Sittingbourne and Milton stated that 'the trade here is derived chiefly from the manufacture and transit of bricks and cement (nearly 6,000 hands being employed in these two industries)' - nearly 45 percent of the total population for Sittingbourne in 1891 according to the figures in the same directory. Given the numbers of unemployed women and children who formed the largest percentage of any population it seems likely that the figure of 6,000 hands would have included Murston, and possibly other parishes of the Hundred, as well as those engaged in the allied industries like barge building and sailing. That 'Kelly's Directory' put brick and cement manufacture first in its description of Sittingbourne and Milton, is indicative of the change that had taken place there in the second half of the 19th century. In the 1862 directory the reference to brickmaking being carried on most extensively was almost at the end of the list of other aspects of trade, after 'the transit of passengers, the market, the supply of the neighbouring district, the shipping of corn (and) the import of coals'. Although all of the others continued to be carried on in 1895, as they had done in previous centuries, they had been overshadowed by the industrial developments that had occurred. (17)

The 20th century: Cement and Barges

During the 19th century the local cement industry prospered, sending cement overseas as well as supplying the home market. By the early 1900s, however, overseas countries, especially America, were developing their own cement making facilities and so the local cement works lost those export markets. Nearer to home, Belgium and Germany were also making cement, which they were exporting to Britain. It was a poorer quality but it was cheaper, and home markets were lost to this foreign competition. It was not only the local cement works that suffered at that time, many of the less economic works elsewhere closed and others amalgamated in 1900 to form The Associated Portland Cement Manufacturers (APCM). This firm even in the 'days of great trade combinations (ranked) among the most important' and controlled eighty percent of the total Portland Cement production on the Thames and Medway. (18)

Locally, Smeed Dean's Murston Cement Works, which in the 19th century had been leased to the Burham Brick, Lime and Cement firm (who joined APCM) remained independent until 1924. This was only possible because of the economic way the company was run and because its different, but complementary, activities helped it to survive. In a report on the cement industry in 1901 it was stated that it was not often that bricks and cement were manufactured by the same firm. It was also helped by the fact that Smeed Dean continued to use chamber kilns, built with their own bricks, which meant that the firm did not have the problem of recouping the high capital outlays faced by many other firms which had installed costly rotary kilns. (19)

Changes did take place, however, in the industrial process. The intermittent kilns, which replaced the old bottle kilns, had drying flats above chamber height next to the chimneys to allow hot air from the kiln being fired to be ducted over the wet slurry to dry it. In the late 1920s a change was made from chamber kilns to rotary kilns, after Smeed Dean had joined the remaining major independent cement manufacturers to form the Red Triangle Group. The new kilns were no longer fired by coke, but by coal which came by rail from a colliery near Canterbury. The old steam engine which had powered the mills of the chamber kilns was replaced by a turbine power plant. In 1931 the Red Triangle Group merged with APCM (Blue Circle) who opened up a new quarry at Highsted, using mechanical excavation rather than the old blasting method. APCM brought some of their staff from other works to Murston and some of the local men were made redundant.

The losses in terms of men was not so great, though, as that of the Smeed Dean barge fleet, most of which was sold off. Regular barge traffic to Murston ceased in the mid 1930s, when goods were shipped instead by lighters, and after the 1960s, by lorries. With the end to the use of barges came also the end to boat building on a commercial scale on Milton Creek. Although other boats were built on the Creek, including during the First World War steam vessels for the navy, barges had remained the most important part of the industry. In the late 1960s the Society for Spritsail Barge Research became interested in the Dolphin Yard, then owned by Bourncrete Products. Eventually a barge museum was set up in an old sail loft, and the refitting of old barges took place using one of the docks once used to build Smeed's fleet of barges. In 1971 a boat building firm 'Constructor Marine' started, launching a 39ft trawler the following year. (20)

The Cement Works

In spite of such attempts there was no large-scale revival of the old industry and in the early 1970s cement manufacture itself came to an end. The decision to close was an economic one made outside the area by a large company, for which the Murston works was only a small part of its operation. APCM announced, in November 1970, that they were going to concentrate their cement production at their Northfleet works. The local newspaper reported that over 200 employees at the Murston works would be left without a job and quoted APCM as saying that it was 'with the greatest regret' that the decision had been taken, that they wished to thank 'all employees at Sittingbourne for their loyal service over many years' and that although 'cement manufacture (would) cease on 31 December ... brick manufacture (would) continue'. The following year the 230 feet high chimney of the APCM cement works was demolished, removing a visual reminder of what had been an important local industry. (21)

The 20th century: Brick Manufacture

Just as the expansion of London in the 19th century had led to the growth of the brick industry in the Sittingbourne area, changes which took place in London meant that by the end of the 19th century the heyday of the stock brick industry was over. Locally made bricks were of a high quality, but they were expensive. The new housing trusts and councils building in the London suburbs were not interested in the stock brick's qualities of strength and durability; they wanted cheap bricks, a market quickly filled by imports from Belgium. The pollution in London which had had a chemical effect on the stock brick, making it more durable, had also meant that the buildings were by then blackened and the builders of the new suburbs wanted red facing bricks to set their houses apart from the older areas of the city.

In the face of falling demand and increased competition the price of stock bricks fell, resulting by 1906 in a cut in the pay of brickmakers. Locally the brickowners were also faced with increased costs as the Milton Creek Conservancy charged a levy on goods entering and leaving the Creek. Instead of helping to keep Milton Creek open, as had been the intention when it was created, the Conservancy Board in fact contributed to the demise of Milton Creek as a commercial waterway. The charges levied by the Board were a financial burden, particularly on the smaller firms, and many of them went out of business at that time. This meant that the amount of traffic using the creek declined. The resultant build up of silt and pollution had the effect of narrowing the channel. Smeed Dean, however, with their diverse activities (not relying on brickmaking alone) and their self-sufficiency (using their own barges and combining the export of goods with the import of raw materials on the same ship), were able to survive much longer. To do this changes had to be made. In 1906 a new 'red' brick plant was opened with a 'Monarch' brick-moulding machine, which could make five million bricks a year, and a continuous kiln. Attached to the kiln were drying and tempering rooms where the bricks could be dried, using ducted hot air, so brickmaking was possible all year round. A second one was opened in 1911, the year in which brickfield owners faced strikes, not only from their own men, as happened at Burley's Murston brickfields, but also, and chiefly, from the bargemen.

Bargemen had been hit badly by a slump in the brick trade during the first decade of the new century as their freight rates were fixed in line with the state of the market. In real terms they were earning less than they had in 1890, the year of the previous strike. Action was taken by London and other Thames' dockers and watermen and local union members were forced to follow suit, although they were amongst the last to come out on strike. The unions demanded higher wages and a ten hour day. As the 'East Kent Gazette' reported, not only did they get a ten hour day but the 'settlement ... represent(ed) a substantial gain to the workers amounting in some cases to an increase of 6/- per week, and in others to considerably more.' The 'gains' following the strike though were not beneficial in the long term as the barge industry continued to decline. The bargemen who remained in 1926 went on strike again, with brick and cement workers, for holidays with pay, but they were not successful. The sale in the 1930s of Smeed Dean's fleet of barges heralded the end of an occupation which had played an important part in the town's economy. (22)

Brickmaking lasted longer, although production changes, developed elsewhere, meant a huge reduction in the workforce as increased mechanization was introduced into the area during the 20th century. In 1926 the Lower Field was rebuilt with an automatic brick plant. A new American 'Auto-brik' machine was installed which was said to be the fastest brickmaking plant in the country, producing 10,000 bricks an hour and replacing the need for 11 hand-making gangs. By 1929 there was also a 560 feet long tunnel kiln, through which cars loaded with bricks ran on a railway track. As a new car was loaded it was pushed in one end by a ram and at the same time the last car was pushed out at the other end with the fired bricks. The brick works closed down for most of the Second World War but restarted afterwards. The tunnel kiln was lit in May 1946 and burnt continuously until September 1979, firing over a thousand million bricks. The 1906 'Monarch' berths were closed down in 1965, and as the old auto-plant was closed a new automatic plant opened, where five men could produce the same number of bricks as it would have taken 78 men in the days of handmaking. The raw materials were brought in (by lorry) from further afield; chalk from Swanscombe, moulding sand from Rye and brickearth from the Teynham area, where it was dug mechanically. However the fuel for firing the bricks, the ash, was no longer brought into the Hundred, but was obtained from the piles of refuse that had been brought in from London a century before; no substitute had been found and in the days of central heating fresh supplies were not available. The changes almost amounted to a reversal of the 19th century system whereby all of the raw materials, apart from the ash, had been obtained locally. That brick making continued at all under the circumstances must have been because of the heavy financial investment in mechanized works for making the bricks, which would justify the cost of bringing in the raw materials.

For a time there was a return to an old style of working. When clamp burning was re-introduced in 1979 the clamps were built in the same way as in the 19th century, although they were fired more quickly using natural gas instead of bundles of wood and sorting was still done by hand. The Murston works remained the only brick works owned by APCM until they bought the brickmaking firm of Ottley Bricks. They kept the name of Ottley Bricks for all the fields, including Murston, but the bricks made at Murston continued to be stamped 'SD' for 'Strength and Durability' and found a market wherever those qualities were still important.

Smeed Dean was not the only local brickmaking firm to continue into the second half of the 20th century. In 1950 Wills and Packham celebrated a brickmaking team which had made a million bricks during the season, and ten years later they finally pensioned off the 'Bellfield Thunderer', a steam engine driving an earth-washing machine, which had been in operation for a hundred years. The firm finally closed in 1969 with the loss of 50 jobs. In 1962 10 Downing Street in London was rebuilt with 100,000 hand made stock bricks manufactured in Sittingbourne and for a time during the building boom of the 1980s the golden yellow clamp-fired stock bricks made at Murston were in great demand for use on the prestigious Canary Wharf development in London. To increase production to meet the new demand the firm re-introduced the faster kiln-firing process, sometimes with disastrous results. Bricks made to be clamp burnt had a higher ash - known as 'soil' - content, and when burnt in the kiln they dissolved into a solid green 'mess' which stopped the machinery and meant that the kiln had to be stopped and allowed to cool, for up to a week, before the workers could go in and clean up. Equally bricks prepared for the kiln failed to 'cook' in the clamps. Another problem the firm encountered was that, although bricks made by the two methods looked identical, when placed next to each other in a wall the actual differences in colour were unacceptable to the Canary Wharf developers, and the kiln-fired ones were returned as unusable. By the early 1990s supplies of local brickearth were reported as running low and it seems unlikely that the local brick industry will survive into the 21st century. (23)

Conclusion
This chapter has been concerned with the major industries which changed the face of Sittingbourne during the second half of the 19th century. The decline in Sittingbourne's former economic specialism, innkeeping, was linked, not to the growth of industry, but to changes in transport. By 1858 the railway had come to Sittingbourne. London could be reached in hours and the town's days as an overnight resting place were over. The boom in brickmaking, with the repeal of the brick tax in 1850, came just in time to save the town's economy. Many of the former inns remain in Sittingbourne High Street. The Lion, the Bull and the George are all still operated as pubs or hotels. At street level little remains of the grandest of all, the Rose. It is occupied by a modern Woolworth's store, but above it the 18th century facade remains intact. The same is true for many of the old buildings, for part of Sittingbourne High Street is a conservation area, as is the centre of Milton. Of the brickfields and other industries, though, little remains.

There is a more tangible reminder of the other major industry which developed in the town during the 19th century, becoming the main employer as brickmaking and the other industries declined during the first part of the 20th century, paper manufacture. It is the history of that industry which forms the main part of the next chapter.

Chapter Four

The Paper Industry and The 20th Century Economy

Introduction

The main industry to be considered in this chapter will be paper manufacture. Unlike the brickmaking and boat building industries little has been published about the local papermaking industry. Amongst other sources, use is made of descriptions published in the local newspaper and the memories of a former employee. The section on the paper industry will be followed by a look at the demise of the fishing industry before the chapter concludes with an outline of the general urban economy at the end of the 20th century.

Paper Manufacture: The Early Years (1730s-1850s)

During the 18th century evidence from the local parish registers show that there was a paper mill in Sittingbourne run by the Archer family. According to an inventory of Robert Archer of Sittingbourne, Paper-Maker, dated 1737 there was amongst other items 'In the Paper Mill' at that time: 'Six pair of moulds; one engine; three presses; four ton of hand rags and 70 reams of paper'. Celia Fiennes described the paper making process she saw in a paper mill she visited in Canterbury in the late 17th century. 'The mill is set a-going by the water, and at the same time it pounded the rags to mortar for the paper ... When the substance of the paper is pounded enough, they take it in a great tub, and so with a frame just of the size of the sheets of paper made all of small wire, ... and they lay a frame of wood round the edge, and so dip it into the tub, and what is too thin runs through, then they turn this frame down on a piece of coarse woollen cloth just the size of the paper, and so give a knock of it, and it just falls off; on which they clap another such a piece of woollen cloth ... and so till they have made a large heap, which they by a board on the bottom move to a press, and so lay a board on top, and so let down a great screw and weight on it, ... this ... leaves the paper so firm they may be taken up sheet by sheet, to be thoroughly dried by the wind.' The mill in Sittingbourne was described in 1752 as 'a Paper - Mill, drying Loft, and Rag-house newly rebuilt ... and Five Acres of Meadow Land ... The Mill Bays are newly repaired; and there is always plenty of fine Water, and Water-Carriage within a quarter of a Mile of the Mill.' At that time it had been owned by William Stevens and the mill is shown on a map of 1769. By the early 19th century the mill was owned by Edward Smith. He was aged 52 in 1841 when he was living, with two servants, in Love Lane, Milton. Handmade paper bearing the watermark E Smith 1820, and the Britannia double foolscap mark, found in a local solicitor's office shows that Edward Smith started making paper in his own moulds in that year. Living in the same area as Smith in 1841 there were ten paper makers. Smith continued to make paper until around 1850 when the mill apparently fell into disuse and the 1851 census includes only one 'former papermaker' living in Milton. (1)

It is possible that Smith had tried to move from making paper by hand to machine-made paper using a Fourdrinier machine. These machines were difficult to operate without highly skilled labour and it may account for the suspending of papermaking operations and for the action Smith took in 1858 to protect his 'machines'. In that year, when a new road bridge was built across the head of Milton Creek which 'obstructed the flow of water to the mill and injured the machinery', Smith ordered his men to demolish the bridge. However, the previous year he had objected to the East Kent Railway Bill in Parliament on the grounds that if the line were constructed as proposed then the mill would be rendered useless for the purpose of papermaking because of the the smoke and dust resulting from the railway, which indicates that paper was hand-made as this requires a clean atmosphere. Whatever the reasons, by the 1861 census there is no evidence of papermaking being carried on in Sittingbourne. (2)

Paper Manufacture: Growth and Edward Lloyd (1860s-1880s)
In the 1860s when the Sittingbourne paper mill of Edward Smith was no longer in use, Edward Lloyd was manufacturing paper at a mill at Boxbridge, on the River Lea on the outskirts of London. From the Boxbridge mill he supplied newsprint (the term used for the paper used for newspapers) for his 'Lloyd's Weekly London Newspaper'. By 1863 he had also purchased the Sittingbourne mill as in April of that year the local paper referred to the 'three immense stacks of straw which stand high above Mr Lloyd's premises, formerly used as a paper mill.' It said that the straw was of three kinds and after it had been 'pressed into a smaller compass by hydraulic power on the premises' it would be 'removed to the mill at Bow'. The report also stated that there was 'little probability that the paper mill here will be put into working order and set in operation for some time to come'. In August 1863 the mill was destroyed in a fire and it was not until 1866 that building work started on new, larger mills. These were 'near the site of the old premises, but nearer to the railway line for facility in transit'. This change in location indicates a different type of paper manufacture from that used by Smith who had been so concerned about air pollution from the railway. In 1867 the shafts were about to be erected and it was expected that it would take a further two years for the mill to be completed, at which time it was thought that about 50 tons of paper a week would be manufactured at Sittingbourne compared to the then 36 tons a week made at Lloyd's Bow works. When the mill was completed a member of the Lloyd family may have been in charge of the operation, as in 1871 Edward Lloyd from London and his wife Mareanne, were living in Lloyds Square, close to the paper mill. (Edward Lloyd Senior's eldest son was Frank Lloyd and it was he who took over the business after his father's death.) The operation in 1871 was still only small scale as, apart from Lloyd, who was a Paper Mill Overlooker, there were only six other paper mill workers, one printer and five labourers, found in the census for that year. (3)

By 1881, though, there were signs of a larger scale operation. The census record for the streets closest to the mill in that year is very faint but it has been possible to identify most of the occupations, although not the names of the workers. Amongst the household heads in that area were 11 paper makers and seven paper mill labourers, with two of each living as lodgers. There was also a storekeeper, a nightwatchman, a gatekeeper, three stokers, two engine fitters and two engineers all employed at the 'Paper Mill'. Living further away were another engineer, two more stokers, a mechanic, a female paper sorter, a paper maker's boy and ten other paper mill workers, giving a total of at least 48 workers. (4)

By then Lloyd had purchased the 'Daily Chronicle' newspaper, (1876), and the following year the firm of G & W Bertram of Edinburgh erected at the Sittingbourne mill the largest ever paper-making machine, capable of making 1,300 square feet of paper a minute. The management of the mill was taken over by Mr Frederick Lloyd, Edward's son, and in 1882, when the mill was rebuilt after a fire, and following the transfer of the full papermaking process by Lloyd from his London mill, the local paper reported that the mill was consuming 400 tons of coal and 80 tons of straw a week! Another fire occurred in 1883 during which three to four hundred reels of paper, each having four to five miles of paper, were destroyed. Fires were a constant hazard, especially the huge stockpiles of straw and esparto grass used to make the paper - rags, which had been used to make hand-made paper at the mill had been in short supply from the 1860s and straw and esparto had been found to be efficient substitutes. The esparto grass came from Spain where Lloyd had the right to cut huge areas of land. At one time local brothers, Isaiah and Ebenezer Shrubsall shipped aboard Lloyd's schooner barge, the Emily Lloyd, on a 5,000 mile round trip to the Mediterranean for esparto grass, possibly the barge had been built locally by the Shrubsall family firm. (5)

In 1884 the mill was enlarged. A new boiler house with eight steel boilers was built, as was a 110 feet high chimney. The newspaper report at the time referred to there being, by then, three large papermaking machines at the mill. In 1888 further improvements were made with the addition of a powerful horizontal engine, two steam travelling cranes and a new papermaking machine. The paper mill continued to increase its workforce during the 1880s. By the 1891 census there were over 140 employees. The different occupations illustrate the paper making process. The raw materials were pulped and other ingredients were added to colour the paper by 'bleachers'. (In 1889 during a fire 200 barrels of resin and 300 barrels of bleach powder were nearly destroyed.) The pulp was then pumped, using steam engines operated by 'furnace stokers' and 'engineers', to the paper making machines. There 'machine men', the highest paid workers, controlled the flow onto a wire mesh. When it reached the end of the wire the paper passed onto wet felts, kept level by a 'press boy'. After this the wet paper was dried by 'dryers', before reaching the 'reeler man'. It was the reeler man's job to cut and label the paper, and a 'reeler boy' had the often dangerous job of collecting the off-cuts from under the working machine, these were then taken to be pulped with the new raw materials. It was not the only dangerous job, in 1884 George Cheeseman, a 15 year old 'dryer-boy', had his arm torn off when it was drawn between the cylinder and the felt rolls as he tried to catch some broken paper. The newspaper noted that this was not his job, but rather the 'dryer man's'. The census also records paper 'sorters', a number of 'clerks', numerous 'labourers' and at 'Paper Mill House' in Milton, the Paper Mill Manager, Thomas E Wenson. (6)

Sittingbourne Paper Mill

In 1890 Lloyds had become a Limited Liability Company with a capital of £250,000 and in 1892 a new mill, within what was now a substantial complex of buildings on the site, was formally opened. The architecture of the new mill was described as being in the Queen Anne style. The main building, approached by a bridge over the water reservoir, was 262 feet long and 156 feet wide. There was a separate boiler house, about 80 feet square, housing five boilers, with room for a sixth, which was at the base of a towering 170 feet high chimney. In the engine room there was a 650 horse power horizontal compound condensing engine which supplied the power, transmitted by a huge fly-wheel of 20 feet in width driving 32 ropes, to the beater and potching sheds and to the finishing house. The bleaching and sizing departments were housed above the engine room and at the end of it was the main pump for supplying water to the various parts of the mill from the reservoir, which was fed by natural springs. Close to the pump were two dynamos used to supply electric light, which superseded the gaslight used in the old mill, however the glazed sections of the roof also provided good natural light. Underneath the beating and potching house was the edge runner department for the grinding up of the material. There were four edge runners there, each consisting of two huge granite cylinders which revolved upon a third, stationary, cylinder. Each of these machines weighed from 18 to 10 tons. The ground material was taken by hydraulic lifts to another department before going to the machines. When the new mill was opened two machines, 118 and 106 inches wide had been installed, and provision had been made for six more. In fact every building had provision for it to be increased in size in the future. From the machine room the paper passed to the finishing house where it was trimmed before being sent off on the giant reels. The new mill was responsible for about a third of the 300 tons of paper a week produced by the Paper Mill as a whole. The report also noted that upwards of 700 tons of coal was being consumed each week at the works, and that between 500 and 600 hands were employed there with newsprint being sent to Australia and to the West Coast of Africa. (7)

Inside Lloyd's 'Daily Chronicle Mill'

Paper Manufacture: Expansion (1890s-1920s)
Unlike the brick and cement industries, which had faced problems in the early years of the 20th century, the paper industry entered a period of growth. This was due in no small measure to the efforts of Edward Lloyd and his son Frank Lloyd, who were at the forefront of new developments in the industry. In the 1890s, following the rebuilding of the mill at Sittingbourne they installed what

was, at that time, the widest machine in England, with a web of 123 inches. It was also the fastest then being used and had an output of 50 tons a week. The cost of the raw materials used to make the paper was, according to account books, between £8 and £10 a ton. Lloyd was always concerned to secure supplies of raw materials and he bought estates in southern Spain and Algeria, with the right to take esparto grass from large areas of land. He was also one of the first to take up the use of wood pulp as a raw material for making paper and purchased a pulp mill in Norway. In 1889 the 'British Colonial Printer and Stationer' produced a supplement which included an engraving which gave a view of each department at Lloyd's 'Daily Chronicle Mill'. (8)

In spite of a major fire in May 1900 by 1902 there were eleven machines at the Sittingbourne mill, the largest (No. 11) had a 'wire' 126 inches wide and 55 feet long producing paper at 550 feet a minute. The price of paper was increasing during the early years of the new century, which was a problem for owners of new newspapers, like Mr Pearson who started the 'Daily Express' in 1900. He considered himself to be lucky, as he was able to buy his 'paper from Mr Frank Lloyd, the only papermaker in the whole world who would enter into a contract to supply (him) with the quantity that (he) wanted at any price'. Lloyd not only supplied his competitors with newsprint but also, according to a report in 1902 of a visit to the Sittingbourne mill, with 'every item ... which is wanted in a printing works, from a rotary machine to cotton waste'. Like Smeed, Lloyd seemed to have a policy of diversification, while still remaining within the overall field of paper manufacture. (9)

As it had been in the 19th century, with the introduction of new raw materials, in the 20th century Lloyds was at the forefront of new developments. Two of its employees, Mr Charles Martin, the mill superintendent, and the chief engineer, Mr Hutchinson, found that by sloping the wire table on which the paper was made the machine could produce good paper at greater speeds. Mr Martin told the American manufacturers of the machines about his innovation and they modified some of their machines. The idea was later patented by a man named Eibel, and he commenced a High Court action against Lloyds for infringing it. In 1911 Frank Lloyd successfully defended the firm, proving that they were using modified machines before Eibel had taken out his patent.

Details of Lloyd's Mill at Sittingbourne were of national interest to papermakers and in 1909 there was a report in a trade journal about the mill. According to this there were 12 papermaking machines, including two machines in No 3 mill 170 inches and 156 inches wide, with the total capacity to make 2,000 tons of paper a week. The mill had a workforce of 1,200 and used 2,000 tons of coal and 2,500 tons of wood pulp every week. Wood pulp, instead of straw and esparto as the raw material for paper manufacture at the mill, was certainly in use the previous year when the local paper reported the arrival of 5,000 tons of wood pulp on a steel steamer. The size of the machines at the mill continued to increase and in 1910 No 15 and No 16 machines were installed, both 175 inches wide and producing paper at 650 feet a minute. The following year United Newspapers Ltd, with Edward Lloyd as Director, was formed to buy Lloyd's newspapers, so keeping them separate from his papermaking business. In the same year Edward Lloyd Ltd was formed with paper mills at Sittingbourne, the largest in the world, pulp mills and a paper mill for making tissue paper in Norway, a London based wholesale and export paper business with branches in Montreal, Melbourne, Cape Town, Buenos Aires and Yokohama and a fleet of barges and lighters. The capital of the new company was £1,270,000 and it was the biggest concern in papermaking the industry had ever seen. (10)

Before the First World War, production at Sittingbourne increased further until there were 17 machines and Lloyd started building a dock for ocean-going vessels at Ridham, on the Swale estuary north of Milton. It was linked to the Sittingbourne mill with a light gauge steam railway. According to a report in the paper the new viaduct, constructed of reinforced concrete, was 2,805 feet long. There was a bridge over The Wall, then it went over Flushing Street, Milton Creek and King Street before curving to cross Gas Road. It then ran parallel to Gas Road, bent left and crossed Cooks Lane and the tramway of Wills and Packham before running straight for 707 feet. (11)

At the mill, during the war, according to a Sittingbourne resident whose mother worked there, canvas haversacks were made for soldiers. After the war, in 1918, Frank Lloyd, who had taken over the firm after the death of his father in 1890, sold off the newspapers and concentrated on papermaking. The papers were sold to United Newspapers and part of the contract was that they would buy all of their newsprint from Lloyds for 30 years from 1920. (12)

The increased production which occurred at the mill in the first part of the 20th century was aided by the geology of the area. When the flow of water from the stream which led into Milton Creek became insufficient, the fresh water needed for the production of paper at the mill was piped from the Meads to the west of Milton and wells were bored into the subterranean reservoir which ran under that part of Sittingbourne. After this the original stream which had flowed along Cockleshell Walk (opposite Ufton Lane), and provided Smith's old mill with its water in the first half of the 19th century, dried up. Once the water had been used in the papermaking process it flowed into the Creek, taking with it paper and other waste from the mill, including, according to Mr Dane who worked in the mill in the 1920s, the acids used to clean the wires. In spite of this, he remembered going home one day with his hair plastered with pulp after swimming in the Creek.

As a First Aid man for the mill he was often called away from his job to deal with accidents, some of which were dealt with at the Memorial Hospital in Bell Road, Sittingbourne, built by Lloyds for their workers, who paid 1d a week into the firm's medical scheme - this rose to 3d a week after the Second World War according to Mr Potts, a boilerman in the mill at that time. Mr Dane left the mill to join the Fire Service during the war and never returned to it. As a First Aid man he had had to be free to attend emergencies and so had been moved round on different jobs and had never had the opportunity to work his way up to the better paid jobs. Others who had started like him as Reeler-boys would have been able to move on to be a Second-boy on a machine, then a First-boy, before being a Press-boy or Machine-man.

Kemsley Paper Mill

In the 1920s there was a shortage of wood pulp and an increased demand for paper which meant that the cost of paper rapidly increased. In spite of the introduction of a three shift system at the mill during 1919 demand for paper exceeded the capacity of the Sittingbourne mill. With no room to expand on the site in 1923 Lloyd started to build a new mill at Kemsley, north of Milton. This was in operation by 1924. The Mill faced south and was 330 feet wide, 800 feet long and 54 feet high. It was a steel, concrete and brick structure - the bricks having been made locally. On one side of the main entrance was the grinder house which was to be linked to Ridham Dock by an aerial steel ropeway transporting the logs for grinding. When this was completed the following year it was the first in England to grind imported timber. On the other side was the Shredder and Potcher House and surmounting the main entrance was a massive brick tower. The main engine in the Power House, capable of 3,000 horse power, not only powered the papermaking machines and the dynamos but also provided steam for the drying process. The Boiler House contained four boilers with plans for ten in all. The coal was conveyed on an endless cable from the coal store below into the furnaces which was mechanically operated, so there was continuous feeding of the fires and only three or four men were needed to look after the whole operation. The coal itself was transported to the Boiler House in trucks drawn by a locomotive itself powered by steam from the boilers - one charge lasting three to four hours. Bales of pulp from Ridham Dock were lifted by a three-ton crane into the Shredder House. From there it passed into the Potcher Floor where each machine had three potchers and three refiners. The liquid pulp then passed into the machine room, the largest machine room for two papermaking machines in the world. (13)

The two machines, 225 inches wide and capable of running at a speed of 900 feet per minute or more in full operation, were the largest in the country. The machines ran almost the whole length of the room with 40 drying cylinders, each five feet in diameter. The Pope reel at the end, onto which the paper was wound, was the first one to be used in England. From the Machine Room the reels of paper were taken to the Paper Store which was capable of holding up to 2,000 tons of paper before it was shipped from Ridham Dock to London or abroad. There were also Stores, an Engineering Shop, a Carpenters' and Joiners' Shop as well as facilities for the use of employees such as lavatories, showers and baths. The water used at Kemsley Mill was pumped from the Meads at Milton, where it had been found using a water diviner, and it was stored in three large concrete ponds, converted from washbacks which remained from the days when brickmaking was carried on on the site, before going to the water tank in the 70 foot high Water Tower over the main

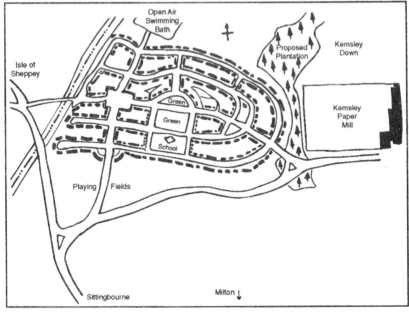

Kemsley Garden Village

68

building. By 1927 when Frank Lloyd died, a third giant machine was being built at Kemsley and a large boiler and generating plant had been completed. The two mills were employing about 2,000 and many, like George Bellingham Junior (my uncle), had moved with their families into the garden village that had been built there.

Frank Lloyd had clearly been influenced by developments in other parts of the country, like Port Sunlight and the new garden towns. The village was designed to house 3,500 and 188 of the planned 750 houses had been built by the summer of 1927. The benefits of the site was made clear in a publicity pamphlet and it is still separated by farm land from the mill. 'The houses (were) of several different designs and (were) grouped in pairs and blocks of three, four, eight and nine. Great care was 'taken to secure a maximum amount of sunlight' and 'the convenience of the housewife' was of 'paramount consideration in the selection and arrangement of all the fittings'. There were 'four grades adapted to the requirements of the different classes of tenants. The accommodation in the first three grades included a kitchen-living room, scullery, parlour and three bedrooms, with an upstairs bathroom and the usual offices, while the fourth grade had in addition a separate kitchen and an additional bedroom.' (14)

Paper Manufacture: Change (1930s-1950s)
Following the death of Frank Lloyd the business was sold to the Berrys, who owned Allied Newspapers and had bought Lloyd's newspapers in 1918, and for whom the mills supplied paper. Sir William Berry told his shareholders that the Sittingbourne and Kemsley plant was the largest in the country and 'larger than any in Canada or USA' with an output 'of 200,000 tons of newsprint a year'. Expansion continued with more machines, including in 1933 the largest in the world at 320 inches wide and making 1,000 tons of paper a week, a new power plant, groundwork mill and building-board machines being built at Kemsley. By 1936 when the mills, which during the intervening ten years had retained the name of Lloyds, amalgamated with Bowaters they were together employing 3,000 and producing 6,500 tons a week. At the time of the take-over Lloyds was the larger company and local workers thought that they were taking over Bowaters, rather than the other way round. Together Bowater Lloyd were at that time the largest newsprint enterprise in Europe with a combined annual output of over half a million tons of newsprint, over 60% of the total manufactured in Great Britain. (15)

During the Second World War production of paper was affected by external restrictions on the quantity of newsprint which could be produced and only the Kemsley mill continued to produce it. At Sittingbourne other papermaking continued, developing products which had been made there before the war, including Kraft. Between 1935 and 1940 Lloyds had supplied 75% of the Kraft liner for a firm of corrugated paper and box manufacturers (which they eventually took over in 1944). During the war, using a workforce increasingly made up of women, the main product at Sittingbourne was containers for war stores, chiefly gun ammunition, made from Kraft liner boards. The containers had two layers of smooth paper with a layer of corrugated paper in between. The first contract for containers for 4.5 inch shells was made in the summer of 1938, and by summer 1945 Bowaters had made 10,542,577 containers and other items from Kraft liner board, including 982,270 containers for 3.7 inch anti-aircraft shells, 8,324,612 for 40mm Bofors ammunition together with 42,599 'Jettison Fuel Tanks'. The latter were made in engineering works at the Kemsley mill and at other firms, the development work having been done by Bowaters. It may have been this armaments work which led to the bombing of Kemsley mill (and village) during the war; some damage was done to the mill, and even more to the village, but many bombs fell harmlessly into the surrounding marshes. (16)

Although in 1948 Bowaters secured a contract to supply newsprint to the United States, following the war there were fears of unemployment at Sittingbourne, which led to the development there of a Waxwrap department and eventually to Flexible packaging. At Kemsley, insulating board manufacturing developed, the straw pulping equipment there was extended, and a bleaching system was incorporated. In 1954 building work started on a new power station and No 6 machine, and in 1955 a report into the town's industry showed that Bowaters were the largest employer, having nearly 5,000 employees of whom around 10% were women, with average wages of £12 a week. In the early 1960s there were difficulties at the mills when the first union trouble interfered with maintenance by preventing weekend work and then machines had to be closed when demand for newsprint was weak. In spite of this in 1961 the labour turnover at Kemsley and Sittingbourne was only 12% compared to 30% at Bowaters' Thames works and 35% at their Mersey plant. (17)

Paper Manufacture: Industrial Pollution
In the 19th century the early complaints about pollution from the mill were concerned with what came out from its chimneys. Apart from the pollution which must have resulted from the numerous fires at the mill, in 1878 the local paper received a letter of complaint about the smoke, fine ashes and sulphuric fumes from the mill. Then in 1892 Milton residents petitioned the mill about the smoke nuisance, the mill put this down to their having to use inferior coal during the coal crisis in the north. In 1895 there was another petition, this time about the foul smell from the Creek during hot weather. Although the Milton Creek Conservancy was set up the 'Smell' did not go away. In 1952 there were complaints about the smell, which resembled that of bad eggs, from the Creek when the tide was low and the wind in the east, something which usually occurred in the evenings. In the mid-1960s there was a big campaign to banish 'The Smell', which included tackling air pollution as the Creek was not thought to be the only cause. In 1974 a survey by P M Bailey of pollution in Milton Creek was a winner in a National Environment Competition. The

report stated that it was the worst polluted area, not only in Kent, but in the south of England. The increase in noticeable pollution was related to the decline in the use of the Creek by marine traffic: that is after barges stopped using it, both those carrying cement and bricks, and those bringing in raw materials for the mill which were not required after Ridham Dock was built. With less use, and no fast flowing stream, the mill having taken the water from it, Milton Creek started to silt up. (19)

According to information from Bowaters at that time, the Sittingbourne mill produced 35,000 gallons of water, with its impurities, per hour. The amount of cellulose fibre was being reduced, due to public pressure, and by 1973 fibre loss was down to less than 1% from the Sittingbourne mill, 3% was common elsewhere. There were however other constituents discharged with the water which could include clay, dyes and acid, depending on the type of paper produced. Pollution from the mill was obviously at its greatest in the upper reaches of the Creek where no marine life survived. It was described as varying in colour from white, through pink to green, to a nondescript colour, 'best described as a mixture of chalk, sump-oil and grease.'

Before the Creek was dredged, layers of pollutants up to six inches deep built up on areas of the Creek bed which were only covered by spring tides, these layers looked and felt like cardboard. Suspended solids were also deposited along the sides of the Creek, especially at bends, so building up the banks and encroaching on the main channel. Areas constantly washed by the tides quickly became coated in a thick greasy deposit which was corrosive, ropes made of natural fibre rotting, sometimes in a matter of weeks. From before the war, efforts were made by the mill to filter the water so as to retain as much fibre as possible for re-use. In the face of increased public pressure in the 1960s, Bowaters, in 1971, installed a Flocculating Clarifier which used chemicals to thicken the solids in the effluent so that the resultant sludge could be removed and so prevented from entering the Creek. Certainly the Creek improved over the 20 years from then; no longer were those entering the area hit by the once characteristic smell.

Accidents, however, can still happen and in August 1991 a fine of £4,000 was imposed after waste was discharged in November 1990, at 'more than 10 times the legal limit'. This followed 'unforeseen problems with new machinery and a breakdown of facilities.' According to a report in the local paper in 1991, the company had spent '£4 million in recent years, including £2 million in the last two years to meet new European Community targets which would come into force in 1993' to prevent pollution. In 1994 it was announced by the National Rivers Authority that a new waste treatment works at Kemsley Mill, which would receive effluent by pipe from Sittingbourne, would ensure that Milton Creek was cleaner than ever. (20)

Paper Manufacture: The Final Decades of the 20th century (1960s-1990s)
In the 1960s, following the drop in demand for newsprint, the Sittingbourne

Mill specialised in coated papers. In 1967 history was made by a new regular rail freight service bringing liquid china clay in bulk from English China Clay's plant in Cornwall to the Sittingbourne mill where it was used to coat the paper needed for illustrated/colour productions. However in the same year more mill workers lost their jobs when another machine closed down, leaving only four working at Sittingbourne. In 1973 Bowaters introduced a computer system, the most advanced in paper making in the world at that time. Then in 1977 the company announced plans to develop and modernise the Sittingbourne and Milton mills. In 1980 though, in spite of a £2½ million project to protect the future of Sittingbourne mill there were layoffs because of lack of orders and the workforce had fallen to 800. (21)

In the late 1980s Bowaters sold the Sittingbourne and Kemsley mills to a New Zealand firm, Fletcher Challenge. The old mill being occupied by the Sittingbourne Paper Company, part of UK Paper. Pulp for the mill still comes from many different countries, lorries bringing in bales produced in Finland, Spain and America. In 1991 the local newspaper quoted Mr Rundell, on behalf of the Sittingbourne Paper Company, as saying that 'the company was in the process of installing a massive high cost new papermaking plant'. It looked as though paper manufacture in Sittingbourne, unlike the other main industries of the past 150 years, would survive into the 21st century. However by May 1992, the national, and international, recession was affecting the paper industry, and the parent company of Fletcher Challenge was experiencing difficulties. As a result plans were announced to close a packaging paper machine at Sittingbourne mill, which produced 50,000 tons a year, with the loss of about 100 jobs. In spite of improvements at Kemsley, including in 1994 a revolutionary new multi-million-pound machine capable of using any recycled paper products as a raw material, the future, of what was still the largest single employer of labour in the town in the 1990s, was looking less secure. The role of the paper mill in the economy of the urban area as a whole, had, though, declined and Sittingbourne was far from being a one industry town as the final section of this chapter will demonstrate. (22)

Oyster Fishing
In 1951 when the last surviving Milton oyster fishermen were interviewed by the local paper they blamed pollution and the effect on the water in Milton Creek with the building of the paper mills for the loss of the local oyster fishing industry. As has already been shown the mill certainly did pollute the water. However the report also said that in 1926 the oyster bed in Standgate Creek was found to be polluted and there was no question of blaming the paper mill for that. It is more likely that the pollution affecting oysters in the Swale came from sewage effluent, as was found to be the case in 1915, when an investigation followed cases of infection resulting from the consumption of shellfish from that area between the mouth of Milton Creek and Conyer Creek. The Redshaw brothers spoke, in 1951, of remembering their father going out with the rest of the fishermen in the early part of the 20th century and one of

them said that "... there used to be 40 boats in the Creek all making a living from some sort of fishing. The oyster bed here used to be one of the best in the country ...". They also said that before the First World War "the fishing was so good they could go out dredging for oysters in the summer and take it easy for the rest of the year". This may indicate a cause, other than pollution, for the decline in the industry. As long ago as 1876, when the House of Commons were investigating the scarcity of oysters, representatives of a local firm, Alstons, blamed overdredging and agreed to a closed time with no dredging in the summer months. The local fishing industry was often threatened during the second half of the 19th century, even before the building of the paper mill. In 1859 men from Strood were charged with unlawfully dredging for oysters in the area. The report of the incident described the fishing ground as being marked out by buoys painted black, inside the area there were buoys of different colours according to the kind of oyster in that area. In 1864 there were fears that the Herne Bay Oyster Fishery Bill would have the effect of putting 70 to 80 people in Milton out of work - the local fishermen did not only fish the local oyster grounds. (23)

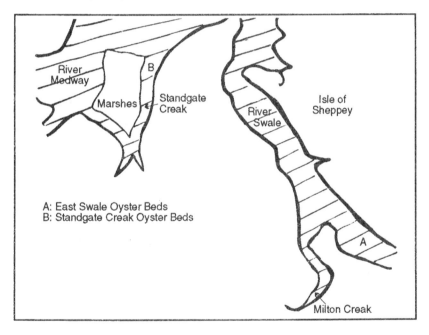

Local Oyster Grounds

At that time oyster fishing was still a major local industry. In the opening section of the local Directory, before any mention even of brickmaking, comes 'the dredging for oysters in the Swale. The free dredgers were incorporated as a company ... the produce is sent to the London market, and employs a whole fleet of smacks and hoys.' A Victorian pot lid showing Ye Old London Cries had one for 'Buy my fine Milton oysters.' Entries in the 1862 Directory include John Hills and Son, Oyster merchants with premises in Milton and London, who had oyster grounds in the East Swale, and James Hodges, foreman to Alston's oyster grounds at Standgate Creek. Ted Bingham remembered both firms being there in the 1870s. He said that fishermen exchanged oysters for eggs with local farmers, so that both had a change of diet, it was called 'dressing the hat'. Local fishermen also caught flounders, mussels, sprats and 'five-fingers' (starfish). The latter was the natural enemy of the oyster and it was important to keep them out of the oyster beds, they were sold to local farmers as manure. Oysters were also at risk from being killed by sand or mud accumulating above them. It is possible that the paper mill did affect the oyster beds in this way, first with the increase of silt in the Creek and then the end of a fresh water input as local streams had finally dried up in the 1950s. (24)

The 1870s saw changes in the local oyster industry. In 1872 The Import Fish and Oyster Company Ltd was formed. They imported young oysters from North America in a steamship which docked at Sheerness. The young oysters were then fattened in beds in the Swale known as the East Grounds, formerly rented by Messrs Hills and Son of Milton. In 1877 350 tons of oysters from Portugal were brought to the Milton beds for fattening. In 1881 there was an advertisement in the local paper for the Milton Fisheries which the Anglo-Portuguese Oyster Fisheries Company had leased the East Grounds from Kings Ferry to Faversham for 21 years with the right to all oysters, mussels, periwinkles, cockles and other fish. The following year when the oyster fisheries were restocked the local paper hoped that oysters would become plentiful and cheap again rather than a luxury as they had become by that time. By 1887 the firm of Hole and Dodd had taken over the oyster beds in Standgate Creek from Alston, with James Hodges as their manager. In the 1895 Directory the introduction to Milton noted that 'the oyster fishery used to be carried on here'. Clearly by then the industry was in decline and although it continued into the 20th century its importance as a main source of employment in the town had ended. (25)

Other Sections of the Urban Economy
Although the industries dealt with in detail in this and the previous chapter provided employment for the majority of the working population during the late 19th and early 20th centuries, other smaller-scale businesses flourished. There was an advertisement in 1859 for the Sittingbourne Brewery which produced Payne's Fine Ales, Bitter Beer, London Porter and Stout. In 1905 the Sittingbourne Steam Brewery, which had been established in the reign of James I, was sold by Vallance to Style and Winch. In Milton the Milton Mineral Works were established in 1869. An advertisement in 1900 catalogued their products as: Soda Water; Lithia Water; Potassium Water; Seltser Water; Lemonade; Zoedone; Ginger Beer; Hop Ale; Orange Champagne and Hop Champagne. (26)

Less pleasant products were made at the Murston Chemical works of Couper and Somerville, close to Smeed's gasworks. In 1867 there was a fire in the creosote boiler and the tank containing pitch, but fortunately the naphtha in barrels was saved. A report of another fire at the works later in the same year refers to it being used for the manufacture of pitch, tar, naphtha and other chemicals. In the 20th century another chemical works was located to the west of Sittingbourne. There were complaints in 1932 about fumes from Bugges Insecticide Works and in 1935 there was a huge fire there. The premises had originally been built by Laurance Seager and during the First World War they were used as a fruit pulping station. After the war they were used by Messrs Keiller for that purpose and for jam making. When Bugges took them over they enlarged them and at the time of the fire they employed 20 to 25 men, mainly ex-service men. (27)

Whitehall Preserve Works (Dean's Jam Factory)

Keiller's were not the only firm in the town to process fruit. Also during the First World War, F G Gooding opened a factory for preserving cherries in Milton, and Bennett Opies factory, engaged in the same operation, opened in Chalkwell Road in the 1920s. It continues to process cherries in the 1990s. The most famous of the firms processing fruit was though Dean's Jam Factory in Bell Road. This started in the 19th century, processing fruit from the extensive farmland owned by Dean, who was also a partner in the brickmaking firm of Smeed Dean, and in 1915 'Dean's Famous Kentish Jams' were being eaten by troops at the front.   In the second half of the 20th century the premises were used first by Sharwoods and then by Freshbake Foods before being closed in the 1980s.

The were small-scale engineering works in the town. In the 1860s Mr Gardiner operated an iron foundry close to Sittingbourne High Street. F Littlewood's engineering firm was established in 1869, he was a brassfounder and brick mould manufacturer who also repaired machinery. At the same time the East Kent Ironworks was operating and in the 1930s it was taken over by the Stevens family who already had an engineering works at Thurrock in Essex. In its early days it made windlass gear for barges. In 1955 the firm opened a machine shop in Crown Quay Lane where it made parts for turbines and papermaking machinery as well as supplying big machine tool user factories. The original premises, in Frederick Street, were used for the foundry and pattern-making shop. Moulds were made from the pattern and the firm was one of the first to use the "freeze" method in this process. (29)

In the 20th century clothing firms opened in the town. The first to do so was a collar factory in Ufton Lane which opened in 1912 and at that time employed 100 hands including girls from the age of 14. In 1961 a new clothing firm, Posner's opened in Staplehurst Road. Clothing continued to be manufactured in that area of the town until the 1990s. Also to the west of the town was Lowes Dog Biscuit factory, which operated until the 1970s, the Export Packing company, which opened in the 1950s and Driclad Ltd, which made special covering for military equipment during the Falklands War. (30)

This brief look at some of the other businesses which make up the urban economy has not included the role of Sittingbourne as a shopping centre. There is a detailed look at Sittingbourne High Street in Chapter Ten.

The second half of the 20th century has seen the development of small industrial estates, like that in the Staplehurst Road area to the west of the town. By 1972 there were three, the London Road Trading Estate on Hollybank Hill, the Trinity Trading Estate which was started in the early 1960s, and the most recent of the three, the Sittingbourne Industrial Park. The following year work started in the Eurolink Industrial Estate following the closure of the cement manufacturer APCM. It is an indication of the changing nature of the urban economy that the firm of Concrete Pipes continues to manufacture concrete products in Milton, one of the many small-scale businesses found on the industrial parks, even though the large-scale concrete manufacturing firm no longer exists. The economy of the town at the end of the 20th century is no longer dominated by single industries as it was by brickmaking in the 19th century and paper making in the early 20th century. (31)

Reminders of the men who dominated the local economy in the 19th century survive in the names of roads, there is Dean Road, Eastwood Road and Smeed Close. Local industries are also recalled in Brewery Road, Forge Road, Gas Road, Kiln Close, Mill Court, Millfield, Mill Way, Oyster Close, Saffron Way,

Tannery Court, and Wharf Way. Finally there is Kings Mill Close, Periwinkle Close, The Meads Avenue, Watsons Hill and Windmill Road, road names which refer to an aspect of the town's economy which survived from before the Norman Conquest until the 20th century, and a study of which makes a fitting conclusion to this section of the book.

Watermills

Like other towns Sittingbourne had a number of windmills, see Chapter Two. However it also had a number of watermills. According to the 1887 'Directory', part of the trade of Sittingbourne came from 'corn mills' and there had been 'six mills' there 800 years earlier when they were recorded in the Domesday Book. References are found in the 15th and 16th century wills to the 'new mille' (1464), 'the water mill of Thomas Iden' (1497), a 'mill pond' (1513) and to 'Pyriwinkle Mill' (1545). A fulling mill is mentioned in Tudor State papers and amongst the local quays listed in a survey in Elizabeth's reign is 'Fluddmill' quay. Writing at the end of the 18th century Hasted noted that there were four corn mills and Perrywinkle Mill, which had been used to manufacture pearl barley. Also as detailed in Chapter Three, there was a paper mill at that time. (32)

Sittingbourne Tide Mill

Like the paper mill, Periwinkle Mill continued to operate in the 19th century. The 1861 Census includes a windmill at Blind Lane near the Chalkwell Tannery; Mead Mill (Mr Watson was the miller there); Periwinkle Mill and

Kings Mill - all three with their own mill ponds but fed by the same stream; Meads Mill at the end of North Street, Milton, near the Vicarage - there were two mills in that area, one powered by water and the other by wind (the latter is included in the Tithe records of the 1840s); and (in Sittingbourne parish) the Tide Mill. (33)

The Tide Mill is likely to have been the 'Fluddmill' referred to in Elizabethan times. In a sale advert of 1838 it was described as a 'Tide and Steam Mill' consisting of a 'very substantial, first-rate water corn mill of four floors, running four pairs of French stones, with gear-work and machinery, capable of grinding and dressing 75 quarters per week; together with a newly erected brick building, with a steam engine of twelve horse power, driving three pair of French stones, and capable of dressing 88 quarters per week.' The advert also noted that the situation of the property was 'one of the best in the county for obtaining wheats or disposing of flour'. By 1861, though, the tide pool was giving rise to complaint. A letter to the local paper said 'the tidal pool ... covers an area of perhaps five or six acres, and is during a great portion of the 24 hours, nothing but a mass of mud, sedge and decayed vegetable matter; and the stench from it, even in the winter ... is at times hardly bearable, and forms an excellent hotbed for fever and ague.' The letter pointed out that there was more severe fever and typhoid in the area of housing near the pool than in the rest of Sittingbourne and Milton. (34)

These houses, like the water mills, are now gone, replaced with roads and factories. It is only at the corner of one road, bearing the name of one of the oldest mills, Periwinkle Close, that any physical evidence survives, with the reconstruction of the water wheel that once worked busily, playing its part through the centuries in the economy of the town. (35)

Chapter Five

The Urban Poor and Important Events

Introduction

This chapter is the first to deal with the more social aspects of Sittingbourne's history. Although most of the rest of the book is concerned with the 19th and 20th centuries, the first section of this chapter, on the urban poor, starts with the way in which they were treated in earlier centuries. It then deals with the official institution for the relief of the poor, the Workhouse, an alternative solution to the problem - emigration, and charitable help for the poor. This leads on to a section on fetes and carnivals, then one on visits from national figures, before the chapter closes with a section on the weather and disasters.

The Urban Poor: the 17th century

The 15th and 16th century wills for Sittingbourne and Milton included bequests to the poor of the parish, however it was the responsibility of the parish in which they lived to provide for them. The account books of the Milton Churchwardens and Overseers in the 17th century show that weekly payments were being made to widows and that their houses were being repaired. In addition to maintaining individual homes the parish also had the upkeep of almshouses. In November 1676 they paid two men 4/9 for one and a half days work and bought 50 laths, tiles, 300 nails, 2 hods of mortar, 75 bricks costing 1/6, a load of loam, a load of straw, thatching rods and a lock to repair Widow Brockwells house and the almshouses. The parish would also be responsible for the costs involved when poor people were taken ill or died. In 1674 Elizabeth Wood was paid 9/- when she was sick and cordials and plaster for her throat cost 3/-. Her nurse, Goodwife May, was paid 4/- and Goodwife James was paid 4/6 for Elizabeth's rent and laying her forth at her death. The four men who carried her to church were paid 4/4 and Mr Turner was paid 2/- for burying her. (1)

It was not only the elderly or sick who were supported by the parish. Sometimes the costs involved in a young person being apprenticed were paid. In 1676 John Elgate was paid £12 for taking Elizabeth Salmond as his apprentice and 8/4 was paid to provide her with clothes: a pair bodis, three white calico hoods, shoes, mending hose and one and a half yards of blue holland for aprons. In the same month, when Mary Gibbs was bound to Goodman Joyn, the cost of her double apparel came to around £2/7/6. It included 7 ells of lorkerum for shifts, an ell of holland material, 10 ounces of yarn, a pair of bodis, a yard of green bay for an apron, one and three quarter yards of double devonshire for two waistcoats, four yards of serge for petticoats, three yards of red Kentish cotton for underpetticoats, two yards of ribbon, four yards of binding, a quarter yard of calico, and two ounces of boan and clasps. Sometimes young people were also given money to have their hair cut. (2)

Younger children might also be the responsibility of the parish. In 1680 Goody Burbow was paid 4/6 a week for keeping Robert Clark's two children for five weeks. Some payments were occasional ones, as in the case of the 3/- paid to Goody Saunders for looking after old Allen about the time he went to hang, watching with him and for providing candles and strong water. In 1668 payments were made to seamen who had been shipwrecked in a storm. Such payments continued in the 18th century. In 1703 payments were made to the poor of the town for what they had lost in a storm. (3)

The Urban Poor: the 18th century
During the early 18th century the parish was increasingly faced with the problem of poor people coming into the area and having to be supported. In 1722 a Scotchwoman was paid to leave the parish with her two children. That was the year in which a new poor relief system came into operation. As a result it was decided in 1724 that the house of Richard Fox should be used as a workhouse. During the next few years many purchases were made for the workhouse including; a porridge pot, a fryingpan, a brine tub, four spinning wheels, a marking iron, candles, a saucepan and a spoon. There was also the cost of food and drink; beef, meat and turnips, four Suffolk cheeses, a bullocks cheek, wheat, boiling peas, milk and 25 gallons of cider. The inmates had to be kept warm, faggots and coals were sent to the workhouse, their shoes were mended and the men were shaved. (4)

The parish continued to provide for the needs of those in the workhouse throughout the 18th century. In just one year, 1766, purchases were made for it of; paper, thread, matches, butter, oatmeal, starch, ginger, sand, nutmegs, sugar, blue, pins, stays, cloth, buttons, hats, a brass kettle, knives, forks, a sieve, tobacco, oil, buckets, bedhinges, a bed mat, a bean hoe, sickles, worsted cloth, four chamber pots, gloves, breeches, shoes and repairs, coal, meal and bread, beer and wine. Clearly not all of these items were for the comfort of the inmates, some related to the requirement that they worked. In 1797 John Hearnden, a weaver, was employed to instruct and keep the children and others at the workhouse employed in the business of weaving. The children at the workhouse were also educated, 19/3 was paid to Widow Page in 1773 for schooling. No doubt they were also punished, a Cat of Nine Tails was purchased in 1786 costing 1/-. They did however receive the occasional treat, as in 1777 when they were given 8d to spend at the Whitsuntide fair or the 2/6 spent in 1788 to provide them with a Christmas present. Although the cost to the parish of the poor was great, the work they did generated income, in 1774 there were receipts from local people for 'work done by the poor'. (5)

The Urban Poor: the 19th century
The regulation of the poor at the workhouse became increasingly strict during

the 19th century. In 1817 it was decided that the poor for the future were to be clothed in good strong warm clothing all alike, which naturally had the effect of making them immediately identifiable when they went out. In 1820 the decision was taken that they would have one meat dinner a week, on Sunday, although it is not clear whether or not this was a reduction or an improvement in their diet. In 1822 a man was employed to keep the workhouse gate, to ensure that those who went out to work went at the proper time and that the children going to school 'go out all together'. Anyone who was not back by 6.30 p.m. in the evening was to go without supper and no one was to leave after supper without permission, unless they lodged out. Those who did not have supper had to be in by 8.00 p.m. (6)

Milton Workhouse

Poor people other that those living in the workhouse were also supported, although rules for them also became tougher. In 1823 it was decided that no one who kept a dog was to get parish relief, and in 1833 the parish stopped paying for bastard children. Sometimes the poor asked the parish for help only occasionally, as when Mary Osborne requested that the cost of her son being apprenticed to a shoemaker be paid or when Edward Loader asked for a pair of shoes which he would pay the parish back for at the rate of 1/- a week. Others might need long term support and it was felt important that the poor should work. However at times of unemployment this was not always possible, in 1829, for example, it was resolved that all able men that apply for relief shall be set work as far as employment can be found. When all else failed the poor were encouraged to leave the area, a fund was set up in 1841 to pay the expenses of the emigration of the poor. (7)

The workhouse continued to be the main way in which the town dealt with the poor. In 1834 the national Poor Law Act appointed commissioners to organise new unions and the building of new workhouses. In 1835 a meeting was held at the old Milton workhouse. At it Sir Francis Head, Assistant Commissioner for Kent, reassured the elected representatives of the 18 parishes in Milton Union that the Central Poor Law Board would support them in the event of objections from the poor to the new provisions. There certainly were objections. Labourers wanted financial relief to continue and at one time they locked Dr Poore, a local magistrate, in the Rose Inn. Soldiers were sent for from Chatham and when they threatened to fire the rioters dispersed. The disturbances didn't last for long and land was soon purchased to build a new workhouse, next to the old one in Milton. There were three categories of poor, the aged and infirm, able bodied men, and women and children. It was decided that younger, well-behaved, married couples could live together, even though this was not the case in all workhouses, as it was felt that, although the workhouse was to be as distasteful as possible to the lower class, poverty might not be a crime. Even so, when families went to the workhouse, although they were in the same building, the parents could not eat or sleep near their children. (8)

In 1838 Milton Union placed an advertisement in the Kentish Post asking for tenders for the supply of goods required for the workhouse. These were: Flour, best seconds; Bread, four pound loaves made of best seconds flour; Butter, good salt, seconds; Cheese, flat Dutch; Tea; Sugar; Salt; Pease; Pepper; Soap, best brown; Blue; and Starch. The workhouse continued to provide for the education of children and in 1840 the parish advertised for a schoolmaster and schoolmistress, aged between 30 and 50, to live at the workhouse. They were to be paid £25 and £15 respectively per annum. The successful applicants may have been Charles Bennett and Mary Jarvis who were the schoolmaster and schoolmistress at the workhouse at the time of the 1841 census. Also living there were Oliver and Elizabeth Aldfoton the Master and Matron and William King the Porter, with his wife Ann. There were 128 inmates, ranging in age from an infant nine days old to one man recorded as being 90 years old. The elderly formed a relatively small proportion of the total, only 22 being aged 65 or over. Nearly half of those living there, 55, were children under the age of 14. (9)

Ten years later in 1851 there was a Governor and Matron, a schoolmistress, a cook and a porter together with 107 inmates and 5 lodgers, all vagrants. There were fewer children, 42, but around the same number of elderly, 25, although most of these were men. There were fewer inmates in 1861, only 76, over a third of whom were children, often several from the same family, only a few of them were there with a parent. Numbers had increased in 1871 when there were 130 inmates and in 1881 there were 142, including 36 scholars, recorded in the census. Life for the residents would no doubt have been tough. As in the previous century, efforts were made to make Christmas time special with a beef and plum pudding treat and gifts of tobacco for the men, tea and sugar for the women and oranges and nuts for the children. The children were also given fruit on New Year's Day and in the summer there was an annual 'treat' although this was not provided by the Union. The children were though still expected to work. In 1900 the Guardians of Milton Union placed an advertisement for a Girls' Industrial Trainer at the Workhouse, to instruct the girls in Sewing and Domestic Work when the girls were not attending Board School. The applicants were to be good plain cooks and to instruct some girls each day in good plain cooking. The salary was to be £25 per annum and £4 per annum in lieu of beer, with lodging, rations and washing subject to deduction under the Poor Law Officers' Superannuation Act. (10)

As well as the workhouse, almshouses continued to be used by the elderly during the 19th century. In 1858 it was planned to build six or eight respectable and convenient houses at the Butts in Milton to replace 'a number of small inconvenient huts' in Water Lane and the High Street occupied by some of the poor widows of the parish. There were also almshouses in Sittingbourne and in 1867 a public meeting was held at which it was proposed that new almshouses should be built for which George Smeed would give bricks and sand and provide an endowment of £20 per annum. The old almshouses at the corner of Crown Quay Lane and East Street continued to exist and in 1889 it was proposed that they should be replaced with new ones although The Spicer Homes, in Bell Road, were not built until the 1930s. As well as 'institutional' provision for the poor, some form of 'outdoor' relief continued, especially at times of distress. Severe weather, in an area where much of the work, both industrial and agricultural, was out of doors, could lead to a loss of income. One such year was 1870 when in the November able-bodied married men with two or more children were given help; 9/- a week if they had two or three children, 10/6 a week if they had four or five children and those with six or more children got 12/-. They received half in money and half in bread or flour, but they didn't get it for doing nothing, they were given work to do and had to work from 7 a.m. to 4 p.m., with an hour for lunch. However the provision of outdoor relief for those with two or three children was soon withdrawn, they had to apply to be admitted to the workhouse if they wanted help. (11)

The Urban Poor: the 20th century
Even in the early decades of the 20th century the threat of being sent to the workhouse was a real one. One resident remembered seeing the impressive figure of the Beadle standing outside the workhouse, as he walked past with his mother on his way to work in the fields, and her telling him to work hard or he would end up 'in there' - he always worked hard! The area, though, had a relatively low percentage of 'poor' in the years before the First World War, with just over two percent in 1909. The Old Age Pension, of 5/- a week, for those aged over seventy was introduced before the First World War, 153

applications for pensions were granted in 1909 and the revision following the introduction of National Health Insurance would also have helped in the declining need for the workhouse. The workhouse gradually became known as Milton Almshouse, and then increasingly it was used as a hospital, coming under the control of the NHS in 1964. The building was replaced with housing in the 1990s, following the closure of the hospital in 1990. Provision for the unemployed continued elsewhere and in 1939 an occupational centre was set up where the unemployed could repair family footwear, and an appeal was made for discarded boots that could be re-conditioned. (12)

Emigration
A new life, in a new land, whether for financial or religious reasons became an increasingly popular solution to problems at home, not only for individuals. As was noted earlier, the local authority sometimes paid for the poor to emigrate, so relieving it of the problem of supporting them.

John Bridge and Caroline Brenchley:
Two local people who emigrated to America during the mid-19th century illustrate different reasons for leaving home. In 1841, John Bridge received a letter from his brother-in-law in Enfield, Connecticut, New England. At that time John was living in Milton but working at the Faversham gunpowder works - a long journey in the days before the railway! The letter told him that there was a gunpowder manufacturer, Loomies, Hazzard and Co in Enfield, who were prepared to pay the fare for John and his family to go to America to work there. He took the opportunity and now Hazzard in America is reputed to have 'more Bridges than rivers'. In the early 1850s Caroline Brenchley was converted to the Mormon faith by Thomas Obray. Subsequently she went to London to look after the blind daughter of a doctor and in 1856 emigrated with that family to America. She landed in Boston and then, on her own, went west with the 'Martin Handart Company'. This was an ill-fated wagon train. It left late in the year and then ran into exceptionally bad weather. Many died on route and Caroline ended up walking most of the way across the Great Plains, finally reaching her goal of Salt Lake City, the centre of the Mormon faith, the following year. There, in 1859 she became the third wife of Thomas Obray, who himself had emigrated in 1854. Perhaps in her case it was love rather than religion that motivated her to emigrate. (13)

Other local emigrants:
For many of those who emigrated from the Sittingbourne area it was, though, poverty which was the main factor involved. In 1870 lectures were being given at the Corn Exchange in Sittingbourne on the advantage of emigrating to the United States. By then some had already left and others were interested in going to Canada and the United States. In the same year there were advertisements in the local paper for books on 'Emigration for Poor Folks', and a letter was reprinted from 'The Times' from a mechanic extolling the benefits of Canada. The following year there was a lecture at the Corn Exchange on 'emigration to California and Oregon and how a Free Passage

thereto may be had'. In spite of the admission charge, many of the poorer people of the town attended the meeting, only to find that many of the advertised speakers didn't turn up and that the 'Free Passage', the thing most had gone to hear about, wasn't even mentioned. Clearly some were prepared to exploit the desire of the poor for a better life. (14)

In 1882 the Cunard Line Steam Ships were taking emigrants to North America for six guineas, including food. In the mid-1880s, during a depression in the brick trade, the local paper reported that workers were emigrating to Queensland in Australia, as well as Canada. Local emigrants often wrote home and in 1888 a letter from Alfred Goodhew, formerly from Milton, was published. In it he gave a glowing report of Sacramento, the capital of California, where he said the pay was good and even the poor owned their own houses and didn't need to pay rent. Advertisements also appeared in the paper encouraging people to emigrate. In 1898 a map of the Klondike Goldfield was published and in 1904 there was a large advertisement saying that free property, farms of 160 acres, awaited those prepared to work in Canada. (15)

As unemployment in the area increased during the years before the First World War emigration increased. By 1911 monthly services were being held at St Michael's for those about to emigrate. In April that year eighty emigrants, the largest party to date, left Sittingbourne. Many of them were single young men but there were also the wives and children of those who had already emigrated. One young man, taking his wife and family, said that he was being 'driven out' as he couldn't 'get enough to live on here'. He was a bargeman and felt that he wasn't being paid enough for the dangers he risked. He said that there was 'plenty of work and money to be had out there' and he was going to go where he could earn what he was worth. The party of emigrants occupied two carriages on the train from Sittingbourne and around a thousand turned out to see them leave. The arrangements had been made by the local firm of Hedley Peters and they sailed from Liverpool on the Corsican. Most of them went to Ontario but some went to Toronto, in Canada, or to Oswego in New York State, where there was already a well established Sittingbourne and Milton colony. (16)

Emigrants continued to settle in Oswego and their deaths there were reported in the East Kent Gazette. In 1926, for example, the 'death of a Sittingbourne man', was announced. He was 'Mr John Bellingham, aged 73 years, ... who formerly carried on business in William Street, as an oil-man, (he) went to America upwards of 14 years ago, and had made his home in Oswego since.' In 1949 a minister from Trinity Methodist Church in Oswego visited Sittingbourne, and the paper said that there had been a large colony from Sittingbourne there for more than 60 years. Ohio was also a popular destination. In 1913 a letter was printed from Alfred Shilling of Freemont, Ohio, saying that he had celebrated Christmas with 50 people, including members of the Cheeseman and Goatham families, nearly all of whom originated in the Sittingbourne area. (17)

The Poor and Local Charitable Activity

At times of serious hardship the wealthier members of the local area provided help for the poor. In 1867 bread, and other articles, were distributed to the poor of Sittingbourne through a relief fund. In 1870, at a time of distress, 520 children were given a dinner of soup and bread. Such occasions are typified by that in January 1871. Subscriptions to the Relief Committee included a quantity of beef from G Smeed, 26lbs of beef from J Millen, a sheep each from T Bensted and T Lake, 20lbs of meat from T Henham, a sack of potatoes from Mr Batch, financial contributions of £2/0/0 each from Mr Dyke, Mr Gascoyne, Mr Grayling, Mr Hulburd and Mr Rayner, of £1/10/0 from Mr Hills and Mr Tonge and others contributed a £1/0/0 each. The relief committee distributed a quart of soup and a loaf of bread to the deserving poor who requested it. On just two days a hundred gallons of soup were distributed. Severe weather again caused distress for the poor in 1881 when children were provided with soup and bread, and in 1909 a soup kitchen was set up in Milton providing for 768 families. (18)

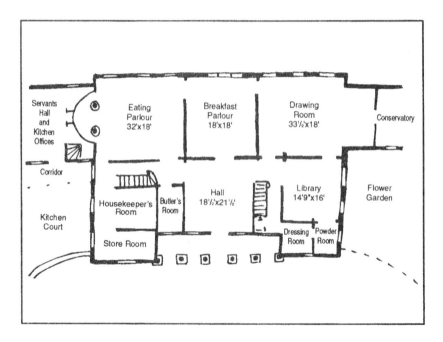

Plan of the Ground Floor of Gore Court House

The poor, both those within the community and those in the workhouse, also benefited from the generosity of George Smeed during the 19th century. The first report of a rural fete being held in the grounds of his home, Gore Court Park, for the inmates of the Union Workhouse, widows, the aged poor and others residing in Sittingbourne and Milton, is found in July 1859. Mr Smeed provided a glass of wine for each of them and tobacco for the men. In the evening they had a pint of old ale and fruit. Other members of the public were admitted to the park on payment of a small sum. That year around 270 poor people and about two thousand members of the public, many getting in without paying, went to the park, and the day ended with a fireworks display. (19)

Two years later the fete, although it was still 'ostensibly for ... inmates of the Union Workhouse and the poor', was becoming a popular event, not only amongst the local townsfolk. The flags were put out in various parts of the town and a large number of visitors arrived by train, including the Sheerness Drum and Fife Band. By the late afternoon nearly all of the local shops had closed. Tea at the Park was provided by a local baker and confectioner, Mr Harms. Ham-sandwiches, cake, bread and butter and tea were provided in a spacious tent for nearly 500 poor people. Members of the public had to pay a shilling for the tea and Mr Harms was unprepared for the huge demand and he was soon 'eaten out' of buns and cakes, and at one time the proceedings came close to mutiny. It took so long to feed everyone that plans for foot races and sack races were upset. The Rifle Corps played dance tunes and 'Kiss in the Ring' seemed to be the most attractive sport of the evening. (20)

The following year there was a procession of the poor from the workhouse to the Park, led by the band of the 16th Kent Rifle Volunteers and the Sittingbourne Fife and Drum Band, with the Milton Fife and Drum Band bringing up the rear. As well as the tea, provided by Mr Harms, the 600 poor and other visitors were entertained by Punch and Judy, a peep show, acrobats, foot races and a donkey race. Refreshments for other visitors were provided separately by Mr Godsmith of the Lion Inn and Mr Bowers of the Ship Inn. Late in the evening a dance was held at the Corn Exchange. The fetes continued to be held each year. In 1864 the children had footballs, trap-bats, tennis balls, cricket balls, bats and wickets to play with. As well as a firework display, the entertainment included balloons going up, the largest over 16 feet in diameter. (21)

Inviting the public into the grounds of one's house was not without its problems. In 1867 the fete took place at Woodstock Park when George Smeed withdrew his offer for the fete to be held at Gore Court following an occasion when members of the public had peered into his house rather than keeping to the footpaths or lawns. He relented though in subsequent years and the fete continued to be at Gore Court Park each year during the 1870s, the highest number attending being ten thousand in 1877. Following the death of George Smeed in 1881 the trustees of his estate were unable to agree on a large scale fete, and only inmates of the workhouse were allowed to have tea in the park, the cost being paid for by voluntary donations. Later in the century funds raised by the local carnival, of which more later, were used to provide an annual dinner for the poor. (22)

Fetes, Carnivals and Special Celebrations
Early Celebrations:
One of the first events reported in the East Kent Gazette was in November 1857. It was a procession to celebrate Guy Fawkes Day. It was held in the evening and the chief attraction in the procession was said to be an effigy of Nena Sahib, attired as a butcher and of rather extensive proportions, with a female figure by his side, although some said that the characters were meant to represent a lady and gentleman nearer home. The effigies were paraded through the town and then burnt at the Butts. Clearly having a well known figure as the Guy was not uncommon as the paper said that two years before an effigy of the Emperor of Russia had been burnt. Celebrations were also held at that time at Christmas. In 1860 Father Christmas was accompanied by carol singers, drums and fifes and masqueraders and a ball was held at the Corn Exchange. (23)

Milton Clock Tower

In March 1863 there was a grand turnout to celebrate the wedding of the Prince of Wales. There were triumphal arches at the railway station and at the entrance to Station Road from the High Street, and the whole of the High Street was decorated with flags and banners. A procession was held led by the Band of the Volunteers. They were followed by the Volunteers, the Sittingbourne Brass Band, the Ancient Order's of Foresters, Shepherds and

88

Druids, and children from local schools and the workhouse. In 1887, the Golden Jubilee of Queen Victoria, a fete was held for Sittingbourne residents at Gore Court Park but Milton decided that it was 'inexpedient to have any Jubilee celebrations' as they had put up a clock and improved their Assembly Rooms in honour of the event. (24)

The late 19th and early 20th centuries:
In the 1890s the two towns co-operated with annual carnivals. They were organised by the Sittingbourne and Milton Masquerade and Carnival Society and the first one took place in 1893. It was held on a Wednesday evening in November and the route went from the station, along the High Street to Snips Hill, then along Murston Road, Shortlands Road and Shakespeare Street, back to the High Street, under the station railway arch to Milton High Street, back along Chalkwell Road and the London Road, up William Street, down Park Road and Dover Street back to the station again. (25)

By 1897 the carnival was drawing visitors from the surrounding villages and towns and the railway had to put on extra trains to bring them in to the town. The procession started just after 7.30 p.m. and it was led by the Chief Marshal, Singler Shrubsole, 'upon a prancing steed'. He was followed by the president of the society and two vice-presidents in an open landau. In all there were sixty entries, including six bands, both fire services and floats from local organisations and businesses. Amongst these there was an entry by John Peters & Sons, a car representing 'a hummock of ice, surmounted by a pole, to which was clinging a Britisher waving a Union Jack', pulled by men dressed as arctic explorers - the race to the north pole being on at that time. One of the bands was that of the Daily Chronicle Paper Mills and they were followed by floats with reels of paper and a machine at work. Other trades and industries represented included butchers, fishmongers, tinkers and scissor grinders, tanners, blacksmiths, rope makers, a local hotel - the Fountain, which had a huge replica of a champagne bottle and the Swale pilots, who had a boat in full sail pulled by a horse. 'Masqueraders and torch bearers marched with the procession on foot (and) most of the large business establishments in the High Street were lighted up for the occasion,' with some properties having fairy lights. It must have been quite a sight. (26)

The following year both towns celebrated Queen Victoria's Diamond Jubilee, but separately. In Sittingbourne a tea for 3,000 children was provided at the Recreation Ground and in Milton 1,500 children processed from The Butts playground to the meads meadow, and Milton Bowling Green was lit with 800 coloured lights. In 1899 a torchlight parade was organised by the combined Sittingbourne, Milton and Murston Fire Brigades in aid of the Transvaal War Fund and the following year there were celebrations following the news of the Relief of Mafeking. As well as the three Fire Brigades, members of the two town councils, various bands, school children and local organisations took part. Floats included one entitled 'Sons of the Empire' - the figure of Britannia was seated at the centre surrounded by representatives of the naval, military and colonial services, and another on which there was 'a little soldier, mounted on a rocking horse, attacking with a lance a thickly-bearded Boer.' (27)

By the early 20th century the local Co-operative Society was organising annual fetes in the summer and children processed through the town. In 1908, for example, there were 5,000 children in the procession with 10,000 attending the fete at the Albany Road Meadow, and in 1914 there were 15,000 people there in the evening. A special celebration was held in 1902 for the Coronation. In Sittingbourne there was a procession from Snips Hill to the Recreation Ground with tea and presentation mugs for 2,500 children and fireworks in the evening. The following year though, there was no carnival in November, because of lack of interest. However, in June 1904, there was a procession to raise money on Lifeboat Saturday, and in the years before and after the First World War there were winter skating carnivals. (28)

During the latter part of the 19th century, a local entrepreneur called George Bowes had taken on the organising of fetes and athletic events at Gore Court Park. The events, particularly on Whit Monday, became very popular with 13,000 attending in 1900 when there was a parachute descent by a lady from a balloon. It was not the first time a balloon had visited Sittingbourne - although the earlier visit was unplanned. In July 1890 a balloon with a small party of gentlemen had taken off from the Crystal Palace. After rising to nearly five thousand feet it had flown over Rochester, Gillingham and Rainham before running out of gas and coming down in a field at Fulston Farm. Bowes continued to organise events during the early 20th century and in 1903 he purchased Glovers in Bell Road. He built an athletics track and a stand to seat a thousand and in July of that year a grand fete was held there, followed by August Bank Holiday sports. (29)

Other entertainments:
As well as locally organised events, performers sometimes visited Sittingbourne. One of the earliest recorded was Emidy's Circus which consisted of equestrian and gymnastic talent. In 1858 the Aztec Lilliputians, accompanied by the Highland Bell-Ringers, appeared at the Public Rooms in Sittingbourne and in 1864 the town was visited by Sanger's Hippodrome and Circus. Excursions were organised to take local people to other places and events. In July 1858 a boat sailed from Crown Quay to Margate. Tickets cost 3/6 and the day trippers had six hours at Margate, however the sea was rough and the ladies on board experienced some inconvenience - the mop and bucket being in constant request. Another trip the following year gave people the opportunity to spend seven hours at Rosherville, later, others ventured further afield, in 1875 there was a trip to Holland, and in 1889 there was an advertisement for a round trip to Canada to visit the Niagara Falls. The advent of the railway gave greater opportunities for excursions and in 1861 there was a trip to see Blondin and in 1864 there was an excursion to the Crystal Palace. In the 1870s there were rail trips to the Lord Mayor's Show in London and to theatre performances there. Dramatic performances also came to

Sittingbourne with annual pantomimes in the Town Hall. In 1882 Messrs Wallace, Roberts and Archer's Company performed Cinderella and in following two years Robinson Crusoe and Little Red Riding Hood were performed. The Town Hall was also the venue for a visit in 1884 from Mr D'Oyly Carte's Company when they presented Patience. (30)

Ancient Traditions:
The increase in fetes and carnivals during the 19th and early 20th century had its effect on older institutions. Both Sittingbourne and Milton had held fairs, a right enshrined in their charters. In July 1860 the annual Milton fair was held on a Tuesday and Wednesday. It had the usual attractions, peep shows and paper toys, gingerbread nuts and 'three sticks a penny', ginger beer and Punch and Judy. According to the local paper the 'three sticks a penny' was well patronised by the Guernseys and 'brickies', while the old woman with her hobnailed boots, short petticoats, and a superabundance of muffler, drove a roaring trade among the juveniles with her 'horses and carriages'. It seems that the carriages were not in very good condition and were likely to tip over if heavy laden. Attendance during the day was small but the fine evenings brought an increase in the number of pleasure seekers. However, by 1864 the paper reported that 'like many other things, this ancient fair and its associations are fast passing away.' By 1872 the annual Sittingbourne Fair, held in May at the Butts, consisted of one stall, a whirligig and a swing, and the Michaelmas Fair, in October that year, had shooting galleries, gingerbread stalls and roundabouts. The paper described it as an 'annual nuisance' and called for it to be abolished. In the same year local children were still celebrating May Day in the customary manor carrying 'their garlands from door to door', but it was not to be long before both this tradition and the annual fairs were to cease - petitions were sent to the Home Secretary in 1881 to abolish the fair. (31)

Peace Celebrations:
There was a fair held after the First World War, as part of the peace celebrations. Once again the two towns had separate events. In Sittingbourne much of the town, both the High Street and side streets, were decorated with flags and bunting. The council had left it to private citizens to arrange this and they were not disappointed. The Convent took first prize. 'Long swathes of patriotic bunting were slung across the front of the building and fixed at various points to the ivy with bunches of sweet peas, roses and other flowers. The front of the porch, the pillars of which were also draped in red, white and blue, bore the device, "Vivent Les Allies", ... flanked on either side by "Vive L'Angleterre" and "Vive La France"' - the nuns there being a French Order. 'After dark the building was hung with coloured Chinese lanterns, and at the upper windows were the illuminated devices, "Praise be to God", "Hail to the Victors" and "Glory to the Dead".' At the other end of the town, in Canterbury Road, the home of Mr Hobbs, bargemaster, had a display of alphabetic flags used in the international signalling code and in Park Road the distinctive

outline of Garfield House was decorated in black, white and yellow, the national colours of Belgium. (32)

In the afternoon there was a procession through the town, led by the police and the Sittingbourne Paper Mill's Band. Others taking part included the Fire Brigade, the Council, representatives of the local churches, children from the local schools, those too young to walk being carried on lorries, nurses from the Red Cross and St John Ambulance Brigade, members of Sittingbourne War Hospital Supply Depot, girls from the Ridham Dock Salvage Depot, as well as tableaux from local businesses and individuals dressed in fancy costume, including 'one young lady who, along with her bicycle, was dressed in beautiful Chinese willow pattern.' The whole of the route through the town was lined with large crowds who then followed the procession to the sports ground in Bell Road. Following the awarding of prizes and the singing of the National Anthem they dispersed to enjoy the various sports and the fun of the fair - which included 'roundabouts, swingboats, shooting galleries, coconut shies, etc'. The children were provided with tea and a Peace Celebration medal and then each of the schools held athletic races. There were also races for adults as well as tug-of-war events between teams from the Fire Brigade, members of the Sports Committee, the Paper Mill, and the Army, as well as others. In spite of showers of rain in the evening dancing took place, with many people in fancy dress, and balloons of fantastic shape were released. As dusk fell the prizes of the sports were presented and the evening ended with a grand firework display, organised by Officer Hedley Peters and members of the Fire Brigade.

Milton also put the flags out, 'though the greatest mass of colour was to be found in the upper part of the High Street (near the Town Hall), where the Decorations Committee undertook to assist the private householders. Here lines of huge naval flags crossed and recrossed the street,' and at the entrance to the recreation ground, where the local children were to be entertained, there 'was a large triumphal arch'. Throughout Milton, including the houses on the Sittingbourne side of the railway, private people had put out decorations. The Park Tavern, in Park Road, flew a large Stars and Stripes and at the home of Mr and Mrs Wade, also in Park Road, the garden and the front of the house were covered with flags and war trophies, including 'a German soldier's cap impaled on a German bayonet'. The procession through Milton was led by the bands of the Milton Christian Mission and the Boy Scouts, they were followed by members of the Council, then the school pageant. The first group of children represented Peace, then came England, Wales, Scotland, Ireland, and the Allied Nations, including one group from the Catholic School representing Serbia. Over a thousand children took part in the procession which was almost three quarters of a mile long. At the recreation ground nearly two thousand children were given tea, as were three hundred adults, including two hundred elderly folk. In a speech, following the tea, Mr Elgar said that over a thousand young men from Milton had served in the war and nearly two hundred of them had given their lives for their country.

Between the Wars:
The same year, 1919, saw the revival of the summer Co-op fete and the following year the Co-op procession included five thousand children. It was followed by a fete, sports and a pleasure fair. Whit Bank Holiday fetes and sports were also taking place again during the early 1920s and the town was visited by Bronco Bill. There was 'a never to be forgotten spectacle' in December 1921 when Santa Claus arrived by plane. Thousands of children, many accompanied by their parents, made their way to Messrs. Burley's farm at Fulston. An estimated crowd of ten thousand lined two sides of the field and prams were parked in an adjoining hop garden. When the plane landed the crowd broke cover and streamed towards it. There was a chance that the plane would be damaged so Santa Claus swiftly got out and went towards a lorry at the end of the field and the crowd followed him. Once he had given out all the toys in his sack he was driven, followed by most of the children, to Moore's Market in East Street, where he opened their Christmas toy bazaar. (33)

Carnival Float (1920s)

The year of 1922 saw the revival of Carnivals, with the first Grand Nursing Carnival, to raise funds for the local Nursing Association. It was held at the end of October and the route started in Murston, ran through east Sittingbourne, the High Street, then through Milton ending up at the Park Tavern in Park Road. The procession was led by the band of the Sittingbourne Paper Mills and the Sittingbourne Motor Ambulance brought up the rear. In between came displays from many local businesses and organisations. The Fire Brigade had two entries, 'the steamer all spick and span, and gaily decorated with flowers, fully manned' and a display on a lorry entitled the "Buckshee Fire Brigade" which caused much fun. The local paper, the Queen's theatre, various schools, including the Sittingbourne Men's Adult School, the Milton Council Gas Department, the Boy Scouts, W J Pullen, the Murston Social Club, the Football and Cricket Clubs, the Co-operative Society and the Allotment Holders' Association all took part - produce from the latter's float being auctioned afterwards. Also in the procession were many individual entries in fancy dress and an entry from Sittingbourne Paper Mills. 'The Paper Mill tableau showed timber in its natural state, then bales of wood pulp, then a reel of paper, and finally, at the end of the car, was a miniature sitting-room, with Mr Gant and a lady seated each side of a fireplace, and the gentleman was reading the finished article, viz., the 'Daily Chronicle'.' (34)

The Co-operative fetes continued to grow in popularity. There were up to twelve thousand at the Albany Meadow in 1923 and there were great celebrations for the Society's Golden and Diamond Jubilees in 1924 and 1934, the latter being held at the Cryalls Lane Sports Field. The Silver Jubilee of the King was celebrated in 1935 with a procession, sports, a beacon fire being lit on Keycol Hill and the planting of oak trees. Two years later a new king was crowned and the Coronation led to many street parties being held. The weather that year was not good and the plans for celebrations on Coronation Day itself were washed out. Different streets held their parties as and when the weather permitted. That for Unity Street and William Street was held on a Friday evening in June. William Street was closed to traffic and trestle tables, provided by Lloyds, were set up and decorated with flowers. Nearly a hundred children sat down to the tea, catered for by the Sittingbourne Co-operative Society. Once the tables were cleared a miniature boxing ring was erected, where little boys donned boxing gloves. However 'when the William Street twin brothers appeared in the ring in a mix-up one of the officials himself did not know who had won and who had lost, much to the amusement of the onlookers.' Later there was dancing to the music of the Harlequins Band, followed by a Punch and Judy show and community singing. The celebration finished 'with a display of fireworks, which left the tired young folks gasping'. 'The outstanding event of the evening was (though) the receipt of a telegram from His Majesty the King from Windsor Castle. ... "The King sincerely thanks the Committee and residents of William and Unity Streets, Sittingbourne, for their loyal greeting and good wishes which His Majesty much appreciated. Private Secretary." One has to wonder just how many such telegrams were sent and where they are now. (35)

The second half of the 20th century:
Street parties were also held to celebrate the Coronation of Queen Elizabeth in 1953, and later the Silver Jubilee (1977) and the wedding of the Prince of Wales in 1981. The Queen's Coronation was also celebrated with a special carnival and in 1981 the clock tower was erected outside of the new Town Hall, Prince Charles giving his permission for the Prince Of Wales Feathers to be used on it. During the second half of the 20th century it was the Labour

fetes each summer which attracted huge crowds when they were held in the Bell Road field - over seventeen thousand attended in 1961. However when the fete moved to the Cryalls Lane field in 1964 numbers declined. Other fetes continued to attract large numbers - a record twenty-five thousand attending the Whitsun fete in the Recreation Ground in 1971. Carnivals also attracted large crowds, after the Second World War they were organised for many years by the British Legion, (the ones before the war having been for the local Nursing Association), forty thousand were on the streets for the one in 1970. During the late 1950s and 1960s the Kent Farm Institute made their presence felt, in 1957 they drenched the crowd and kidnapped the Carnival Queen, and there were an increasing number of complaints over their behaviour before their final fling, throwing silage over the crowd, in 1966. (36)

Sittingbourne Clock Tower

There were also the visits from circuses throughout the century. One resident remembers them coming during the early decades. The cages of animals were driven through the High Street, up Bell Road to Bowes Park. Men from the circus had long poles with a tin on the top so that people watching the parade from upstairs windows could drop money in. Another resident remembers the circus parades in the 1950s when elephants and dancing bears made their way through the streets. (37)

Visits from Famous People
The Duke of York:
It was not only fetes and carnivals that attracted the crowds, they also turned

out when important visitors came to the town. One of the greatest such events was the visit of the then Duke of York, later to become King George VI, in 1921. The Duke drove along the road from Rainham, and at Keycol Hill the staff and some of the patients from the hospital lined the road. 'Eleven o'clock was striking as the Prince entered (Milton) High Street and halted at the Town Hall, with a thousand Milton school children massed around, and with the famous Milton "Grenadiers" ... drawn up in line, with a background of girls dressed in white. In the centre of the roadway were a group of pretty girls in white, engaged in a Folk Dance,' ... 'It was as though the Prince had stepped into a little bit of Milton history two or three hundred years ago'. The Prince was then driven to Sittingbourne through crowded streets. He was met by members of the Sittingbourne Urban Council at Cheapside - near the entrance to the Paper Mill. He then visited the brickfields of Messrs. C Burley where he was shown the process of hand brickmaking. As he left the brickfield he inspected the Borden Grammar School Company of Cadets, the Sittingbourne Fire Brigade, the Boy Scouts and the Girl Guides before he passed on to the Paper Mills. The Mill Band played the National Anthem and the Prince then inspected a 'guard of honour, composed of 333 of the ex-Service men of the Mill'. During his tour of the Mill the papermaking process was explained to him and he 'saw paper being made for many of the principal newspapers in London, including the "Daily Chronicle", "Evening Standard", "Daily News", "Sketch", "Daily Express", "News of the World", "Tit-bits", "Sporting Life", "The People" and others.' (38)

The Duke of York in Milton High Street

On leaving the Mill the Prince was motored up Dover Street, Park Road and Tunstall Road to Whitehall in Bell Road, the home of Mr and Mrs G H Dean. The Prince was entertained to luncheon in a pavilion. Amongst the many guests were local notables including Mr Burley, Lord Harris, The Reverend Doubleday, Captain Donald Dean, Mr G R Butcher, Mr Leslie Doubleday, Mr Goodhew, Mr F Austen Bensted, Mr Gardiner, Mr Packham, Mr Wills, Mr Hedley Peters, Mr Frank Filmer, Mr Andrews, Mr Grant, Mr Bowes and the Chairmen of Sittingbourne and Milton Councils. One of the guests, Mrs Boulding, remembered the Prince being 'locked' in the toilet, which had been specially installed, at a cost of £150, for his visit. In the afternoon he visited the Smeed Dean brickworks. 'The Royal party saw a brickmaking machine at work ... but the wind blew the dust about in great clouds, and time was pressing, so that the visitors hurried on. The Cement Works, with their range of kilns attracted attention. ... As a souvenir of the Royal visit Messrs. Smeed, Dean and Co. issued a very fine book of photographic illustrations of their great Works, copies of which were accepted by the Prince and members of the party.' (39)

Other Visitors:
It was not only royal visitors who drew the crowds. In 1937 nearly four thousand turned out to see Sandy Powell, a very popular radio star at that time, when he came to Sittingbourne to choose the Shopping Week Beauty Queen. Another radio star, and later TV star (Dixon of Dock Green), Jack Warner, also drew great crowds in 1953 when he opened the Conservative Fete. In the 1960s pop stars and TV soap stars drew in the crowds, Tommy Steel, pop and film star, was besieged for autographs when he appeared at a benefit football match in 1962, and in 1967 Coronation Street star, Elsie Tanner, signed autographs at the Co-op in East Street. Another pop star visited the town in 1986, Band Aid superstar, Bob Geldof, was given the honour of 'Freeman of Swale' at a ceremony at Sittingbourne Town Hall. Then in 1989 came another royal visitor. Princess Anne, the grand-daughter of the Duke of York, visited the town. Her arrival, by helicopter, at Westlands, was watched by 1,350 pupils. She was then driven to the Swallows where she was met by over two hundred children, including Brownies and Guides. 'Inside the leisure centre, more than 150 guests representing the council, local sports groups, voluntary organizations and the main contractors for the centre were among the reception group.' Princess Anne was shown around the development and unveiled a plaque to officially open the centre. As well as viewing various groups who used the centre in action she also detoured to visit old folk from Age Concern. From the Swallows she was driven to Michelsons tie factory in Staplehurst Road. As well as touring the factory and meeting staff she was presented with a cheque for the Save the Children Fund. The Princess then returned to Westlands and met the headmistress and pupils before leaving for Kensington Palace. Westland pupils were also presented to Princess Anne in 1991, when she opened a Save the Children shop in Sittingbourne High Street, they had raised over £4,000 for the fund of which HRH is president. (40)

Politicians:

The town has also been visited by its fair share of political figures during the past century. Before the First World War, Votes for Women was a national issue. In 1908 members of the Women's Freedom League visited Sittingbourne and held an open-air meeting at the Cattle Market - presumably when there were no cattle there! Later in the same year a militant Suffragette addressed a meeting of the Sittingbourne Women's Adult School in Trinity Hall. More than two hundred women attended together with one lone male reporter - who sat near the door. The Policeman who patrolled the area in case of trouble, an uncommon sight in that area at that time, was not needed as the meeting passed without incident. After the Second World War the town was visited by leading members of the main political parties. In 1950, at a meeting at Sittingbourne Town Hall during an election campaign, Harold McMillan criticised the then Labour government. There were stormy meetings during the election campaign of 1951 when Harold McMillan, then Prime Minister, again visited the town. A bye-election in the constituency in 1964 attracted attention from national politicians, with visits being made by Edward Heath, George Brown and James Callaghan. Then in 1976, Margaret Thatcher, at that time leader of the Opposition, spoke at a local Conservative dinner. (41)

The Weather and Other Disasters

Before the First World War:

Severe winter weather was often a disaster for the lives of individuals and local businesses, especially during the 19th and early 20th centuries when much employment was out of doors. Ways in which distress at such times was relieved has already been described. Fortunately such events have been rare, although the mid-1870s to mid-1880s were clearly a bad time. In 1875 there was a remarkable fall of snow, fifteen to twenty inches deep, which blocked the Sittingbourne to Sheerness railway line. The line was blocked again in 1881 when the heaviest snow storm for forty years was experienced, with drifts of snow six to eight feet deep. Two years later it was gales which caused problems with the 220 foot long, glass and slate roof of Number 1 Machine Room at the Paper Mill being blown in, fortunately there were no fatalities. There was heavy snow again in 1902, a hundred men cleared it from Sittingbourne streets and twenty five horses and carts removed it and tipped it into Milton Creek. Severe winter weather could also bring pleasure for some - there was skating on the dykes at Kemsley following a sharp frost in 1892 and after a severe frost in Milton in 1908 the most popular rink was the sheet of ice covering about four acres on Mr Cornford's farm near Milton Church. (42)

Disasters were not only natural, sometimes they were man-made. Strike action could cause distress for local people - the strike by bargemen in the 1890s was described in detail in Chapter Three. National strikes in the 20th century also had their effect. In 1911 there was a strike which closed the Port of London and railways services were disrupted. There were fears that the Paper Mill would close and the local fruit industry was affected, as were shopkeepers whose supply of goods were disrupted. The following year, during a strike in the coal industry local trade was paralysed. There was though an even greater disaster which affected local people in 1912, the sinking of the 'unsinkable' Titanic. Nearly 1,500 lives were lost, including Mr Richard Henry Rouse, aged 53, a labourer who had lived at New Road, Milton. Fortunately, Miss Kate Buss, daughter of Mr and Mrs Buss of Shortlands Road, Sittingbourne, on her way to California to marry Mr Samuel Willis, whose father also lived in Sittingbourne, was rescued by the Carpathia. (43)

Since the First World War:
In 1922 there was a more local disaster involving a boat. A steamship carrying 4,500 tons of Canadian wood pulp going to Ridham Dock struck one of the buttresses of King's Ferry Bridge. The damage to the bridge was so great that it had to be closed. A temporary raft bridge was built, but rail passengers from the island to the mainland had to use a ferry from Sheerness to Port Victoria, near Rochester. Three years later it was again the weather which led to tragedy when a tree, uprooted in a whirlwind, killed a motorist at Snips Hill. In 1926 the area was affected by The National Strike. Workers at the Paper Mill went on strike and there were no train services, although Maidstone and District buses continued to operate. (44)

Gales and floods left a trail of havoc in February 1938. At that time the floods in Milton were the worst in living memory. The Creek overflowed at about 9.30 p.m. on a Saturday evening and 'within a few minutes the neighbouring streets and houses were flooded to a depth of several inches'. The rise in the water level was so rapid that residents hadn't been able to take any precautions. The front room of Number 3 Bridge Street had four feet of water in it within minutes and the resident had to retreat upstairs. Customers in the Waterman's Arms were marooned and the beer in the cellar of the Crown and Anchor was ruined. The flood extended as far as the King's Arms in High Street and an underground cable tunnel was flooded, putting telephones out of action. The following year a snowstorm left a trail of damage with crashed chimneys and delayed trains. (45)

The whole country suffered in 1947 during a record freeze. Sittingbourne was thought to be the coldest place in the country, with 32 degrees of frost and the Paper Mill was put on short time because of a shortage of coal. Greater distress was caused in 1953 when the area suffered disastrous floods. Two hundred houses in Sittingbourne and Milton were affected and three families were made permanently homeless. All of the land at Church Marshes was flooded when water poured over the top of the sea wall. Bus passengers near Iwade were marooned all night. The driver of a following taxi reported that 'in a matter of seconds the water rushed across in a huge tidal wave and swept up over the bonnet of the bus, forcing it to halt in front of me'. The taxi driver, his passenger and two motor cyclists, whose machines were swept from under them, got into the bus, where 'the water started to come up through the floor boards.' The people in the bus 'got up on the backs of the seats' and when the water got 'higher and higher' they 'broke open the ventilators in case (they) had to climb up on the roof.' Gifts came in from all over the world for the victims of the flood. The following year Milton Creek was frozen for three days, the last time that had happened had been in 1893. (46)

In 1968 there were the worst floods since 1953, over three inches, (8cm), of rain fell in under eight hours and train services were disrupted. The following year the area was battered by two blizzards within five days of each other and in 1973 torrential rain flooded houses on the newly constructed Grove Park Estate. There were floods again in 1978 when the sea wall was breached at Upchurch and Tonge. The Creek burst its banks at Crown Quay and the iron foundry at Gas Road was cut off by the tide. The following year the area was affected by a severe frost. Torrential rain in 1983 led to flooding at the junction of Sittingbourne High Street and Bell Road and there was chaos in 1985 during arctic conditions in the area. (47)

The worst year for disastrous weather in the town's history has though to be 1987. In January that year there was the heaviest snow for decades. The Isle of Sheppey was cut off and panic buying led to many shops being without food, especially bread. The snow was so severe that council snow ploughs were snowed in, passengers were stranded when both buses and trains got caught between drifts and Milton Creek was blocked by iceflows. In April, storms left a trail of havoc and a walkway at Westlands School was demolished. Worse was to come. On a Thursday night in October 'hurricane winds brought devestation without warning ... the storm felled thousands of trees (and) demolished buildings.' 'Communications and industries were at a standstill. Telephone lines were dead. Everyone was without electricity, there was no water in many areas and even gas supplies were affected.' 'Roofs and tiles were ripped off in the gales, chimney pots crumbled and a number of trees wrecked houses. People were left homeless.' Fortunately nobody died or was seriously injured. The council set up emergency reception centres and additional staff and machinery was brought in to clear up the roads, many of which, including the main A2, had been blocked. (48)

At the height of the storm in Sittingbourne, wind speeds touched a hundred miles an hour - described by one resident as sounding like an express train coming straight at you. A couple living in the Avenue of Remembrance had a narrow escape when a copper beech tree fell onto the roof of their house. A cricket shed at the nearby Borden Grammar School was blown from its base and hurled thirty yards before turning over near a busy road. On the Friday, following the hurricane, local schools were closed and many rail services were brought to a standstill because of trees across the line. 'It was (though) at the Albany Road Recreation Ground and the nearby cemetery that the full force of the terrifying storm was most evident. About one third of the trees in the recreation ground were uprooted (and) twenty trees fell in the cemetery causing extensive damage ...' (49)

The cemetery and the recreation ground had both been started in the 19th century, a time of rapid urban growth, and it is with the effects of that growth in terms of public buildings and organisations, that the next chapter is concerned.

Chapter Six

Urban Growth

Introduction

This chapter looks at the way the urban area grew from the mid-19th century to the late 20th century. It is divided into four separate time periods, in each of which different issues are dealt with; sanitation & health, housing, public transport & public buildings and public service organisations.

The mid-19th century: Sanitation and Health

In 1858 a petition was sent to the General Board of Health requesting an inquiry into the sanitary condition of Milton. A report in the East Kent Gazette at that time paints a vivid picture of Milton in the mid-19th century. Twenty years earlier an Act had been passed which gave the Milton Commissioners power to raise money by means of rates or by borrowing money to; pave streets, make sewers and drains, light streets, erect privies, remove nightsoil, provide fire engines and prevent nuisances. By 1858 they had partially paved Milton by means of lagging, kerbing, channelling and macadamizing the carriage ways, they had erected a gasworks and there were 36 public lamps. However there was no system of public sewers in any part of the town; the houses and privies usually drained into cesspools, the overflow from which found its way by means of open channels into the streets, and in times of rain was washed down the side gutters, the smell from which was much complained of. There were three public water pumps and one fountain, although many of the houses and some of the poorer cottages had pumps of their own. Refuse was usually washed away by the rain, only occasionaly being collected by a cart. A local farmer collected the nightsoil (the solid content of toilets) and cesspools containing nightsoil were emptied about twice a year. Typhoid was very common and in 1854 there had been a serious cholera epidemic. It was not a pretty picture. (1)

Sittingbourne, situated higher and further from the creek tended to be healthier but was no better off in terms of the provision of a sewage system or water. An anonymous circular, reported in the local paper in 1860, described Sittingbourne as 'past praying for, a sink of abominations, reaking with impurities, a very hot-bed of disease, and where the inhabitants are so sunk in squalor, as to be walking about merely to save the burial fees'. The newspaper though wanted proof that the 'heaps of offal and vegetable matter, the black pools and stagnant gutters, in the midst of which our fellow-townsmen eat, drink and lie down', as claimed in the circular, actually existed, saying that although 'the consumption of soap amongst the brickmakers is not what it should be' one wouldn't 'find a stronger, healthier or more cheerful set of men'. Nuisances did though clearly exist, in 1865 a letter was sent to the local paper complaining of two or three piggeries in the town where tubs of stale blood and heaps of manure were to be found all within a few yards of houses tenanted by respectable people. There was also the nuisance caused by brick burning close to houses and in 1869 there was a court case at which the decision was made that it could not be done within 112 yards of the plaintiff's residence. In 1866 there was a cholera outbreak in Sittingbourne with eight or nine victims from East Street in just one week. Both Sittingbourne and Milton suffered from a common problem, that of the tide pool of the corn mill at the head of Milton Creek. The cottages known as The Wall, which were built on its banks and where there was 'more fever of a severe and typhoid character' than in the rest of the town, ran across the boundary between the two parishes. (2)

The mid-19th century: Housing
It was though Milton which suffered the problem of flooding from the Creek. In 1863 houses were flooded in Flushing Street as far as the Kings Arms in the High Street. In 1851 Milton was still slightly larger than Sittingbourne, however many of the new roads that started to be built during this period were in Sittingbourne. In 1860 Station Road and the road from the station to The Wall, described as the 'darkest and dirtiest road' in the town, were included in Sittingbourne Parish. Then, in 1864, 41 acres were purchased from Captain Vallance and once the brickearth was removed it was intended that a new estate should be built. The main road through it would start at the High Street, near Station Street, and end at Tunstall Road. This was Park Road, and in 1869 it, together with William Street and Eastbourne Street were adopted by Sittingbourne parish, which meant that the parish were responsible for their upkeep. In the same year the British Land Company Ltd asked the parish to take responsibility for Shortlands Road, Milton Road, Cooper Street, Harold Road, Goodnestone Road, Bayford Road and Shakespeare Street. However only Shakespeare Street was accepted, so the builders had to maintain the roads, paths and drainage of the others until the parish thought them of sufficient utility to take them over. (3)

Taking on the responsibility for roads was no light matter, the upkeep could be difficult and expensive. In 1869 the Sittingbourne Improvement Commissioners faced the problem of disposing of water which built up under the railway arch near the station making Milton Road almost impassable in winter. To solve the problem they cut away the hill, lowering the level of streets and underpinning shops and houses, so that the water would drain away to the reed pond, all of which cost over a hundred pounds. It is unlikely that the occupants of shops and houses in Milton Road would have owned their own properties, they would have been paying rent. However people were being encouraged to become property owners, in 1858 there was an advertisement for the Faversham, Sittingbourne and Lathe of Scray Permanent Benefit Building Society which offered to advance sums on mortgage, the money to be repaid over five to fourteen years. (4)

During the mid-19th century much of the new building development in both Milton and Sittingbourne was related to the growth of the brickmaking industry. In 1864 George Smeed planned to erect cottages near Milton church in anticipation of brickmaking operations there, and the development of the Murston Road area in the east of Sittingbourne was the result of the Smeed Dean brickfields in that area. (5)

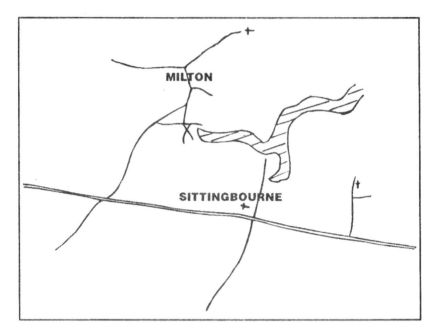

Sittingbourne and Milton in the mid-19th century

The mid-19th century: Public Transport & Public Buildings

The growth of the Sittingbourne area was also affected by the arrival of the railway. In November 1857 the East Kent Railway between Chatham and Faversham was formally opened. A special train left Chatham at noon and arrived in Sittingbourne just after 1.00 p.m. It was greeted by around a thousand people and there was a triumphal arch of evergreens and flowers and a banner with the words 'Welcome to Sittingbourne'. After staying for a quarter of an hour, when speeches were made, the train went on to Faversham where it arrived at 2.00 p.m. The train made the return journey in the evening but the line was not opened for passengers until the following year. From the 25th January 1858 there were to be six trains each way every day except Sunday when there were three. By June that year the branch line from Sittingbourne to Sheerness was nearing completion. The bridge, for both road and railway, at Kings Ferry, was made of wrought iron plates resting on brick piers, and the company had the right to charge tolls for those crossing it. The total length of the water-way between the abutments was 530 feet and there were ten 40 feet openings between the piers for the passage of vessels. In addition the one in the middle was 60 feet in width and over it was a drawbridge to allow masted vessels through. At Sheerness the station was close to the pier and there was a branch line running to the dockyard. (6)

The first Sittingbourne to Sheerness train ran on March 3rd 1860. It took 25 minutes and had to go slow along the section through a cutting where there had been land slips. It was planned to solve the problem by planting grass and lichens. Later that year the line from Chatham to Victoria was opened. The increased use of the line led to improvements at Sittingbourne. In 1861 a passage was made under the rails at the station and the railway company applied to take possession of a public road and footpath near the Latimer Chapel so that they could extend their premises by purchasing adjoining property. It was in that year that the first serious rail accident occurred. The 9.55 a.m. express down train was approaching Sittingbourne at 40 miles an hour when, a mile and a half from Sittingbourne station, the tyre of one of the wheels of the brake-van went off the rails. This led to the third class carriage turning on its side and the legs of a naval warrant officer were trapped. The left leg was literally torn from his body and his right leg was crushed and mutilated in a most frightful manner, portions of it were strewn along the line. He died later. (7)

Following the opening of the railway in 1857 a meeting was held to consider the establishing of a Corn Market in Sittingbourne. The meeting was held at the public rooms in Crescent Street and Mr Eley of Tonge presided. Mr Gordelier, who ran the public room they were in, proposed that it should be used, extending it if necessary, as it was near the bank. Mr Lake said that he realised that if new rooms were built Mr Gordelier would suffer financially but that the present room gave no attraction to the town. Mr Knight of Bobbing proposed that a new building be built in a field near the railway station but Mr Dean objected to this, saying that property in the vicinity of stations was of little value in most towns, and he proposed a site on the High Street in the centre of the town. This was agreed upon and the following year tenders for the building were requested and the lowest, £1,090/16/3 was accepted, the foundation stone being laid by William Lake in August 1858. It was decided by a meeting of shareholders that market day at the Sittingbourne Corn Exchange should be on Wednesday, and the first market was held on January 12th 1859. (8)

The building included a balcony and it was formally opened with a Grand Concert on 25th January 1859, but before that a lecture was given there on January 13th. This showed that fears that the 'lofty pitch of the Corn Exchange would cause unpleasant reverberation or echo were unfounded'. There was an audience of around 300, the only drawback was the draught made because the new doors wouldn't close fully. In 1860 the building was improved by the addition of a triple dialled clock. Whilst Sittingbourne was engaged in building a new prestigious hall, which was 'a great ornament to the upper part of town', Milton was making do with its existing Town Hall and Assembly Rooms. The latter were in such a state of disrepair that they were no longer able to be used by the public and in 1863 a meeting was held to plan repairing them. (9)

The mid-19th century: The Cemetery & Public Service Organisations
The increase in the number of houses, over 150 between 1851 and 1859, and the resultant increase in population soon meant that the existing church yard at Sittingbourne ran out of space for burials. In 1859 discussions were held about opening a cemetery, two sites were proposed, Step-stile field adjoining Bell Lane and a field adjoining Ufton Lane. The latter was chosen but there were problems with its purchase and in the end land owned by Mr Smeed in Tunstall Lane was purchased at a cost of £600, £200 an acre. In 1860 the Burial Board met, they agreed to construct a mortuary and accepted a tender of £1,430 for building work in connection with the cemetery. The foundation stone for the chapels at the cemetery was laid in May that year. In October an advertisement was placed in the local paper giving the burial fees for the new cemetery. These included £1 for a grave space of 9 feet by 4 feet in perpetuity, £4 for a 9' by 8' vault, 7/6 for digging and filling an adult grave, 10/6 for erecting a headstone, and 1/- for ringing a bell at the funeral. There was in addition the fees for services and if the burial was of a non-resident then the burial fees were double. (10)

Sittingbourne Cemetery

106

There were local developments within the postal service. In 1858 a new Money Order Office was opened in Milton. There was clearly an increase in the use of the post, in 1861, for example, over 4,000 letters passed through Sittingbourne Post Office on Valentines' Day. A significant amount for a town, including Milton, with a population of around 7,000 according to the census held that year. In 1864 Sittingbourne Post Office was improved, it stayed open until 10.00 p.m. and a dentist operated there every Friday! Also in 1864 a new Police Station was built, at the bottom of Park Road, and Petty Sessions were held in the Court House there from January 1865. (11)

Sittingbourne Police Station & Court House

Both Sittingbourne and Milton had gasworks which supplied their respective parishes. Milton's was publicly owned, having been built by the Commissioners in 1846 but Sittingbourne's gas works was privately owned, by George Smeed. Not all of his customers were satisfied with the service he provided. In a letter to the local paper in 1860 one customer complained about the smell of ammonia, asking if they were paying to be poisoned and saying that it was not even 'cheap and nasty' as it was dear! Milton also, by 1863, had a fire engine. It, together with engines from private fire insurance companies, the Kent and the Phoenix, attended a fire at the Chalkwell tannery in that year. In 1869 there were calls for a new Fire Brigade in Sittingbourne after a fire at Cheapside when there were problems because hoses would not fit the gauges on the engine. (12)

The late-19th century: Sanitation & Health

Improvements were made in the water supply for Sittingbourne in 1870. Pipework was laid from water works at Keycol Hill to the town. However there was still no adequate sewage system and the new water supply, in some cases, may have had an adverse effect on the health of residents. In a letter to the local paper in April 1871 reference was made to the use of wells as cesspools once houses had piped water. This meant that other wells, still in use, became contaminated with sewage and the risk of cholera increased. William Street, for example, had no piped water and the wells on the east side were not fit for domestic use because wells in Park Road which did have piped water were being used as cesspits and the sewage was contaminating the underground supply. (13)

Milton did have a sewer, completed in 1859, the overflows from the cesspools went into it and it flowed, untreated, into the Creek, from which some residents still drew water. Provision for emptying cesspools and carrying away nightsoil was left to private enterprise. Although there was some improvement in the disposal of sewage by the end of the century the main sewer outfall was still considered to be too close to the town. A report in 1870 referred to the prevalence of epidemic diarrhoea, like enteric fever, which was caused by the condition of excremental filth which prevailed in the area, and resulted in far more deaths than cholera. It was not only human excrement which was to blame, in 1879 the Milton Urban Sanitary Authority passed a bye law requiring any manure deposited in any open space within a hundred yards of a dwelling house or workshop must be removed within 48 hours. (14)

By 1879 there were problems between Sittingbourne and Milton over the water supply. Although the 1870 report into the sanitary condition of Sittingbourne and Milton had stated that they formed almost a single town, and recommended that they join together for sanitary purposes, this had not happened. When Sittingbourne opened the water works at Keycol Hill Milton bought water from them. In 1879 Milton wanted to buy an equal share in the water works, Sittingbourne wouldn't let them. A Commission of the Local Government Board was set up to investigate the dispute. They decided that the three local boards, Sittingbourne, Milton and Rural should not unite. Sittingbourne was to keep control of the Keycol water works but Milton was to pay half of the cost of erecting the works and laying the mains to the junction with their pipes and a third of the annual working expenses in return for the right to a water supply in perpetuity. In 1896 the Keycol works were enlarged but problems between the two towns continued. In 1899 Milton refused to meet with Sittingbourne Council to discuss the water and sewage disposal question. (15)

The two towns did co-operate though over the provision of a hospital. There had been earlier hospital provision in the area, especially for those with infectious diseases. In 1599 there was a request for financial help for the 'hospital or spittle house at Key Street, for diseased persons'. In 1607 the

Canterbury Sessions ordered that Anne Radolphe of Tonge, a maiden aged 15, greviously visited with the falling sickness should be kept at the Key Street hospital for as long as Tonge Parish paid the yearly sum of 50/-. In the 18th century Milton Parish had a building at Kemsley known as the Decoy. In 1736 they paid 10/6 to Elizabeth Wright for nursing smallpox victims at the Decoy and a girl from the Workhouse was taken there. In 1832 a Commission had said that Milton should have a Cholera Hospital. However it was not until 1882 that the 'Sittingbourne and Milton Joint Infectious Hospital, at Keycol Hill, was opened to the public. (16)

Keycol Hill Hospital

It was intended that the building should accommodate 24 patients in eight wards, contained in two pavilions connected by open corridors, with a central administrative block. As it was an 'infectious' hospital the sanitation arrangements were very important. There were earth-closets, fitted with Moule's patent apparata, separated from the interior of the building by 'air-passages' to prevent the possibility of the return of foul air. Stoves headed the wards and fresh air was admitted through a grating in the external wall under the head of each bed. There was a separate mortuary and a disinfecting chamber.

The late-19th century: Housing
Provision of amenities, such as sewage, came from the payment of rates - Sittingbourne having formed a Local Government Board in 1873. The second half of the 19th century seems to have been no different to our own times.

Some ratepayers didn't pay their rates or paid them late. In a letter to the paper one ratepayer complained that arrears were not collected before the next payment was asked from those, such as he, who paid their rates on time. The number of ratepayers increased during the last part of the 19th century with the building of more houses. (17)

By 1881 there was an additional 28 streets, compared to 1851, in Sittingbourne parish and 17 more streets within Milton parish, although a number of these, including Park Road and William Street were partly in Sittingbourne parish. The boundary between the two parishes in fact ran through numbers 73 & 75 William Street, at the latter the front bedroom was in Milton and the back bedroom in Sittingbourne. Some streets in Milton had been renamed, Water Lane had been changed to St Paul's Street and Love Lane had become Mill Street. Streets in Milton and Sittingbourne had also been given name plates, 'fixed at conspicuous places at the corners of each' street. In Sittingbourne it was decided in 1881 that there would be no more streets known as Terraces. Lloyd's Terrace was renamed as Lloyd Street and Albion Terrace, together with Malcomb Place, became part of Canterbury Street. (18)

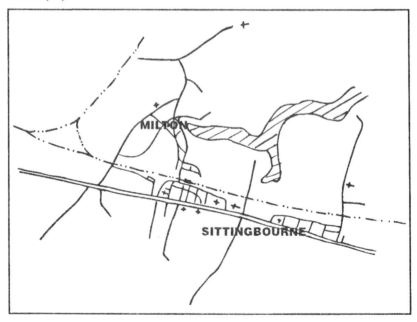

Sittingbourne and Milton in the late-19th century

Property ownership continued to be advocated. In 1889 there was an advertisement which said 'Why pay rent when in five years you can live in your own house rent free by joining the Provident Association of London Ltd.' Some of the better off residents clearly bought houses as a form of investment.

In 1884 James Kemsley purchased two timber built freehold cottages in West Street for £265, and the following year he bought two houses in Station Street with a rental of £36 per annum for £420. In 1891 the development started of the Rock Estate, south of the London Road, an area which during the bargeman's strike had been a favourite parade ground of trades unionists. (19)

With the increase in the population came demands for public open spaces. In 1879 a ten acre site in Sittingbourne, close to the cemetery and adjoining Smeed's hop garden, was purchased at a cost of £2,200 as a recreation ground. The provision of grass and a fence cost a further £700 but, as there was no public footpath through it, it had the advantage that it could be closed at night. Another amenity was introduced in Milton. In 1880 an old house at the bottom of Milton High Street was pulled down and the following year a new building opened there, the 'Hundred of Milton Coffee Tavern'. (20)

It may not have been the best choice of site as flooding continued to be a problem for residents of houses in lower Milton. In 1875 there was a particularly bad flood. The cellars of the Jolly Sailors Inn, Flushing Street, were completely filled with water which spoilt every barrel; wheat and flour at Mr Goble's mill was damaged; a chemist's shop was inundated with water getting into the poison cupboard where one parcel containing 20lbs of arsenic was speedily dissolved and everything that come into contact with the arsenical liquid was spoilt and in a private house a man who was asleep downstairs woke to find his bed floating about. Sittingbourne residents were not without problems of their own. They were beginning to be bothered with gipsies. There were four tribes, the Lees, Rossiters, Bakers and Harrises living at Snips Hill in the 1870s. (21)

The late-19th century: Public Transport & Public Buildings
The last part of the 19th century saw increased use of the railway, not only by passengers. In 1871 a letter to the editor of the local paper complained of the lack of accommodation at Sittingbourne Station for carmen and others who loaded goods into railway trucks. It said that the road at the side was too narrow for carts to pass, so causing jams, and the through trains frightened the horses. The freight side of the railway business sometimes had other problems - in 1873 the body of an infant, decomposed, was found in an uncollected box at the goods department of Sittingbourne Station. It was a goods train shunting near the station which caused a serious train crash in 1878 when it went, by mistake, onto the London track. An express train from the Kent coast hit it. The second, third and fourth carriages mounted above the first carriage and the engine. The front end of the first carriage was jammed against the engine, five people were killed and forty to fifty of the three hundred passengers on the train were injured. A few weeks later a new points system, controlled by a signalman, was introduced, which if it had been in operation could have prevented the accident. The London, Chatham and Dover railway did not have a good record of safety and in 1898 it was amalgamated with the South Eastern Company. (22)

The following year there were talks about the proposed building of a railway between Sittingbourne and Maidstone, but they came to nothing. Throughout the second half of the 19th century the link between Sittingbourne and Maidstone was maintained by an omnibus service, operated by James Gambell. This operated once a day, except Sundays, leaving in the morning and returning in the afternoon. By 1895 it was timed to coincide with trains from and to Sheerness. Passengers for London, who did not want to use the train, could travel by John Prentis's hoys, from Milton's quay, every alternate Sunday, returning from Hartley's wharf, Horselydown, the following Saturday. (23)

Sittingbourne High Street, showing the 19th century Town Hall

In 1870 improvements were made to the Assembly Rooms in Milton. The building up to the commencement of the second floor was substantially rebuilt and whole front and sides were re-stuccoed. The rooms could accommodate three hundred and a new clock was put in the belfry turret. Under the Assembly Room was a meat market and it was hoped that the Saturday market would recommence. A series of entertainments were held at the Assembly Room when it re-opened. In 1879 it was decided to use them as a Coffee Tavern, although this may have not lasted long as the new tavern was built the following year. Part of the ground floor of the Town Hall, formerly used as a potato and fruit store, was converted into a meeting room in 1886 and in 1873 the interior of the Court Hall was renovated. (24)

In 1878 improvements were made to the Corn Exchange in Sittingbourne when it was taken over by the Local Board and it re-opened as the Town Hall. Repairs had to be made though in 1894 when a large portion of the ceiling fell down, fortunately there was no report of anyone being injured. (25)

The late-19th century: The Cemetery & Public Service Organisations
With a greater population the number of injuries and deaths in the town increased. In 1875 the Burial Board purchased additional land. In 1889 classes were being held by the St John's Ambulance Association. The Keycol Hospital when it opened had an ambulance and in 1898 Sittingbourne had one of its own. The towns were still served by a number of fire brigades. There were problems in 1872 when the hose of the fire engine that arrived to deal with a fire didn't fit the hydrant. Members of the towns' brigades were all volunteers and in 1889 the Sittingbourne Fire Brigade were represented at the Lord Mayor's Show in London. In 1897 it was proposed that Sittingbourne should have a steam fire engine and a fund was launched for the estimated cost of £300. The following year they took over the Kent Fire Office engine and appliance, which were given as a free gift to the town, and the new fire engine was christened. In 1899 public subscriptions were requested to buy a new manual fire engine for Milton to replace their current engine which they had had since 1829. (26)

Improvements were made to the postal system throughout this period. In 1870 Sittingbourne Post Office was connected to the telegraph system, although initially messages continued to be received at the railway station and it was not until 1879 that there was a direct link from the Post Office to London. A new branch post office was opened in East Street in 1885 and in 1892 there was a new main post office in Sittingbourne High Street. The offices next to the Bull Hotel which had been used for 15 years were small and inconvenient and premises lower down the High Street, formerly used as an outfitters, were converted. Interior walls on the ground floor were removed to form a long room in the centre of which was a long polished mahogany counter. There was a post box inside as well as outside the building, the system for handling money orders was improved and when a telegram message had been written it was placed in a small lift to be conveyed to the office above. Behind the main room was the sorting office with provision for eight clerks to work at the busiest times, such as Christmas. On the upper floor, as well as the telegraph office, where it was proposed to employ female staff, there was a room for the local Inland Revenue Officer and a flat for the caretaker and his family. It was considered to be one of the most complete Post Offices in Kent and, according to the paper, only one further improvement was required, a lamp outside to show the importance of the building. (27)

The lamp would have been a gas lamp, and the building itself was lit by gas. In 1899 there was an advertisement for the Sittingbourne and District Gas Company Penny in the Slot Metre - no deposit, no rent, free fitting, each light costing less than a farthing an hour. However by that time electric light was beginning to be used, In 1899 electricity was used as motor power at Packham's brickfields and the Co-op in East Street introduced electric lighting, both inside and out. One other improvement to the public amenities of the town occurred during this period, the Sittingbourne Free Library, for both lending and reference, opened. In 1887 the books of the Sittingbourne and Milton Book Society were offered to the town as a free public library. A catalogue of the books was submitted to Sothebys and they characterised it as a valuable library. A meeting of ratepayers decided to adopt the Public Libraries Act and a building in Crescent Street was altered in 1888 to provide for 4,000 volumes. Then in 1897 a further 700 volumes were added to the library. (28)

Sittingbourne Memorial Hospital (based on a line drawing on the Opening Ceremony Programme)

The first half of the 20th century: Sanitation & Health
The early years of the 20th century saw the inauguration of the Sittingbourne Sewage Works (1904) and the opening of Milton Water Works at Highsted (1906). The water works had two wells, 102 feet deep, which had been excavated by pickaxe and shovel. Engines pumped water to the reservoir, 79 feet in diameter and 18 feet deep, at the top of the hill. The work had cost £12,800 and a further 10/4 a day was required to provide water for six to seven thousand people. The year before there had been a scare in the Park Road area when water from the Sittingbourne works had green vegetation in it, the company, apologising, said that it should have gone through the waste valve

and not into the mains! It was not until the 1930s that the water and sewage systems of the two towns were finally amalgamated. The Highsted and Keycol water works were linked in 1932, Highsted being improved in 1938, and a new joint sewage works was opened in 1934. (29)

In 1913 Sittingbourne had a new motor ambulance, the first in Kent, a gift to the town from Mr and Mrs G H Dean. By that time there was support for a cottage hospital in the town. A letter to the editor of the East Kent Gazette in 1911 suggested that the King Edward VII Memorial Fund should be used for that purpose. However it was not until 1930 that the Sittingbourne Memorial Hospital, in Bell Road, was finally opened. It was not in memory of the king, but of Mrs Frank Lloyd, and was a gift to the town from Mr Lloyd and his daughter. Meanwhile a new sanatorium had been opened, in 1915, by the Sittingbourne and Milton Joint Hospital Board at Keycol Hill. It was a single storey building with accommodation for 20 men and 20 women, and was considered as one of the best in Kent. (30)

The first half of the 20th century: Housing
The urban area continued to grow, with more houses and more streets. In 1919 there was a scheme for a hundred new houses, 50 of them at the Bell Road end of town. Then in the 1920s the Lloyd family built the new paper mill at Kemsley and with it a garden village. (See Chapter Four) Private housing also continued to be built during the 1920s. According to a report made by the Housing Inspector in 1925, of the 1,965 houses in the district, 237 had two or more families. There were 26 families living and sleeping in one room and 40 cases of overcrowding. The council's remedy to the need for further housing in the town was to support the owner-occupier scheme, whereby the council would grant a subsidy of £75 a house and advance 90% of the valuation of a house. The council believed this would encourage individuals to build new houses, so reducing overcrowding without the need for the council themselves having to build houses. There was an advertisement in that year for a five-roomed bungalow with bathroom for £450 and in 1927 'model villas' in Ufton Road and Rock Road were being advertised. (31)

The scheme had some success, houses in Glovers Crescent and Trotts Hall Gardens being sold to tenants, but it did not solve the housing problem and by 1930 the South Avenue Housing Estate, 'Sittingbourne's new garden suburb', had been built by the Council. It was planned to build 130 houses of the non-parlour type, in pairs and blocks of four or six. They were built of local red bricks and had bay windows in the living room. The ground floor consisted of a living room, with a fire and oven and built-in dressers with glazed doors; a scullery with a gas cooker; a larder; a bathroom and a coal store. Upstairs there were three bedrooms with built-in cupboards. The houses were the first in Sittingbourne to have electric light and the rental was low, 9/6 a week including rates. (32)

The housing problem was still not solved and in 1932, although 530 houses had been built in recent years, including nearly 200 at Vicarage Orchard and Barrow Grove, built by Milton Council, and a further 174 at Elm Grove and Quinton built after amalgamation, there were still 853 applicants for houses and the council were concerned over slums and high rents in Milton. Private developments took place. In 1933 semi-detached houses on the Westlands Estate, with garage space, were being advertised for £430, and two years later Wraights developed the Hawthorn Orchard Estate. In 1935 there was the possibility that Gore Court Park, the 19th century home of George Smeed, could have been developed as a housing estate, but the Council decided to reserve the land for public use and it became King George's Playing Fields. (33)

Following the Second World War housing became a high priority for Sittingbourne Council, especially on the 36 acre Ufton Lane / College Road site, where Prisoners of War were used to help in the building work. The need for houses to be built quickly led to the use of prefabricated Nissen huts at Kemsley to house 60 families. By January 1948 the Council had finished its building programme, but there was still a housing shortage, with 900 on the Council waiting list, then in August a new housing estate off the Canterbury Road opened. (34)

As in the 19th century, some local people experienced problems with gipsies. In 1938 there was a street battle between local residents and caravan dwellers. A man driving a greengrocer's van was attacked by eight men. Miss Mable Featherstone rushed from her hairdressing shop on the corner of Shortlands Road, brandishing a pair of curling tongs, and dragged the man to safety. In spite of the bravery of that lady, local women were afraid following the incident and locked their doors - in those days doors were usually left unlocked! (35)

The first half of the 20th century:
Public Buildings/Authorities & Public Transport
An attempt was made in 1902 to bring about the amalgamation of Sittingbourne and Milton but it failed, largely because of a campaign in Milton to keep 'Milton for the Miltonians'. However, by the early 20th century Milton was suffering from the fact that its name was a common one, there being 20 other Milton's in the country. In spite of adding 'next Sittingbourne' to the postal address letters continued to go astray. In 1907 Milton Council decided to change its name and, in view of its past royal connection, decided on Milton Royal. However when it applied to the County Council to make the change it was told that the Secretary of State could not agree to the use of the word 'Royal' and the word 'Regis', meaning 'of or belonging to the King' was suggested as an alternative. In November 1907 the change in name from Milton to Milton Regis was approved by Kent County Council. (36)

By 1926 Milton Regis Council were investigating the purchase of land, the Tannery in Chalkwell or Westfield, London Road, for a new Town Hall. The building they were using had been built in 1803, the council had purchased it in 1886 but it had no room suitable for public meetings as the upper room had been condemned in 1916 because the joists were rotten. Then in January 1927 a proposal was put to Sittingbourne Council that they should amalgamate with that of Milton. There were many points in favour of the scheme. It was clear that although the towns had previously been distinct they now practically constituted one town. The boundary between the two crossing, as it did, streets, and even through houses, caused significant problems, not least in the provision of water and sewage disposal. Some streets had two or more sewers and water mains and both towns went to considerable expense to pump sewage to their respective sewage works which could without cost drain easily to the others. It was clearly economically inefficient to have two town halls, two fire stations etc., when one would suffice. Also if they were united into one town then their joint size would give them greater status than they each had on their own. People living in both towns worked in the other, and yet it was in Sittingbourne that all the public amenities, library, swimming baths, cinemas, and the railway station were situated. Sittingbourne Council accepted the recommendation and invited Milton Council to a conference. A referendum was held in Milton, 783 voted in favour of amalgamating with Sittingbourne but 1384 voted against. (37)

In 1929 though it was finally decided that the two towns would amalgamate under the name of Sittingbourne and Milton, Sittingbourne having objected to the original choice of Milton and Sittingbourne. Five years later Milton Rural District Council merged with that of Faversham to form Swale. In 1937 the new Sittingbourne Urban Council put forward plans to acquire land for a new Town Hall, offices, Library and Fire Station. The intervention of the Second World War meant that these plans were shelved. However in 1948 they proposed to use land behind the existing Town Hall, between the High Street and Remembrance Avenue, moving the Cattle Market to land nearer the railway, and including in the scheme a public gardens. (38)

Although the railway continued to be important, during the first half of the 20th century it was bus services which dominated public transport in Sittingbourne, especially in the 1930s. The increase in the number of buses using Sittingbourne High Street by 1930 led to an appeal for a bus shelter. Then in 1931 a new company, the Venture Motor Bus Company set up a business in competition with the established firm of Maidstone and District. Their application for a license was rejected when M & D objected. Maidstone and District were losing business to Venture who were cheaper and more popular, carrying 3,062 passengers to and from London in August that year and over one and a half thousand passengers on their local buses on just one Saturday. Venture appealed against the decision and they were backed by the local council and the local MP, but their appeal was rejected. In 1932 there was criticism of the Road Traffic Commission for refusing to grant new bus licenses but Maidstone and District continued to dominate the local bus services. Then in 1935 there was a controversy between them and the council over the congestion caused by their buses in Sittingbourne High Street. There were no bus shelters or waiting accommodation and the council wanted M & D to provide a bus station at the rear of their East Street offices. (39)

The first half of the 20th century: Public Service Organisations
For most of the first part of the 20th century Sittingbourne and Milton continued to have separate Fire and Ambulance Brigades. In 1901 Milton acquired a new steam fire engine and in 1928 a new fire station was opened in Crown Road and a new fire engine was dedicated. The men of both brigades continued to be volunteers, and in 1921 Chief Fire Officer Hedley Peters spoke out in favour of retaining the voluntary system rather than employing professional firemen. When fires occurred the distinctive 'crack' could be heard as the maroon was exploded by the Sittingbourne Fire Brigade as a signal for the men to gather and high up in the air the ball of smoke could be seen, curling away like an inverted mushroom. In 1906 the Sittingbourne Brigade won the Premier event at the South-Eastern District Championships at Crystal Palace. In 1938 the two Fire Brigades finally merged into one. During this period two new ambulances were dedicated, the first, a motor ambulance, in 1924, then one belonging to the St John's Ambulance Brigade in 1932. (40)

There were developments in the provision of both gas and electricity during the first half of the 20th century. In 1900 a Public Notice was issued that the County of Kent Electrical Power Distribution Company Limited had the right to construct works, lay down wires and other apparatus and to break up streets in Sittingbourne and Milton. In spite of this auspicious start to the new century it was not until 1926 that Milton Council applied to the Electric Power Company to provide electricity for the town, by that time Sittingbourne and Milton were the only towns in the area not to have it. By 1929 electricity cables had been laid, however in 1934 the council voted in favour of gas rather than electricity for street lighting. A new gas holder had been erected in Milton in 1929, in 1930 new gas showrooms and an office were opened in Milton and two years later a new modern gas works were opened in the town. (41)

In 1911 another new post office was opened, this time at the top part of Sittingbourne High Street, near the Baptist Tabernacle. Ten years later the Sittingbourne Telephone Exchange moved to new premises. The improved facilities at the exchange meant that people no longer had to turn the handle of a magneto generator to call the exchange they could just lift the receiver. The local directory for the 1920s included the telephone numbers of local subscribers. Often several had the same number, with an additional figure given. This was the number of times that the particular phone would ring - presumably those with the same number could easily listen in to other people's conversations! (42)

There were also improvements in the provision of library services during the period. In 1901 they were occupying rented premises and a number of the books were ones which had once belonged to the Literary and Scientific Association. The Free Library was not the only one operating in the town. In 1911 there was an advertisement for Thomas Ash and Sons, The Library, High Street, which had been brought up to date with the newest books and charged 2d a week per book or by subscription. In 1930 the Public Library extended its opening hours to from 3 to 5 p.m. and 6 to 8 p.m., except Wednesday which was early closing day in the town. The following year the council debated whether or not to employ a full-time librarian and accepted the County Council Library Scheme, which led to the closure of the Milton, Kemsley and Murston Library Centres. Following the joining of the County Scheme £2,000 worth of new books were purchased and in 1934 the council recommended demolishing Milton Old Town Hall and building a Public Library and toilets on the site, although this was not opened until 1939. In 1949 the Sittingbourne Library moved from Crescent Street to rooms over Burtons in the High Street. (43

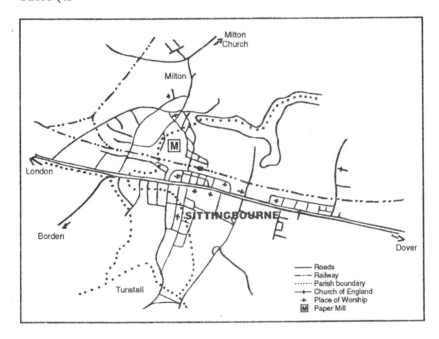

Sittingbourne and Milton Between the Wars

The library was to move again during the second half of the 20th century. Before moving on to that period it is worth looking at two entries in the East Kent Gazette. In 1931, following the census which showed that there were 10,087 males and 10,088 females in Sittingbourne and Milton a cartoon said that the town had: two Town Halls; two Fire Brigades; two Waterworks; two

Surveyors; two Gas Undertakings BUT only one surplus woman, and rumour has it that she has emigrated! (44)

In 1935 the paper looked back on the urban developments during the twenty-five years of the reign of King George. The Council had built more than 700 houses including roads such as Trotts Hall Gardens, Glovers Crescent, Elm Grove, Bobbing Road, South Avenue, Barrow Grove and Vicarage Orchard as well as subsidising the private building of a hundred others. In addition Kemsley Village had been built and roads had been improved, notably Bell Road, which had been transformed from a narrow hedge-lined lane into a desirable residential district. Cromers Road had been constructed, replacing an old bridle path and together with the Avenue of Remembrance, built under the Unemployment Relief Scheme, improved access to the town. Roads had also been improved with the addition of 'Belisha Beacons'. Open spaces had been provided, the Meads Playing Field, Chilton Playing Field, Gore Court Park (King George's), and, thanks to the generosity of Mr and Mrs Andrews, The Grove sports ground. The unified town would benefit from a new Sewerage Scheme, improved water supply, banishing the anxieties of the recent drought years, up-to-date fire pumps, a well-equipped motor ambulance and a re-constructed Swimming Baths, with constantly clean water. New schools had been built (see Chapter Seven) and as well as the new Cottage Hospital a Health Visitor and Child Welfare Centres served the area. (45)

The second half of the 20th century: Sanitation & Health
By the mid-20th century most of the problems over sanitation had been overcome, although there was opposition in the 1960s to the addition of fluoride to the water supply, part of a national debate on the issue. In 1972 the Church Marshes Sewage Works in Milton were extended, although as has been noted in Chapter Four, the location of the sewage outfall was linked to problems with the smell from the Creek. The sewage system itself, in the late 1980s, suffered problems with sewage overflowing and serious flooding in certain areas of the town. It was, though, the question of hospital cover for the town that dominated the period. In the mid-1970s over 600 people a year had operations at the Memorial Hospital, but in spite of this it was announced in 1976 that the hospital was to close. There was a campaign against its closure and in 1978 it was given an £82,000 facelift. However, six months after it reopened plans were announced that it was to close for five months, perhaps for good. The hospital, however, remained open through the 1980s, over a thousand operations being performed there during 1984. But the fight was eventually lost and the surgery closed in July 1988. There were fears in 1991 that it would be demolished, but in the end it was incorporated into a new building housing a psychiatric unit. There were also changes occurring at Keycol Hospital. Although in 1981 plans to build a geriatric and day-care centre were abandoned, in 1985 improvements were being made to the facilities so that patients from the Milton Hospital (the old Workhouse) could be transferred there. In the 1990s Keycol Hill was chosen to be the site of a children's hospice, Demelza House. (46)

The second half of the 20th century: Housing

A huge amount of housing development took place during the second half of the 20th century. Whereas the emphasis in housing development in the 19th century was on private developments, and council housing dominated the first half of the 20th century, in this period there was a greater balance between the two. This section will then be split into three parts, council housing, private housing and other factors relating to housing.

Council housing:
There was a flurry of council building during the 1950s. In 1950 work was well underway on the Homewood estate and what was referred to as Sittingbourne's miniature 'Garden City' - the Canterbury Road estate was due to be completed by 1953. In 1953 the first houses to be completed on the North Court Estate in Milton were officially opened. By 1957 the thousandth council house since the war was built, the largest of the post-war estates was Canterbury Road, with 418 houses and flats. As well as North Court and Homewood Avenue, Manor Grove had been built and work had started on a new estate at Staplehurst Road. The council at that time were planning to build a hundred more houses, then no more. The following year, though, Government restrictions on capital expenditure cut the housing programme from 164 to 56. In 1959 older council houses were improved. £60,000 was spent on improving 327 homes, including putting in inside toilets. (47)

By 1960, of the 7,000 houses in Sittingbourne, 2,000 were council properties. The 1960s was the final decade of major council building, another 500 council houses were built by 1967, when tenants faced rent increases because of a £29,000 budget deficiency. During this period, in 1965, Sittingbourne was one of the first towns to adopt a special method of 'systemized' building of council houses in Glebe Lane and Cedar Close, much to the dismay of local brickmakers. In 1967 a council development in Murston Road included 30 houses, 30 one-bedroom flats in three storey blocks and 14 three-bedroom maisonettes. In 1973 the council took over control of Kemsley and in 1981 the houses there were improved so that they were better than newer council-built properties. Flats on the Murston Road estate were converted into maisonettes in 1985 and in 1988 plans were announced to change the face of council housing with the setting up of a new housing association. (48)

Private developments:
In 1959 there were private estates at Ufton Court, Pigeon Orchard, Gaze Hill, Staplehurst Road, Windmill Road, Highsted, Beechwood Avenue, Regis Park and Park Drive, - detached four-bedroom houses with integral garages on the latter costing £2,850! The Fulston Manor Estate was built during the early 1960s and in 1965 Wards Construction planned to build 155 houses between College Road and Borden Lane. The late 1960s was a time of expansion, in February 1969, 929 new houses had been built in the previous 12 months, a further 560 had been started and there were 454 under construction. There were also plans for 56 detached three and four-bedroom houses and

121

bungalows off Highsted Road with complete pedestrian and traffic separation. (49)

In 1970 plans for a mini-estate at the top of Park Road were approved but the access of the planned Grove Park Estate on to the A2 was attacked. The estate went ahead, by 1973 seventy five percent of the residents there were commuters and the following year they fought plans by the council to buy private houses there for the use of council tenants. In the early 1970s house prices rocketed and the council was under attack for not releasing more land for housing. Plans were announced for a new mini-town in north Milton and in 1978 work began on the giant housing scheme. (50)

Church Milton Estate

In 1983 150 houses were built in Peregrine Drive and Gaze Hill and in 1985 the Church Milton Estate opened. However there was anger in the early 1990s when the residents there discovered that their gardens were contaminated by lead. Other small scale developments continued, such as the redevelopment of the Bell Road Jam Factory (Deans) site, but the building of large scale private estates ended with the slump in the building trade. (51)

Other Factors:
Along with the building of new houses, both private and council, came the demolishing of old roads in the town centre. In 1953 it was proposed that nine houses in King Street and four in Gas Road be demolished as all were subject to flooding, however at that time there was a problem in rehousing the

families. By 1955 a five-year slum clearance programme was planned, which would mean that 305 houses would have to go, and the families be re-housed. In 1960 32 premises on New Road, Milton Road and The Wall were cleared and in 1962 the council compulsory purchased Cross Street, Lorne Place and Berry Street, work on demolishing the latter starting the following year. Sometimes houses were demolished, not because of the condition of the properties, but to improve traffic flow through the town. Houses and streets, including Pembury Street, Dover Street and Spring Street all made way for the one-way system. The slum clearance programme was causing problems by 1967 as council house building was not providing enough new accommodation to house those who were losing their homes. (52)

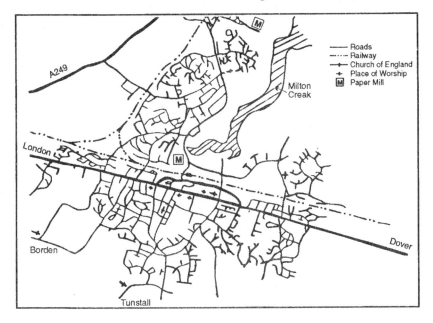

Sittingbourne in the 1990s

However houses continued to be demolished, 80 houses in Eastbourne Street, Queen Street, Faith Street, Princes Street and Milton Road were purchased by the council in 1970 prior to their being demolished, although this did not happen for some time - those in Eastbourne Street were still standing in 1974. Empty houses could cause problems, residents of Shakespeare Street complained of being overrun by rats because of the number of boarded-up houses. An alternative to clearing older houses was to improve them and that was what happened in Frederick Street, Gibson Street, Arthur Street and parts of Hawthorne Road and Laburnum Place where residents were given grants to modernise their homes. (53)

Many of those who lost their homes during the slum clearance programme were elderly and the period saw the building of council homes and flats for the elderly. The first block of flats built was Churchill House in Milton in 1966. This was followed by Johnson House, and in 1970 a warden controlled home in Pembury Street. Ten years later Tannery Court, a sheltered housing scheme was built and in 1985 two blocks of flats were built in Frederick Street - Mockett Court and Freeman Court, both named after local community workers. (54)

In spite of the vast increase in the number of houses in Sittingbourne, there were still those who preferred not to live in them, and the provision of suitable locations for gipsies and travellers was a problem throughout the period. In 1958 there was un-authorised caravan camping on railway land in the Crown Quay Lane area and in 1963 there were fears of a gipsy invasion as more were staying during the winter on APCM land in Murston. In May that year the gipsies were evicted but some moved to Milton, and the council considered providing a permanent site at the Murston Sewage Pumping Station. Evictions from Bowater's land occurred the following year and land at The Wall, Milton, was used as a camp site. The problem flared again in 1966 when caravans were parked on waste land near Musgrove Road and a private firm was used to evict them, the following year there were complaints against their being in the Princes Street area. (55)

In 1976 Murston residents won their fight to prevent a gipsy camp being set up near their houses and in 1980 plans to put 15 permanent gipsy pitches on Gas Road were shelved, although later a gipsy site was set up at Murston. In 1982 there was a mass eviction of up to 60 caravans from Church Marshes, north of Milton, and various village sites were considered, with the decision to use Hooks Hole Quarry in Borden being approved in 1984. The gipsies, however, continued to use Church Marshes, in 1984 they were blamed for damage done to Milton Church Hall, in 1987 children gipsy children stoned health worker's cars at Church Marshes and the site became a battleground when police were attacked in 1988. The same year saw the eviction of gipsies from Mill Road but the problem continued into the 1990s with caravans moving on to closed industrial sites before being evicted. (56)

The second half of the 20th century: Public Transport & Public Buildings
The late 1950s saw the electrification of the railway and Sittingbourne station was enlarged to cope with the additional traffic. It was expected that the amount of traffic would double with more trains for city workers, 37 a day to and from London. However fears that Sittingbourne would become a dormitory town were unfounded. Rail links to the Isle of Sheppey were also improved with the opening, in 1960, of a new Kings Ferry bridge over the Swale. Local bus services to rural areas declined as private transport increased and local villages were sometimes served by a post bus. (57)

The civic building scheme, planned before the Second World War, finally became a reality. In 1960 the council approved a scheme for new council offices on the corner of Central Avenue and Remembrance Avenue and in 1965 these were completed ahead of schedule. With the opening of the new Assembly Hall there the old Town Hall in the High Street closed, the site being sold for re-development. The final event there was an exhibition of dolls from around the world. In 1973 the local Council joined with Sheppey and Faversham under the name of Swale and in 1977 it was granted the status of a Borough with the right to elect a Mayor, the council eventually took over premises at the corner of East Street and Crown Quay Lane, where once almshouses had stood. In 1994 there were fears that Swale would lose its identity if it had to merge with Maidstone under a new local government system, however in 1995 it was announced that the existing councils were to remain. Although there was a significant amount of new building during the period the old was not forgotten and in 1958 Milton Court Hall was renovated, with its use being changed to that of a museum in 1972. (58)

The second half of the 20th century: Public Service Organisations
The civic building scheme in Central Avenue included Revenue House, the first building to be completed, a new Police Station, Post Office and Library. The need for a new library was apparent in 1951 when the old one was becoming congested. In 1953 a new, temporary, building was opened in the car park behind the High Street Town Hall, and the following year a Junior Assistant was employed so that the library could remain open at lunch-time. The Public Library had competition at this time from a commercial operation, Chain Libraries, which had premises in the High Street, a stock of 5,000 books and also served as a social centre. (59)

In 1958 a new, permanent library, costing £10,000 was opened by the author, H E Bates. In his speech he said that the inspiration for the family in his best-seller 'The Darling Buds of May', had come when he had been on his way to Sittingbourne on a previous occasion and he had stopped at a village shop where he saw a whole family, mother, father and seven or eight children pile into a very dilapidated truck. The building was extended in 1971, at a cost of £50,000. The library in Milton High Street was though closed in the 1990s and plans were made for a museum of Sittingbourne & Milton to be located there. It was in 1961 that the new Post Office opened in Central Avenue, in spite of objections to the low site, requiring steps down to it. When the Post Office was opened there was already a new Telephone Exchange on the site. Work had started in 1958 and it was expected at that time to provide over 2,200 subscribers compared to the 1,353 at the exchange at the old High Street Post Office. More lines were required in the mid-1960s and in 1966 plans were announced for an extension providing 800 new phone lines. (60)

The Police Station also moved to a site in Central Avenue in the 1970s leaving the old building at the bottom of Park Road to be used as a court house, although by 1995 the future of the old building was in doubt. There were also moves to new premises for the fire and ambulance services. A new Ambulance Station opened in 1963 on St Michael's Road, although the road itself did not officially open until the following year. It was not though until 1981 that a new Fire Station was opened, also on St Michael's Road. It had been next to the Baptist Tabernacle, and prior to that in Crescent Street.

By 1957 over 23,000 homes had electricity and in spite of the great changeover to North Sea gas in the early 1970s, the first house was connected in November 1971, the second half of the 20th century was increasingly dominated by the use of electric power. (62)

Chapter Seven

Religion and Education

RELIGION - Introduction

In this part of the chapter the main religious denominations will be considered separately. In each, individual buildings will be dealt with in chronological order. Only a brief general history of each can be given. No attempt is made to provide a guide to the surviving buildings although more detail, when available, will be given of those which no longer exist.

Anglican Churches

Before the Norman Conquest (1066), the present day area of Sittingbourne, including Milton and Murston, was one large parish - Milton. The parish church was located in the marshes north of Milton, on the site of the present church.

Holy Trinity Church, Milton

Holy Trinity Church, Milton:
In 1052 an attempt was made, according to the Milton legend, to rebuild the church on a new site nearer to the town centre. The old site was cleared, however, every time stones were laid on the new site they were mysteriously moved during the night back to the old location. A watch was kept but no one was ever caught. It was believed that the hand of God, the great architect, was

at work and so the new church was erected on the original site. The main building material used was flint and the present chancel dates from that time. In Norman times there was also a south transept which included more Roman brick and sandstone. Milton was one of the wealthiest churches in the Canterbury diocese and soon after the Norman conquest it was given by William I to the Abbey of St Augustine in Canterbury. (1)

A sacristy was added to the chancel during the first half of the 13th century, this was a small chapel with a room above where an Anchorite, or Hermit, lived. During the 14th century alterations were made. The church was enlarged, the Norman south transept was incorporated into the south wall and the tower - the largest parochial church tower in Kent and the third largest in England - was built. In 1450 a chantry chapel was added by the wealthy de Northwode family. Jane, co-heiress of Norwood, married Sir John Norton, who became Sheriff of Kent in 1514, and his marble tomb stands in the chapel. Mass would have been said in the chapel for the founders and their relatives until England broke with Roman Catholic church during the reign of Henry VIII. At that time there would have been a great chancel screen, carrying a rood loft, dividing the nave from the chancel. In 1514 John Godyn left in his will, 'a bushel of malt to the gilding of the rood loft.' In 1516 Thomas Berry made a gift to the church of 6/8 for 'the making of the new frame of the bells'. In the 17th century the four existing bells were recast at Whitechapel to make five new bells. Also during the 17th century the church was extensively repaired, but by the mid 19th century it was falling into disrepair. However, the idea of pulling it down and replacing it with a new church closer to the centre of Milton was rejected by parishioners. (2)

In 1888, although the church was little used, (St. Paul's having been built in 1863), it was decided to restore it. As well as general and structural repairs the Tower Screen, the seven foot high panelling and the box pews were all removed. Red tile was laid and new pews were fitted. During the 20th century stained glass was put in the East window and the Tudor communion rail, the tower and the roof were all restored or repaired. An oak reredos was added to the high altar in 1933 and in 1970 a new Tower Screen was erected.

St Michael's Church, Sittingbourne:
During the 11th century when Lanfranc set up Rural Deaneries there was no mention of Sittingbourne. The original church, consisting of a nave and chancel, dates from the Norman period. During the 13th century the chancel was doubled in length and in the following century the side aisles and the lady chapel were added, the latter being built on a crypt. The tower, which had been started in the 13th century, was completed in the 15th century and at that time the cross aisle was extended and a rood loft erected. Fifteenth century wills refer to the High Altar and ones dedicated to St Mary, St Christopher, St John Baptist and the Holy Cross in the chapel of St John; to the chapel of the Blessed Virgin Mary; the light of St Katherine; the light of St Michael; the chapel of St Nicholas on the south side of the choir of the church and the light

of St Clement; the light of St James; the Image of the Holy Cross; and the Image of the Blessed Mary. The images may well have been frescoes, wall paintings, as ancient frescoes were discovered during restoration work in the 19th century. There was also a shrine on the exterior of the church known as 'Our Lady of the Buttress' which was discovered in 1962. (3)

St. Michael's Church, Sittingbourne

During the 17th century, when the then five bells were recast to give six, there was an oak church porch or stile outside, but this disappeared in the 18th century. The church suffered badly from fire in 1762 and was never restored to its former grandeur. Some improvements were made in the 1860s when a memorial stained glass window was installed with a reredos beneath, seats were fitted and the cross aisle was restored. However attempts in 1873 to restore the roof of the nave nearly led to the collapse of the whole building - the tower in fact seems to have been built without foundations! In the late 19th century the number of bells was increased to eight and in 1923 a peal of 5,056 changes was rung. In the 1880s the church opened a Mission Room in East Street and in the 1960s St Michael's House, a social centre, was opened behind the church. (4)

Holy Trinity Church, Sittingbourne:
In 1860 it was proposed that a new church be built in the west of Sittingbourne and a design was drawn up by Mr Wimble, architect, of London. In 1663 the Rev Graham was appointed and the new 'church' used a building in Pembury

Street, there not being enough funds for a permanent building. In 1865, when £1,300 of the estimated £3,600 had been raised or promised, a start was made on the boundary walls and, although unfinished, the church was officially opened on 2nd October 1866. The building in Pembury Street was used as a school room and for social / fund-raising events. In 1869 Queen Victoria approved the assignment of a district to Holy Trinity, which meant that weddings could take place there, and a bazaar was held at Gore Court Park in aid of funds. In 1871 a letter was published in the local paper from Thomas Lake of Tonge. He referred to having 'seen three large buildings erected in Sittingbourne as Dissenting places of worship while the half finished structure at the top of the town represent(ed) the effort of the Churchmen of this district to provide for the spiritual wants of the rapidly increased population in the locality in which it is erected'. (5)

Holy Trinity Church, Sittingbourne

An appeal was made to the general public for funds and in 1873 the building was finally completed, the original building having been extended by 23 feet and side aisles added. In 1879 an organ was installed, replacing a harmonium, and a reredos was erected below the East window. Plans were made to replace the single bell with a peal of six bells in 1895 but it was found that major alterations would need to be made to the tower to support their weight and the plans were never carried out. A vestry was added on the north side of the church in 1898 and in 1902 the Lady Chapel was built. (6)

Holy Trinity, as did many churches, played a major social as well as religious role in the community. In 1906 Holy Trinity Hall opened with a concert at which the Holy Trinity Glee Party sang and the Trinity Men's Club was started in connection with the Trinity Institute. The church was innovative, leading the way in using lay persons to do readings, in setting up a 'Children's corner' and having a Good Friday Procession of Witness. Plans to unite Holy Trinity with St Mary's in the 1950s were not realised, however with falling numbers in the 1970s the church was linked with Bobbing. In 1994 the 125th anniversary of the church was celebrated with a Victorian Weekend. (7)

St Paul's, Milton:
In 1859 funds were raised by public subscription for a new church in the centre of Milton. The new church was built in 1863 on a site in Waterlane, later called St Paul's Street after the new church. The ground, given by the Archbishop of Canterbury, although swampy, was convenient, being at that time in an area of high density housing. The building was of brick, in a Gothic style, the builder being George Chrisfield. According to the local paper the church had 'no pretensions to architectural beauty' the style being 'a kind of nondescript'. The front was plain, but the back 'had a better appearance with a large Gothic window'. The interior was 'bare of ornament' and a pair of large doors opened directly from the street, letting cold air in. There was seating for 700 with a nave and two side aisles, separated by octagonal pillars, (as in the churches of Holy Trinity, Milton and Sittingbourne), and the church was lit by gaslight. After the opening service a hundred children of the Sunday School processed with flags and banners through the town. The building was demolished around 1950. (8)

St Mary's, Milton (Park Road):
With the increase in the population of south Milton came calls for a church to serve the Park Road area of the parish. In 1898 a bequest of money provided a grant of £2,000 for the proposed church. Work on the building started in 1901 and it was consecrated in 1902. In 1925 the population in the north of Milton parish (Kemsley) had increased and the parish was divided, with St Mary's parish south of the railway line and Milton parish to the north. In 1938 the church buildings were increased when a hall was built on the west end. (9)

Roman Catholic
During the Medieval period, as well as St Michael's Church there were two other Roman Catholic places of worship for pilgrims travelling along the road from London to Canterbury. The Hermitage of Shamel was located to the west of Sittingbourne, at the foot of the hill leading from London Road to the High Street, where a stream crossed the road. It certainly existed in 1255 when Henry III issued a writ to find out how much it and the four houses held by Brother Silvester, Hermit of St Augustines, were worth. This hermitage was dedicated to St Thomas and there was another religious house to the east of the town, Swainstree, on Snips Hill. (10)

An Act of Parliament in 1549 replace the Catholic Mass with the Prayer Book service still used in the Church of England. Local wills dating from this time no longer include gifts for the different saints at St Michael's, nor for priests to say masses for their souls. The change from Roman Catholic to Anglican was though a slow one. The reign of Henry's daughter Mary saw a return to Catholic worship, but with the accession of Elizabeth I in 1558 the priest at Milton was deposed and laws passed against Catholic priests. In 1587 a priest was arrested in Sittingbourne and later executed in Canterbury. Some local families continued in the Catholic faith, the most notable being the Roper family of Lynsted, the chapel in their house being finally closed in 1775.

A Roman Catholic revival occurred in the late 19th century and in 1881 a Mass was celebrated in a house near Sittingbourne railway station. In March 1892 a series of lectures were given at Sittingbourne Town Hall against Catholics, but later in the same year a chapel/school together with a house for a priest was built on the London Road, and the first public Mass was held on the 20th November that year. In 1893 an open air service was held with the Litany in Latin and the following year the property known as Schamel was opened as a Catholic Convent school. (11)

Catholic Church

The foundation stone of a new Catholic Church was laid in 1901 and it was opened and consecrated the following year. In 1905 an 'Angelus Chime' of eight bells was first heard and in 1910 the first Requiem Mass to take place in Sittingbourne since the Reformation was performed. Corpus Christi processions took place and in 1929 the route was extended so that the public could get a better view, one resident remembers seeing the girls from the Convent School in their white dresses scattering rose petals. In the 1930s the Assembly Hall in West Street, formerly used by the Liberals, was opened as Whitefriars Hall, the Carmelite Order returned from exile and took over the church in Sittingbourne and the Carmel Hall in Ufton Lane was opened. (12)

Non-Conformist Churches
Methodists:
There is evidence that non-conformist congregations met in Sittingbourne and Milton in the 18th century. Probably the oldest, and certainly the most widespread in terms of churches in the local villages as well as the urban area, is the Methodist church. In a lecture on Early Methodism given in Sittingbourne in 1907 references were made to John Wesley visiting the town in 1768, 1771 and 1784. In 1863, when the original Wesleyan Methodist Church in the High Street was being demolished to make way for the new building, a house which had stood in front of the chapel, was also demolished. At that time the local paper reported that 'John Wesley is stated to have preached on several occasions in one of the rooms belonging to the old house'. The new 'handsome and commodious edifice' erected at that time by L Shrubsole of Faversham, to a design by J Wilson of Bath, was 'built in the Italian Gothic style' with 'a square tower in front, with four pointed gables of open stone work'. There was a spire on top and a vestry at the base, entrances in the tower led, via stone steps, to the galleries. The ground floor was entered through a vestibule to the right of the tower and, including the galleries, the building provided seating for seven hundred. The ceiling was slightly arched and divided into square panels, with oak mouldings and carved bosses. The rostrum, or pulpit, was unusual in that it was large enough for four people. Below it stood the communion table on a platform, separated from the ground floor by a light oak rail. The floor was covered with a 'handsome Brussels carpet of the fleur-de-lis pattern'. The building had gas lights and a central heating system. There was a large Gothic window in the tower end and the five windows on each side of the main body of the church had blue and crimson stained glass in the quatrefoils. In 1875 the building was enlarged with the addition of an orchestra and a minister's vestry, then in 1899 the foundation stone was laid for new buildings adjoining the church. In 1859 the Wesleyan Sunday School met at a building in East Street to which a new ante-room had recently been added and in 1903 the first Evangelical Mission was held at the Wesleyan Methodist Chapel at Snips Hill. (13)

These buildings were much smaller than the Wesleyan Methodist church in the High Street. It was the largest place of worship for Methodists in the urban area, but Wesleyan Methodists were not the only Methodists to worship locally. In 1859 the Bible Christian Society opened a new chapel at St George's Street, Snips Hill. In 1879 there were plans for them to have a new chapel in East Street but the memorial stone was not laid until October 1887. The Bible Christian Society became the United Methodist Church in the 20th century and in 1920 the Ex-Bible Christians at the United Methodist Church in East Street celebrated their centenary. (14)

In 1868 another group of Methodists, the Primitive Methodists, planned to build a chapel in Shakespeare Road. This was erected the following year but by 1871 was already too small and it was planned to build a new one, using the old one as a schoolroom. It is not clear whether or not the plan was carried out at that time but in 1883 a 'substantial and commodious chapel was built', in front of the old building, by Messrs High and Monk to a design by the architect W L Grant. Seating was provided for 250 and local businesses made contributions, including a gift of the cocoa matting from John Peters and the provision and erection, at cost, of the palisading in front of the building by Tett and Hussey. (15)

Methodist Church Sittingbourne, High Street (Pre-War)

Primitive Methodism was also strong in Milton. There was already a chapel there in 1860 and in 1863 a bazaar was held to reduce the debt on the building. Another bazaar was held there in May 1877, this time to raise funds for a new chapel in St Paul's Street, which was built in 1878. In 1885 the Milton Primitive Methodist Mission Band performed at the 'old' chapel, now called a Mission Hall, in St Paul's Street. (16)

There was also a Wesleyan Methodist chapel in Church Street, Milton, and there were close links between the different Methodist churches, both in the urban area and the surrounding villages. In 1898 the Guild Band performed during the interval of a lantern lecture given at Sittingbourne Town Hall, as part of the Wesley Guild Winter Lectures. The local methodist churches finally amalgamated in the 1960s with the Wesleyan Methodist Church in Sittingbourne High Street becoming the main place of worship. It was not though the same building that had been opened in 1863. That had been destroyed in February 1944 (see Chapter Nine on the Second World War for details) and a new church had been built on the site in 1952. The foundation stone laid in October 1951 was part of the original building and contained a copy of the East Kent Gazette for that year. (17)

Milton Congregational Church

Congregationalists (URC):
Congregationalists as well as Methodists worshipped locally in the 18th century. In 1910 the History of Paradise Chapel, Milton, was published. It stated that in 1789 there were no dissenting places of worship in Milton, the first chapel being erected in 1790. This building was 'a simple square building abutting right on to the footpath, with cottage-like windows fitted with folding shutters'. In the 1840s, when the Rev Parrett started his ministry, the meeting place was a wooden building in Crown Road. Then in 1856 something happened which led to a rapid increase in the church's membership. At that time legally everyone had to pay rates to the Church of England. Many non-conformists, dissenters, objected to this and when the Rev Parrett took a stand and refused to pay the rate his household goods were seized and put up for auction. Non-conformists from Sittingbourne, where Church rates had been

135

virtually abolished, came to support Rev Parrett, as did many from Milton. His furniture was bought and returned to him and a collection taken to cover the legal expenses. As a result the payment of Church rate ended in Milton and in 1860 a new chapel was built in Crown Road, meetings being held in the Milton Wool Warehouse during its construction. It was a neat Gothic structure with a small tower and spire at the east end with a large schoolroom and vestry attached. Three years later there were over three hundred children attending the Sunday School and a new schoolroom had to be erected at the side of the church. In 1894 there was a split in the congregation with a new church worshipping, first in the old Primitive Methodist chapel and then in a new iron building called the 'Bethel Mission Hall'. The two congregations were reunited in 1909. In the 1840s there had been talk of uniting the Congregational churches of Sittingbourne and Milton but they could not agree on a common place of worship. They were finally united in the 1970s when the Milton Congregational Church closed, the building subsequently falling into disrepair and eventually being demolished in 1992. (18)

The new United Reform Church used the old Sittingbourne Congregational Church building in Sittingbourne High Street which had been opened in 1863. For 20 years before that time the 'Free' Church had met at the Latimer Chapel in the Butts, Sittingbourne - they celebrated their 51st anniversary in 1892. After the new church was built they continued to use the Latimer Chapel as a Sunday School until 1878 when they built a new Sunday School room in Crescent Street. After the First World War the Congregational Church opened a War Memorial Institute for Young People in Berry Street at the rear of the Crescent Street School Rooms. In the 1920s the Congregational Church had its own Tennis Club, as did other churches, including the Baptist Tabernacle in Sittingbourne High Street. (19)

Baptists:
The Baptist Church dates from the greatest decade of church building in Sittingbourne, the 1860s. In April 1866 the Rev Spurgeon, a leading English Baptist, preached at St Michael's in aid of a fund for building a new church. Later in the same year the Baptist Sunday School was formed and a site chosen. The Rev Spurgeon returned in 1867 to lay the memorial stone and the building was opened in October that year. It was a plain brick structure with seating for five hundred. There was provision for a gallery to be added later if required and the builder was Luke Phillips junior of Milton. (20)

In 1881 the Rev Doubleday was appointed pastor - he was to remain as pastor for the next 40 years. It was a time of expansion. In 1884 a Sunday School building was added to the west side of the church. In 1886 extra seating in the church was provided with the erection of a gallery and in January 1897 the memorial hall and rooms were opened. As well as increasing facilities at their main place of worship the Baptists also opened Mission Rooms in Flushing Street, Milton, and at Bayford Road, Sittingbourne, where the increase in numbers attending the Sunday School in 1901 led to the premises being enlarged. (21)

Baptist Tabernacle, Sittingbourne

There were always close links between the Baptists and other evangelical organisations and in 1909 Herbert Booth, son of General Booth founder of the Salvation Army, led an evangelical mission at Sittingbourne Baptist Tabernacle. Towards the end of the 20th century there were plans to sell the High Street site and move to another location, Bell Road being a likely choice, as yet though these plans have not been realised. (22)

The Salvation Army:
The Salvation Army started in Sittingbourne in 1884 with parades on Whit Monday and the opening of Barracks in Shortlands Road. All did not always go smoothly in those early days and the local paper recorded that when James Millen, a new recruit, asked Arther Costen to stop smoking during a service at the hall he was attacked. Costen later appeared in Court and was fined for riotous behaviour. In 1914 a breakaway group, the Milton Christian Mission, used the old St Paul's Schoolroom in Kingsmill Road, Milton, as a place of worship. The Salvation Army also met in Milton, in Bridge Street and around the time of the First World War they held meetings at the Ebenezer Gospel Hall in West Street. (23)

The Salvation Army Band started in the late 19th century under Bill Shilling and is remembered by Sittingbourne residents as playing outside a pub at the junction of Bell Road and East Street during the early decades of the 20th century. At that time the Sittingbourne Songster Brigade had been formed under the leadership of William Beeching. The Salvation Army is known, not only for its music, but also for leadership in the temperance movement. When it came to Sittingbourne there was already a well established temperance movement - developed no doubt to counteract the high levels of drunkenness amongst brickfield workers. In June 1857 the Sittingbourne and Milton Temperance Society held their Annual Festival on Whit Monday. The following year 40 people 'took the pledge' following Temperance meetings and the Wesleyan Methodists formed a Band of Hope, the junior branch of the temperance movement. The Baptists also had a Band of Hope and in 1887 a Temperance crusade was supported by the Church of England as well as the non-conformist churches, Holy Trinity, Sittingbourne, had a Band of Hope in the 1890s. (24)

Other Non-Conformist Groups:
Those active in the area include the Mormons, the Pentecostalists and the Jehovah's Witnesses. The Mormons, also known as the Church of Jesus Christ of Latterday Saints, were very active in the area in the second half of the 19th century. Their evangelistic campaigns led to many local people emigrating to the USA (see section on emigration in Chapter Five). Their local meeting place was in Pembury Street and district conferences were held there in the 1890s. The Pentecostalists started locally in the 1920s when the local branch of the Assemblies of God baptised believers in Tonge Mill stream. In 1929 Pastor Jeffries had two houses knocked down in Berry Street and built the Welcome Hall. The church became part of the Pentecostal organisation in the 1940s and in 1970 they moved to a new home, in East Street. The Jehovah's Witnesses are a more recent addition and the local group meet in the Kingdom Hall behind Sittingbourne High Street. (25)

Most of the buildings used by the off-shoots of the main religious groups detailed in this brief history no longer exist. Also long gone are the Gospel Hall found in William Street for a few years at the turn of the century and the Ebenezer Gospel Hall in West Street which survived until the 1920s. (26)

Links between the churches were strengthened in the 1920s with the formation of the Sittingbourne Brotherhood (and later Sisterhood), a non-political, non-denominational Christian organisation. During the depression they organised soup kitchens, as did the Salvation Army, and they founded the local branch of the Lifeboat Association. In 1933 a Peace Gathering of Youth was held at the Football ground in which 25 Sunday Schools and other juvenile and adult groups took place, and in 1974 the first inter-denominational Procession of Witness on Good Friday took place. (27)

EDUCATION - Introduction
Unlike the previous section, where there was sufficient information to consider different denominations, and even individual buildings, separately, in

this section no attempt will be made to give detailed histories of individual schools. Instead, different schools will be referred to within a chronological outline of education in the local area, set in the context of the growth of, and changes in, the national system.

The 19th century: Elementary Education before 1870

In 1870, when the first Elementary Education Bill was introduced into Parliament, the situation in Sittingbourne and Milton was typical of much of the country. Both parishes had church schools, known as National Schools, and a number of private educational establishments, of variable standards. St Michael's National School in Sittingbourne was the oldest school, having been started in 1812 to teach children of the poor of either sex, reading, writing and arithmetic and the principles of the Christian religion. Funds for the school came from annual subscriptions, an annual collection at the church and weekly 'pence money' for each child. Children from the ages of six to fourteen attended the school which, until the 1840s, was held in a boarded off section of the church. Then in 1846 the St Michael's National Schools, for Boys and Girls, were built at the Butts, to the north of the church, in the same area as an Infant School, funded by the Vallance family, which had been built in 1839. (28)

In 1866 the Canterbury Diocesan Board of Education gave a grant of £60 to the fund for enlarging Sittingbourne National Schools to provide accommodation for 160 children in each school (Boys and Girls). By that time the Milton National and Infant Schools were well established, with annual treats being held in July. There were though far more children than could be accommodated in the National Schools. Some of these attended private schools such as Mr E Grigsby's Day School for Boys at his home at The Wall, J Bigwood's 'Sittingbourne Academy' or 'French House', an Establishment for Young Ladies and Gentlemen run by Mr and Mrs White. (29)

The 19th century: Elementary Education after 1870

The 1870 Elementary Education Act sought to complete the existing voluntary system, retaining efficient schools but filling up gaps to provide education for all children from five to thirteen. Districts were allowed a year in which to provide sufficient places through voluntary schemes, otherwise School Boards would be set up and schools provided using money collected by increasing rates. In Sittingbourne members of the Church of England, led by the Bishop of Dover, met in October 1870. An additional 300 places were needed in the Parish and the choice was either to 'extend and increase the National Schools in Sittingbourne, on the same principle as that on which they (were then) conducted; or else throw up their hands and go in for a rate-aided school'. The majority were in favour of continuing the 'National voluntary system of education, based upon religious teaching' - 'the moral effects of these schools were obvious to all'. As a result of the meeting a committee was set up and a subscription started to raise money for a new National School. (30)

Non-conformists in the town were also opposed to increased rates and secular education, so a meeting was held by Methodists at which it was decided to enlarge the building then used as a Sunday School to provide accommodation for a Day School. The Memorial stone for this was laid in May 1873 and the Wesleyan Day School opened in January 1874 for around 150 pupils, the Headmaster being Mr Roper. Eighteen months earlier, in May 1872, Holy Trinity National Schools opened in Spring Street, to the north of Holy Trinity Church. The building cost £900 and could accommodate 300. The opening of this school led to a fall in numbers and then the closure, in March 1873, of the Infant School at the Butts which had been maintained by the Vallance family. As well as the new schools being built, both St Michael's National Schools and the Milton National Schools were enlarged. The latter could not though provide sufficient accommodation for all the Milton children and in October 1875 a School Board for Milton was set up. They took over the running of the National Schools at the Butts, Milton, although the school retained its name. (31)

Holy Trinity School (ISP)

In spite of the efforts of Sittingbourne in providing new schools, by 1877 the increasing population, together with new bye-laws which meant that attendance at an efficient school for children from five to thirteen was compulsory, was causing problems. A report showed that of the 1624 children of school age, 881 were attending Public Elementary Schools and 76 were at Efficient Private schools. Of the rest, 164 were at inefficient private schools and 503 were not attending school at all. A letter to the editor stated that teachers at certain voluntary schools were refusing to admit children without shoes or stockings or who didn't know the alphabet, in violation of the Education Act which meant that they could lose their public grant. The problem of 'unacceptable' children was particularly acute in Milton. It was felt that the 'waifs and strays' lowered the standards of schools and therefore their income, as the grant schools received depended on how well the children did in the annual Public Examinations. Also, it was felt that 'ignorant and undisciplined children' lowered the moral tine of schools and it was hoped that Milton would erect a school especially for the 'gutter' children. (32)

In 1879 the Education Department issued a final notice that if places were not found for over 350 children then a School Board would be set up to take over education in Sittingbourne. However in 1894 the National System of Elementary Education was still in operation in the town and as no fees were charged the School Board was unnecessary. Two new schools, an Infants School at the Butts and St Michael's Mission Room had been built. The latter provided for 124, the three St Michael's Schools had an average attendance of 462, Holy Trinity Boys and Girls had 377 children, Holy Trinity Infants had 105 and the Wesleyan School a further 398. Elementary Schools in Milton, being run under the School Board system, were suffering in the 1890s, from bad behaviour and poor attendance. As well as the former National Schools, Boys, Girls and Infants, at the Butts, Milton, there was also Grovehurst School, a mile north of the town. In 1896 Mrs Turner resigned from that school as there were 64 children attending the school and she hadn't been granted another teacher. (33)

The population of Milton parish had been increasing, especially to the south of the railway line. Schools had been built there, but not by the Milton School Board. In September 1894 Schamel, a private residence in West Street was purchased for conversion into a convent and boarding school for young ladies, and in 1896 a Roman Catholic school with 141 places was built, however only 30 to 40 children from Milton attended it. There were over 300 Milton children attending Sittingbourne schools and in 1897 it was decided that a new infant school should be built in the Ufton Road area of the Rock estate. In 1898 the School Board borrowed money to build this school, and to enlarge the Butts Boys School. The increased provision of Elementary school places in Milton may have affected Sittingbourne schools, as in 1900 staff numbers at St Michael's Schools were reduced because fewer children were attending. (34)

School Log Books give an idea of elementary schools. The school terms were different in those days with the schools being open in August and closed for four weeks during September, for hop-picking. The employment of children meant that attendance during much of the year was poor. On August 15th 1873 the Holy Trinity Log Book noted that attendance was poor as 'the harvest has commenced and many of the children are employed'. In October 1863 many children were absent from St Michael's School as they were 'picking potatoes at 10d a day' and it was not until the end of October that the school was full when the boys who had 'been in the brickfields since March, returned for the winter'. Other absences were occasional, such as for the annual fair in October or when a ship was launched. Sometimes provision was made for such events as in 1873 when Holy Trinity closed for a half day in May when 'a circus came into town'. (35)

When they were in school the children wrote on slates which were provided by their parents. The range of subjects taught included geography, history, science, arithmetic (including mental arithmetic), grammar, recitation, dictation, composition and, of course, scripture. This was an important subject in these Church schools and the children were often taught it by the vicar, and they were also expected to attend services on holy days such as Ascension Day. The children were arranged according to standard rather than age within classes. Classes were large at times of full attendance. In 1863 St Michael's was 'suffering for the want of another teacher - one assistant teacher with 100 boys present renders the work of teaching very laborious and not sufficiently effective.' (36)

Teachers did have help from some of the older, brighter children, but not all such children proved to be suitable. In 1903 Daisy Flick, a monitress at Holy Trinity, 'dressed in a style not suitable for a teacher in school, an example which is having an effect upon the children. On Monday morning she had two large brass balls in her hair and a string of pearls round her neck, besides bows etc.' A Pupil Teacher at St Michael's in 1863 came late to lessons, 6.45 a.m. instead of 6.30 a.m., neglected his home lessons and had not learnt the dates connected with his English history. (37)

There were also problems with school buildings. In 1863 the School Committee of St Michael's were concerned with how the school could be better ventilated and how the closets could be rendered less offensive. They also had problems with the behaviour of the children - early in October 1863 George Gold was cautioned for annoying the girls during dinner time and two weeks later two boys were not allowed to sit all afternoon, also for annoying the girls - education may have changed in the last hundred years, but children clearly haven't! (38)

The 19th century: Private and Higher Education
As well as the main national and local authority schools, private schools continued to flourish in the late 19th century. In a four month period from September 1893 to January 1894 there were advertisements in the local paper for Twyford School, Crescent Street, Sittingbourne; a preparatory school for young gentlemen held in a room attached to the Baptist Chapel; Sittingbourne College, Sandringham House, Albany Road; Park Villa School, Park Road; Bickerton School, Milton and the High School for Girls and Kindergarten, 17 Station Road, Sittingbourne. By 1898 the latter had moved to 77 High Street, Sittingbourne. The Principal was Mrs Potter, Mr Potter was the Music Master and there were two Assistant Mistresses. The subjects taught were English,

Book-keeping, French, Latin, Mathematics, Drawing, Painting, Modelling, Pianoforte, Violin, Singing (Solo and Class), Harmony, Dancing, Drilling and Repousse Work. The Misses Mantle's School in Park Road offered a similar range of subjects suitable for young ladies, although not book-keeping, mathematics or Latin, but in addition they prepared boys for local examinations, probably the entrance examination for Borden Grammar School. (39)

Borden Grammar School (Pre-1930)

Borden School, as it was first called, was founded as a boys' grammar school by the Barrow Trustees in the 1870s. Under the provision of the 18th century will of Farmer Barrow, money had been left for the well-being of the people of the locality. The first building, in a seven acre site in Borden parish, provided by the Trustees, cost less than £11,000. In spite of a local campaign against the school by those who felt that the poor of Borden should have benefited from the Trust, the school opened on 14th October 1873 with 23 pupils, nine from the parish of Borden. It was intended that local children should attend daily but that there would also be boarders from further afield. A legal controversy with the Charity Commissioners in the 1880s meant that the first governors resigned, then the agricultural depression during that decade meant that the Trust's income declined and in 1892 the Headmaster took a 50% reduction in salary. During the 1890s the school became increasingly dependant on public money and had to take in more scholarship boys. (40)

The 19th century: Adult Education

It was not though only children who were educated in the area. From as early as the 1850s evening classes were being run. In 1857 Mr Grigsby had an evening school at his house at The Wall during the winter months. In 1866 the night school at St Michael's was given a grant of £2 10/- and in 1869 a night school was operating in the Pembury Street Sunday School Room of Holy Trinity Church. By the 1880s Examinations of the Science and Art Department, South Kensington, were being held in Sittingbourne following classes in freehand and model drawing, geometry, perspective, mathematics and the Principles of Architecture. In 1892 such classes, organised by the Sittingbourne Science and Art Committee, under the Technical Education Scheme, were held at the Town Hall. In 1895 they were also holding classes for examinations in shorthand, cookery and ambulance. At that time there was a separate Technical Education Committee in Milton holding French classes. However the County Council gave a grant for Technical Education to Sittingbourne not to Milton and by 1896 the classes were run by the Sittingbourne and Milton Technical Education Committee. Classes were usually held in the evenings in the Town Hall, Sittingbourne, and woodwork joined the list of classes in 1896, with cookery at the Crescent Street schoolroom in the afternoons. The range of classes held continued to increase, with Poultry rearing, dressmaking, flower culture, nursing and beekeeping in 1898 and woodcarving, basketwork, gardening and physiography in 1899. (41)

The 20th century: The Early Years

The opening years of the 20th century saw a second major Education Act, (1902), one designed to provide 'an educational ladder ... (to) enable the clever child of a labouring man to rise to high positions in the land, if he has the ability to do so. The Elementary School leads up to the Higher Grade School, and that in turn leads to the University.' The act meant that ratepayers had to pay for education and that Voluntary schools which did not reach new standards would have to be replaced with new Council Schools. The Act angered non-conformists and the Sittingbourne and Milton Passive Resistance Committee was set up. They objected on grounds that the Act: violated conscience - making them pay for instruction which was unscriptural; ignored the rights of citizens - taxation without representation (School Boards tended to be dominated by Churchmen); was detrimental to the interests of education and that there was no moral sanction for it as education had not been an issue on which the government had been elected. Their campaign took the form of not paying the part of the rate used for education. They were taken to court and in October 1903 an open air protest meeting was held outside the Baptist Tabernacle as resisters left the Police Court. The following month an auction was held to raise funds on their behalf. (42)

One of the first benefits of the Act in Sittingbourne was the establishment of a new school of Higher Education for Girls. The County School opened in October 1904 at 75 High Street with 28 full-time girls receiving secondary education and 48 older girls, pupil teachers at Elementary Schools, receiving part-time education. Miss Freeman was the first Head Mistress and in 1905 the school was recognised by the Board of Education. Negotiations took place with the head of Sittingbourne High School for Girls, which from the 1890s had been operating at 77 High Street, and in 1906 the two schools amalgamated. In the same year the Head of Borden School left, taking most of the boarders with him, and Mr Murdock commenced his 30 years as Head Master establishing it finally as a Boys' Grammar School. (43)

Canterbury Road Council School

Following the Education Act of 1902 there was a review of Elementary Education and the report by Kent County Council in 1905 showed that there were ten schools in Sittingbourne and Milton: Holy Trinity; St Michael's; St Michael's Mission Room (Infants); Milton Council Schools (Butts); Ufton Lane Infants; Grovehurst; St Paul's Infants; St Peter's Roman Catholic; Pembury Street (Infants) and the Wesleyan School. The last two schools were found to have unsatisfactory premises and in 1907 the Kent Education Committee decided not to recognise the Wesleyan School as an Elementary School after the end of November 1908. This led led to the building of Sittingbourne's first Council School at Gaze Hill, which was opened in June 1909. Mr Roper, who had been Headmaster of the Wesleyan School since it opened in 1874, took over the new school and was Head there until he retired in 1919, after more than 50 years as a school teacher. The following year (1920) repair costs for the Pembury Street Infants School became too high and it closed in March. (44)

The 20th century: Secondary and Adult Education

The early 1920s saw the setting up of the Sittingbourne and District Education Board which was responsible for Elementary Schools, maintained Secondary Schools and Further Education. By the end of that decade Borden Grammar School had a new home in a new building in Remembrance Avenue, Sittingbourne. Their old building became the home, in 1930, of the Kent Farm Institute. This establishment remained there until the mid-1960s - its most memorable contribution to the life of the area being possibly its entries in the local carnival. The building was used subsequently as a Teacher Training College, the first one in Kent for mature students. Then in 1978 it became the Adult Education Centre for the area. (45)

Adult Education classes had been held throughout the 20th century. In 1904 they had transferred from the Town Hall to a room in Brenchley House. In 1919 an Adult School for Men opened at the Butts and in 1938 a building on the playing field of the County School for Girls was used as a Technical Institute in the Evenings (and as an annex to the school during the day). Classes were held in commerce, shorthand, typewriting, woodwork, domestic science, dressmaking, physical training, keepfit, Greek dancing and art & craft - some of the latter classes being held at Borden Grammar School. In 1973, when Brenchley House itself became vacant the Adult Education Centre took it over for five years. (46)

Brenchley House had been the home of the Girls Grammar School (formerly called the County School), until its move to a new building on Highsted Road in 1958. It was then used by the Sittingbourne East Girls School until they moved to a new School in 1969. The East Girls School was the last of the four new secondary schools to be built in the town following the 1944 Education Act, which raised the school leaving age to 16. The building of the first two, one for boys and one for girls, on land to the south of the London Road west of the town, was underway in 1946. In 1957 a further Secondary School for Boys opened, on the Canterbury Road to the east of the town, this soon became known as St John's. By that time the Westlands girls' school had also become overcrowded. In 1956 two classes of eleven year olds were given two teachers and were taught in rooms at the Butts Infant School, before moving to Brenchley House as the new Sittingbourne East Girls School. (47)

In 1979, when this school finally moved into new premises on the same site as St John's and became known as Rowena Girls School, the two secondary schools to the west of the town were united as Westlands, the first local co-educational secondary school. It was not until 1993 that plans were announced for the combination of St John's and Rowena into a Community College. This came at a time when Sittingbourne was reverting to the use of a Secondary School Selection Test (11+), following twenty years of 'Comprehensive' education. In this system children went from Primary School to one of the 'comprehensive' Secondary schools - that is, having children of all abilities - for two years, at which time the most able children transferred to one of the two Grammar schools - Borden for boys and Highsted for girls. The main exception to this system was the final secondary school to be built, Fulston Manor, which kept children from eleven through to 16+. It was built to the south of Sittingbourne on the grounds of Highsted School and opened in 1977. It was the first local school to go 'Grant Maintained' in the early 1990s. (48)

The 20th century: Primary Schools
The location of the new Secondary Schools reflect the growth of post-War housing in the area, and the same is true for the location of new Primary Schools. One of the first was Barrow Grove, which was proposed in 1947 and was opened by the early 1950s. Increasingly in the 1950s the old schools became overcrowded, even with the transfer of children to the new Secondary schools at eleven. When South Avenue County Primary Infants School was opened in 1958 it alleviated the problem caused by children attending St Michael's Mission School being transferred to the Butts. In 1962 a new Roman Catholic Primary School opened in Windsor Drive and the following year Middletune Junior School in Milton, which had opened in 1958, was extended. To the south of the town a new school in Minterne Avenue opened in 1965 and to the east Landsdowne Road Primary School opened in 1969 on the Vincent Park Estate. In 1970 Minterne School was extended to provide an Infants department and during this decade other schools were built, including Grove Park which opened in 1974 and a Special School, St Thomas' which was built in Milton. (49)

The Convent 'Schamel', Sittingbourne

In 1973 the older, pre 1903, schools were given facelifts. Holy Trinity was affected in the same year by the introduction of a one-way system in the town. The decline in population in the town centre led first to the closure of St Michael's Primary Schools in 1958 and then in the 1985 to the closure, in spite of a campaign by parents of the remaining 68 children, of Holy Trinity. The buildings were eventually taken over by the ISP providing for children with emotional and behavioural problems. In 1993 the oldest surviving Primary School, Canterbury Road, suffered a major fire but it was soon rebuilt. (50)

One final change occurred in the educational institutions in the town in the same year when the Convent School left the premises it had occupied for nearly a hundred years for a site out of the town. (51)

Chapter Eight

Local Politics, Sport and Social Life

Introduction

This chapter is divided into four time periods, mid-Victorian (1857-1889), late Victorian and Edwardian (1890-1910s), between the Wars (1920s, 1930s) and the Post-War period (late 1940s-1990s). In each period there will be sections on local politics; sport - football, cricket & other sports; and social life - improvement societies, fraternities, pastimes & cinemas. No attempt is made to give a full detailed history of every organisation mentioned, rather it is intended to give a broad picture of the interests and activities of inhabitants in each of the time periods.

The mid-Victorian Period: Local Politics

In the mid-Victorian period there were two main political parties, the Liberals and the Conservatives. One campaign illustrates the situation during the period. During the 1868 election campaign both Mr Henry Tufton, the Liberal candidate for East Kent and Mr E Leigh Pemberton, the Conservative candidate, spoke at meetings in Sittingbourne. Of the two it was the Liberal meeting that was best supported, especially by influential townsfolk such as Mr Smeed, and which received the greatest coverage in the local paper. Tufton's support came mainly from the more urban parishes whereas Pemberton was more popular in the rural area. The number of electors was small and there were no local polling stations, instead polling booths were set up in the Bull Meadow. A hundred electors, supporters of Tufton, had a sumptuous breakfast at Smeed's home, Gore Court, and then processed to the town accompanied by a brass band wearing blue caps and sashes and preceded by a man dressed entirely in blue. In spite of such a fine start to the day, shortly before polling closed red ochre and flour and rotten eggs were thrown by the crowd that had gathered and stones were thrown at the windows of the Bull, water was thrown from the windows onto the crowd and several fights broke out. Locally Tufton got the most votes but not in East Kent as a whole and it was Pemberton who was elected. In July 1881 the Sittingbourne, Milton and District Liberal Association held their first meeting, with F G Lloyd as their chairman and in 1884 they organised a great demonstration in Sittingbourne in favour of the Third Reform Bill to extend the franchise to working classes in rural districts. The following year a local Conservative Association was formed. (1)

The mid-Victorian Period: Sport

Football:

In 1869 it was proposed to have a local Football Club and in April that year a match took place between twelve members of the Gore Court Club and twelve of the 16th Kent Rifle Volunteers. It was not though until the 1880s that football really became established in Sittingbourne and this can be closely linked to the provision of a recreation ground - the ten acre site had been offered by Mr Twopenny in 1879. The total cost for its purchase, laying grass, putting up fences etc came to around £3,000 and in 1881 a concert in aid of the Recreation Ground Fund was held at the Town Hall. The Sittingbourne Undaunted Football Club certainly played on the Recreation Ground in November 1881 when they had a match against Elm House School, Key Street, and they were still playing matches there in February 1883. During the same period Sittingbourne United also started playing at the Recreation Ground. They had matches there against Faversham which were reported in the paper in both 1885 and 1886. In those days the players wore high necked, long sleeved shirts and coloured jerseys. Their shorts came down well over the knee and they wore heavy shin guards and spiked shoes. In October 1886 it was proposed to form an association of footballers to be entitled Sittingbourne Football Club with a total of 50 players, many coming from Sittingbourne United which was to lapse. The new club's first match was played against Sheppey Rovers in November 1886. The following year another club was formed. The Nil Desperandum Football Club played its opening game at the Recreation Ground on a Wednesday evening in September 1887. (2)

Cricket:
A number of cricket teams had been playing locally for many years before football was played. In 1857 both Milton and Gore Court played matches. The Gore Court Club had started in 1839 and their first recorded match was at Cobham in July 1847. In 1860 the team united with the Sittingbourne Club, matches were to be played at Gore Court and the new team practiced at the ground at the back of the Bull Inn. However the following year the club was dissolved and a portion of property was sold to defray the outstanding liabilities. The Gore Court Club continued to play, with Smeed allowing them free use of the Gore Court Park Ground in Bell Road from 1882. There were plans in 1863 for a separate Sittingbourne Club and other local teams were formed including 'Sittingbourne Paper Mills' (1878), Sittingbourne United, Borden School and the Sittingbourne Etceteras. (3)

Other Sports:
The oldest local sport still being played in the mid 19th century has to have been bowls. Milton Bowling Green is believed to date back to the 16th century and records from the 17th century show that the local churchwardens were paying for work to be done on the green. The same accounts refer to Butts, where archery would have been practiced and in 1875 the Gore Court Archery Club had seventy members. There was also a tennis club at Gore Court and a Lawn Tennis Tournament took place at the Bull Meadow in 1887. Athletics was well established locally with not only the Bank Holiday Sports at Gore Court Park but less formal events such as a foot race of ten rods between Charles Marden aged 72 and Miles Probert aged 63 in a meadow at the rear of the Plough in 1859. Regular gymnastics practice occurred in 1867 and in 1862

a prize fight was attempted near the Sittingbourne junction with the Sheerness railway line, but the police broke into the ring during the first round. With the advent of bicycles the Sittingbourne Bicycle Club was formed in 1879 and two years later the Gore Court Bicycle Club was formed. Another sport played locally was quoits and in 1886 the Sittingbourne and Milton Quoit Club played a team from the Paper Mills at the Milton Arms pub. Water sports also occurred occasionally, there was a rowing match on Milton Creek on Boxing Day in 1880 and there was a swimming match there in May 1884. Sometimes more rural sports invaded the town, as in 1876 when a stag hunt, which had started at Hollingbourne, made its way through the Bull meadows, along the High Street, down Station Street, Milton Road, over the Creek and out to Elmley Ferry where the stag was eventually caught. (4)

The mid-Victorian Period: Social Life
Improvement Societies:
The Victorian period was one in which self-improvement was seen as an ideal, and many clubs and societies were formed with this in mind. In 1857 two lectures were given on Phrenology at the Public Rooms and a meeting was held to form a society to have lectures during the winter months. In the same year a lecture on a poem was given at the National Schoolroom to members of the Milton Mechanics Institute. In 1859 a Literary and Scientific Institution was formed in Sittingbourne. They opened a reading room at the Corn Exchange which was open from 10 a.m. to 10 p.m. daily, except Sundays, and which had daily and weekly newspapers as well as the best periodicals. The Institute also planned to have lectures, a chess club and classes for languages, music and the sciences. In 1861 lectures were given at the Public Rooms on Mesmerism and Electro-Biology and in 1863 the Public Rooms were hired for six months by the newly formed Sittingbourne Literary Institute, and they opened a reading room there. A reading room was also one of the amenities provided at a Workmen's Hall in the East End in 1866, like the Institute they opened a library but they also provided refreshments at moderate prices. (5)

By the early 1870s the Sittingbourne Institute was suffering from the fact that the building they used, although quiet, was not attracting passers by, however in 1873 they held a Floral Fete at Gore Court Park. In 1875 the Sittingbourne Institute Library was enriched by 333 books and the following year it was decided to open an institute in Milton. The new institute held a concert in the Milton Assembly Rooms in 1877, the same year in which the Sittingbourne Institute finally closed. Meanwhile a new society, the Sittingbourne Scientific Association had started holding meetings as had the Sittingbourne Mutual Improvement Association. The rooms used by the Sittingbourne Institute were taken over by the Sittingbourne Club in 1878 and they planned to convert the former Latimer Chapel, at the Butts, Sittingbourne, and open it as the Sittingbourne and Milton Working Men's Club and Institute. By 1879 the Workmen's Hall was open from 5.30 a.m. to 11 p.m., the club had 283 members and held a Tea Party for men and their wives and sweethearts. The following year the Workmen's Club was given the books of the defunct

Sittingbourne Institute and in 1881 a billiards tournament was held there and members went on an excursion to Calais on the August Bank Holiday. By 1887 the Workmen's Club were playing other clubs at billiards, bagatelle, whist, cribbage and chess. Meanwhile other clubs and societies had started in the town. In 1884 a Debating Society started, the following year the Sittingbourne and Milton Mutual Improvement Society met at the Crescent Street Schoolroom and a Middle Class Club met at Mr Gorham's rooms in Pembury Street where they had a large billiard room with a full size table, a reading room and a quiet room for games. (6)

The Workmen's Club & Swimming Baths

Fraternities:

There is no doubt that most of the improvement societies would have been for men only, certainly the advert for the formation of the Lecture Association was addressed to 'Gentlemen'. However there are a number of other societies which existed, or were formed, during the second half of the 19th century which are still seen as men only organisations, or fraternities. In 1857 fifty members of the Society of Comical Fellows celebrated their 14th anniversary at the Smack Inn at Milton. The following year there was a meeting of Court No 2293 of the Ancient Order of Foresters at the Good Intent Inn in Milton. In 1859 a meeting was held at the Bull Inn in Sittingbourne, admidst fears of a French Invasion, to set up a Volunteer Rifle Corps. The new Corps assembled at the Corn Exchange twice a week, went through their exercises and paraded along the High Street, led by a band and accompanied by many young and noisy admirers. In 1862 a new rifle range was opened for the 16th Kent (Sittingbourne) Volunteer Rifle Corps. By 1882 the Volunteers numbers exceeded a hundred, the highest since they were started and the following year they became part of the First Volunteer Battalion of the Buffs (East Kent Regiment). During 1861 the Ancient Order of Foresters opened a new Court at the Wesleyan School room in Sittingbourne, called Court Resolution and the Men of Kent Lodge of the Order of Druids celebrated their 18th anniversary. In 1873 the Foresters, Odd Fellows and Druids Fete at Gore Court Park attracted 6,000, including members from Sheerness, Chatham and Canterbury. The Royal Ancient Order of Buffaloes held their first banquet in Sittingbourne in 1886 and by 1889 they had a hundred brethren. The same year saw the Loyal Orange Lodge holding meetings in Sittingbourne and a new Forester's Hall being opened in Milton. (7)

The Masonic Hall

In 1869 a Warrant was granted for a lodge of the Free and Accepted Masons to be held in Sittingbourne at the Latimer Chapel. It took the name St Michael and when it was consecrated the bells of the church were rung and a dinner was held afterwards at the Bull at which the Volunteer's band played. Masonry was on the rise in Kent at that time and membership was far from a secret affair, in fact the paper reported the names of those taking office each year. In 1878, when the Workmen's Club moved into the Latimer Chapel building the Freemasons met in St Michael's schoolroom and the following year they moved to a room in the Town Hall. In 1883 a Warrant was granted by the Prince of Wales for a Royal Arch Chapter to be held in connection with St Michael's Lodge and then in 1888 a Masonic festival was held at Sittingbourne. The High Street, Crescent Street, Station Street and West Street were all gaily decorated and the Union Jack was flying on St Michael's Church. The premises of the Sittingbourne Club in Crescent Street were given for the use of the Masons for the day and crowds gathered to see a procession from there to St Michael's for a service, although they were disappointed that the Masons were not in full regalia. The day ended with a banquet in the Town Hall. The following year a purpose built Masonic Hall was opened in Albany Road by Earl Amhurst, the Provincial Grand Master of Kent. (8)

Pastimes:
Temperance organisations also flourished in the town. In 1858 a musical entertainment was given by the Sittingbourne Temperance Society at the Wesleyan Schoolroom. In 1872 the Lodge of Good Templars, an anti-drink temperance organisation, was established. The initiation fees were 1/6, with weekly subscriptions of 1d for men and $^1/_2$d for women. Local Churches had their Band of Hope groups which often had musical bands. Other musical groups were also formed. In 1860 the twenty members of the Sittingbourne Fife and Drum band were making rapid progress under the instruction of Mr Jay and in 1882 the Sittingbourne and District Musical Society gave their first concert at the Town Hall and St Michael's Change Ringing Society held their first annual meeting. Singing was also popular, in 1861 Tonic Sol-Fa Singing classes were held in the Public Rooms and in 1875 members of the Free Church Tonic Sol-Fa Class gave a concert. Workers at the Paper Mill formed musical groups, in 1880 members of the Musical and Dramatic Club gave an entertainment at the Milton Assembly Rooms and in 1885 the Vocal and Instrumental Society gave a series of concerts there. There were other drama groups although some may have not lasted long. The Sittingbourne Amateur Dramatic Club gave an entertainment at the Corn Exchange in 1868, yet in 1885 the 'newly formed' Sittingbourne Amateur Dramatic Club performed the Lady of Lyons at the Town Hall. As well as Balls being held at the Town Hall lovers of dancing had the opportunity to attend Quadrille classes at Berry Street in 1871 and at the Milton Assembly Room in 1887. Interest in gardening increased during the period. Both a Horticultural Society and a Gardeners' Mutual Improvement Society held shows in 1874, soon after they were formed, in 1888 there were requests for allotments under the new Allotments Act and two years earlier a Poultry and Rabbit Society was established. (9)

Cinemas:
There were no cinemas during this period, although there was an early forerunner in the Magic Lantern Show given to entertain 400 children at the Baptist Church in 1872. (10)

The late-Victorian & Edwardian Period: Local Politics
Locally, even though the area had a Conservative MP, it was the Liberals who dominated the political life of the town. In 1894 a women's branch of the Liberal Association was formed for Sittingbourne and Milton. Then in 1906 there were great celebrations when finally the area had a Liberal MP and the following year there was a formal opening of the Sittingbourne Liberal Club.

Their supremacy was not to last for long as in the 1910 election the Liberal candidate, Napier, was beaten by the Conservative, Wheler. Although by that time the size of the electorate had increased it was still, for the North-East Kent Parliamentary Division, only 14,649 out of a population of 76,887. There was though clearly local interest in politics as, also in 1910, the Sittingbourne Parliamentary Debating Society was holding meetings. (11)

The late-Victorian & Edwardian Period: Sport
Football:
Football continued to be popular during the late-Victorian and Edwardian Period. In 1899 it was announced that Sittingbourne Football Club was to become a Limited Liability Company and three years later, in 1902, they celebrated their first major trophy win. The deciding match was played against Ashford at Ramsgate. Sittingbourne quickly took the lead, although many of their supporters missed the first goal as the special railway excursion train arrived late. Those who had not gone to Ramsgate knew that the 'Black and Reds' had won when two maroons were fired from the Fire Station. A large crowd, including the Sittingbourne and Murston Band and members of the Fire Brigade in full uniform, awaited the return of the team at the railway station and there was a triumphal procession through the town to the Bull Hotel - the club's headquarters. A few years later though there was a cash crisis at the club and the paper reported that the popularity of football was on the wane. It was not until 1910 that the club were able to announce a profit, after four years of loss, which had been achieved by cutting costs through withdrawing from the South-Eastern League and playing only in the Kent League. Smaller clubs also had financial problems, in 1905 a concert was held in aid of Milton Town Football Club. Many of the smaller clubs played one or more teams in the Thames and Medway Combination before the First World War, including Sittingbourne, Milton Regis, Daily Chronicle, Murston Rangers and Borden Grammar School. (12)

Cricket:
A number of local teams also played cricket throughout the period, including, Gore Court, Sittingbourne Wednesday, Daily Chronicle Paper Mills, Borden Grammar School and Sittingbourne Co-op employees. In 1892 it was proposed that there should be a new joint Sittingbourne and Milton Club and in 1905 it was proposed that there should be a Cricket League. Then in 1908 Gore Court Cricket Club celebrated its 70th anniversary. (13)

Other Sports:
One of the major innovations in sport in Sittingbourne occurred in the mid-1890s with the building of a swimming bath. A number of possible sites were considered in 1894. One possibility was one of the ponds at Mede Mill Milton, but the owner objected, another was a site near Adelaide Dock, but it was felt that the objectionable smells around Milton Creek would make it unpopular, so at that time Bayford Moat seemed the most likely site. The Baths came a step nearer in January 1895 when the Lloyd Brothers made the magnificent

gift of £1,000 towards the cost and in May that year a site at the Butts in Sittingbourne was purchased. The Baths finally cost just over £2,000, of which over £1,600 was contributed by the Lloyd family, and they were opened in 1896. A Swimming Club was quickly started and within a month had a hundred members, the following year they held their first Annual Aquatic Sports. The Swimming Baths was designed to also be a gymnasium and in the winter months it was converted for that purpose, with both gymnastic classes and roller skating taking place there. In the summer of 1901 there were water polo matches and the following year swimming classes were held for ladies. Children were also taught to swim and in 1905 it was decided that during the summer holidays those children who could swim would be able to use the baths without a teacher for 1d. During the winter rolling skating increased in popularity and in 1910 there were fancy dress roller skating carnivals and a hockey match on skates, on what was Kent's only municipal rink. (14)

Hockey on grass was a new sport at that time. The Gore Court Hockey Club was founded in 1908 by Mr Jackson. He was secretary of the Cricket Club and got the use of the Cricket Club's outfield as a pitch. The men in those days wore hob-nail boots, knee-length baggy shorts and shirts like a football kit. Unlike football though there were also women hockey players who wore ankle boots and ankle-length skirts. Other established sports also continued during the period. In 1900 a new pavilion was opened at Milton Bowling Green and the Bell Inn Bowling Club was also playing matches. In 1906 the 29th Annual Open Tournament of Gore Court Archery and Lawn Tennis Club took place. The club claimed to be the oldest Lawn Tennis Club in England and had eight courts in use for the 225 competitors in the tournament. (15)

Athletics was also popular. Local firms like the Paper Mills had their own annual sports and the Whit Monday Bank Holiday Athletics Event was thought to be one of the oldest athletic festivals in Kent. For many years it was organised by Mr G W Bowes and in 1903, following difficulty in continuing to use Gore Court Park, he purchased the Glovers estate, near the junction of Bell Road with Highsted Road, and turned a meadow there into an athletic ground. Around the outside there was a cinder cycle track, 24 feet wide in the finishing strait and 18 feet in other parts. It had a slope inwards of 33 degrees and the surface was made of fine ash, sifted chalk and cockleshell. Inside the cycle track was a grass running track about five laps to the mile, with a separate 120 yards strait course for the sprint. There was accommodation for 14,000 spectators, with a grandstand providing seating for 400 and changing rooms underneath. There was also an octagonal bandstand with a 60 feet by 30 feet dancing platform as well as permanent covered stalls for tea parties and a ladies lavatory. Bowes Park was considered to be one of the finest athletic centres in the south of England. Unfortunately for Mr Bowes in 1905 Gore Court Park reopened for Amateur Athletic Sports on Bank Holidays and the numbers of spectators was split between the two sites. The following year Glovers, including Bowes Park, was sold and in 1906 the paper commented after the August Bank Holiday Sports there that 'with so many attractions for holiday folk - far more ... than ... (when the sports were) held at Gore Court Park ... (they) do not secure such large gates'. (16)

The late-Victorian & Edwardian Period - Social Life
Improvement Societies:
The Workmen's Club continued to flourish during this period. In the early 1890s they started a cycling club and in 1898 they were registered under the Friendly Societies Act 1875. At that time they provided papers, a lending library and games and membership was open to any person over the age 18 for an annual sum of 5/- or 1/6 a quarter. In the same year the inaugural meeting of the Sittingbourne and District Mutual Improvement Society was held, although in general there was less interest in improvement societies than there had been in the earlier period. (17)

Fraternities:
In 1890 the annual meeting of the Provincial Grand Royal Arch Chapter of Freemasons in Kent was held at the, then new, Masonic Hall in Sittingbourne. Nearly 20 years later, in 1909 the Provincial Grand Lodge of Freemasons, Kent, met at Sittingbourne and were given a tour of the paper Mills and the following year Brother Herbert Black, Past Master of St Michael's Chapter was appointed as Assistant-Grand Director of Ceremonies in the Grand Mark Lodge of England. In the early 1890s a new Foresters Hall was opened in East Street. The front of the hall was a classic design with cement and artificial stone dressings. There was seating for 700 and the facilities included a stage, a kitchen and a dressing room. The Buffalo and Oddfellow organisations continued to operate and the YMCA held meetings for a few years during the mid-1890s. Finally, just before the First World War, a new Institution opened, the Bargemen's Brotherhood. (18)

Pastimes:
Music and singing continued to be popular. In 1890 the Sittingbourne Amateur Instrumental Society was formed and in 1892 the String Band of the Paper Mill played at a Garden Party held at Milton Bowling Green. The Sittingbourne Choral and Orchestral Society were using the Pembury Street schoolroom to practice in in 1895, in 1897 there was a Free Church Musical Association, in 1901 a choir was formed by the Education Department of the Sittingbourne Co-operative Society and in 1898 the temperance White Ribbon Choir gave a concert in Sittingbourne Town Hall. There was also a White Ribbon Band, which had been going for ten years in 1905, and in that year the Milton Town Brass Band was being reorganised. However the Sittingbourne and District Musical Society, formed in 1882, was experiencing financial difficulties in 1907 as there was little public interest at that time. Dancing classes were held at the Girls High School at 77 High Street in 1900 and later in the same year there was a dance held in connection with the Sittingbourne and Milton Shop Assistants Recreation Society. Local gardening clubs continued to hold annual exhibitions and in 1898 there were plans for additional land to be made available at Gaze Hill to meet the demands for

allotments. In the Edwardian period new clubs were formed, in 1902 there was a Homer Society, for homing pigeons, the Sittingbourne and District Photographic Club was formed in 1905 and in the same year the first meeting was held of the Old Bordenians Club. In 1909 over sixty boys joined the new children's organisation, the Boy Scouts, and a cycle patrol was formed. The following year the Sittingbourne Model Aero Club was formed following interest when a plane flying from Paris to London had to make a forced landing at Fulston Farm. (19)

The Queen's Picture Hall

Cinemas:
The Edwardian period saw the arrival of films in Sittingbourne. In 1904 there was a Cinematograph entertainment at the Foresters Hall given by the Co-op Education Department and in 1905 there was the first visit of Biograph Animated Pictures to the town, with a show at the Town Hall. The following year, under the management of G W Bowes, Jury's Imperial Animated Pictures were shown at the Town Hall and then in 1910 the Drill Hall in East Street held cinematograph entertainments. Later that year the old Wesleyan School building in East Street was converted to a cinema and opened as the Empire Picture Hall in July. Two year later, in 1912, the former Vallance and Payne's Brewery in the High Street was also converted and the Queen's Picture Hall opened in the February with seating, costing 2d, 4d, 6d and 9d for reserved seats, for 450. Then in 1913 the first 'All Coloured' programme was shown at the Empire and in 1914 there were plans for a picture theatre in Milton - although the First World War put paid to that. (20)

Between The Wars: Local Politics

The period after the First World War saw the rise of the Labour Party and women began to play a greater part in politics, in 1920 Milton had their first lady Councillor. The following year motor cars were used for the first time to take local electors to vote. By 1923 the local Labour Party had rooms in East Street and they adopted Rev Stanley Morgan as their Parliamentary Candidate. The General Election took place in the December and the Conservative, Major Wheler, was elected. The following year there was another General Election and he was re-elected, with an increased majority. Four years later, in 1928 following the death of Major Wheler the Conservatives adopted Mr Maitland as their candidate and he was elected, though with a reduced majority and in 1934 a new Conservative Club building was opened in Milton. Mr Maitland, who was later knighted, remained as the local MP throughout the inter-War period. In April 1939 he spoke at a Conservative Club meeting at the Bull Hotel in favour of the Government's conscription measure and he also spoke to members of the local British Legion on the danger of war. The following month, speaking at the AGM of the North-East Kent Conservative Association, he said that he did not think that there would be a major war, he believed there must be peace through strength. (21)

Milton Conservative Club

Between the Wars: Sport

Football:

In 1919 Sittingbourne Football Club, which, unlike Sittingbourne Athletic Football Club, had not played during the war, was revived and a fete was held to raise funds for the club. In 1926 they won both the Kent League Cup and the Thames and Medway championship and in 1927 there were plans to form the club into a Limited Liability Company with capital of £1,000, in 5/- shares, so that it could enter the Southern League. The following year the club opened a new grandstand and dressing rooms at the Bull Ground and there were appeals for financial support. Although they joined the Southern League they did not do very well in it, it was in other competitions that they found success. They won the Kent Senior Shield in 1927 and 1928, and in 1928 and 1930 the club celebrated winning the Kent Senior Cup final, however there were no triumphal processions through the town as there had been in 1902. Success did though help their finances and in 1931 there was the good news that their debt, which had been £2,300, had been wiped out. However in 1935 they were again in financial difficulty. Competitions on the Grand National and the Derby had been made illegal and this had been the way in which they usually raised money, so an appeal was made for 8,000 sixpences to pay for the rent of the field. Two years later the Club planned to run two teams and hoped to celebrate their jubilee the following year by clearing their debt. (22)

Other local teams playing during this period included Sittingbourne Paper Mills who were in Division 1 of the Kent League in 1929, and who had a second team which along with Murston Rangers played in the New Brompton and District League. In the same year Murston Social Club had a team playing for the Sittingbourne Charity Cup. Ten years later Sittingbourne Wednesday and Sittingbourne 'Black-and-Reds' played with Sittingbourne in the Kent Senior Cup, Lloyds played in the Kent Amateur Cup, Sittingbourne Reserves and Old Bordenians played in the Sheppey Charity Cup and Lloyds had other teams in Division II of the Kent League and the Faversham League. (23)

Cricket:
Gore Court Cricket Club was also revived after the First World War and in 1929, after having had free use of the Gore Court Park ground in Bell Road for 46 years, the club opened a new ground at the Grove. In the same year there was also provision for cricket to be played at Kemsley with the opening there of a Sports Ground and Cricket Pavilion. A number of cricket clubs had teams during this period, many being linked to occupations, they included United Newspapers, Sittingbourne Paper Mills, Sittingbourne Civil Service, Swale Division of KCC Police, Sittingbourne Co-op Employees, APCM and others such as Kemsley, Milton, Murston Social, Borden Grammar School and the Kent Farm Institute. Finally, just before the start of the Second World War, Gore Court Cricket Club celebrated its centenary. (24)

Other Sports:
After the war a Ladies Swimming Club was formed and so was Sittingbourne Bowling Club, with a new green being excavated in 1922. The Milton Bowling Green continued to be used although in 1939 it changed from being a crown green to being an association green, following the construction of a larger green. There were attempts in the 1920s to set up a golf club. Initial

plans to lease Lynsted Park fell through and then in 1928 it was hoped to acquire Wormdale on the Maidstone Road. The Golf Course was finally opened there in June 1931. In the same year the first AGM was held of the Sittingbourne and District Table Tennis League and in 1938 Sittingbourne offered a home to a Table Tennis Champion, a Polish Jew from Austria, who had been on tour in England when Germany annexed Austria and he couldn't go back to his own country. Other sports popular during the period include tennis, with local churches having teams, hockey, darts, boxing, riding, rifle shooting, cycling and motor cycling. (25)

Improvements were made to Sittingbourne Swimming Baths with the installation of a filtration plant in 1930 which meant, according to the paper, that there would be no more 'Dirty Water Days'. The baths continued to be used for roller skating, including rick hockey, during the winter until 1934 when a new indoor bowling green was installed for the winter months. The local council increased the provision of open spaces for sports during this period with, not only the acquisition, thanks to George Andrews, of The Grove, but also with the opening of a new playing field between the end of Chilton Avenue and the South Avenue housing estate, the first playing field to be opened with a grant from the Kent and National Playing Fields Association. Then in 1935 the Council decided to buy Gore Court Park for £3,250 to preserve it as an open space, and it was opened two years later as King George's Playing Field. (26)

Between the Wars: Social Life
Improvement Societies:
The Workmen's Club continued to be active during the period between the wars, in 1926 the members took possession of the freehold of the Club's premises and they held their 55th AGM in 1934. They would have continued to play in inter-club competitions, as they had in the Victorian period, and other clubs such as Sittingbourne Paper Mills, the Liberal Club, APCM, the Territorials, the British Legion, KCC, Sittingbourne Conservatives, Kemsley and the Co-op were also playing a variety of games including billiards, whist, double and single cribbage and double and single darts. (27)

Fraternities:
Meeting were still held by the Freemasons at the Masonic Hall, although there is no mention of them in the local paper during the period. The Bargemen's Brotherhood, which was started just before the First World War, were given a building which had been used at the Whitehall Hospital during the war to use as a meeting place in Crown Quay Lane, and it was opened in 1920. In the same year the Sittingbourne United Lodge of Good Templars moved from Bayford Hall to meeting in a room at the Wesleyan Church. In 1921 a new organisation started in the town, the Sittingbourne Brotherhood, they met at a hut at the football ground and aimed to have 500 members by the end of their first year. Three years later a new Rotary Club was started in the town, it had its inaugural dinner at the Bull Hotel in 1924. (28)

Pastimes:

After the First World War many clubs and societies were reformed, including, the Sittingbourne Orchestra, the Sittingbourne and District Musical Society and the Homing Pigeon Society. The Chevron Orchestra performed at the Town Hall for Chevron dances and whist drives and a new, non-political club was established, the Cedars Club, which had 150 members by 1921. There was an increase in membership of the Boy Scouts, with a rally being held in Sittingbourne in 1921, and a company of Girl Guides was formed in Milton in the following year. Dancing was popular throughout the period. In 1922 the Sittingbourne Folk Dancing Class did well at competitions at Maidstone, in 1938 there was an advertisement for the White Rock Ballroom which had a new milk bar and soda fountain and the following year the elimination heats of the Kent Amateur Ballroom Dancing Championships were held at the Paper Mills Club House. There was though a decline in popularity for some traditional forms of music. In 1932 the Sittingbourne and District Musical Society, celebrating their 50th anniversary, put on the Messiah, but audiences was poor, there being less enthusiasm for oratorios than when the club was formed. Other forms of entertainment were taking over. In 1923 a lecture was given to the Sittingbourne, Milton and District Radio Society at their rooms in Berry Street and in 1929 there was an advertisement for Marconi Televisions. (29)

Cinemas:

In 1919 a Charlie Chaplin film, 'Shoulder Arms', was being shown in Sittingbourne. The 1920s was the age of Chaplin and the silent movies, then in 1930 came the first week of 'Talkies' at the Queen's with the showing of 'Broadway Melody'. In 1934 there were plans for the Plaza in East Street to be rebuilt and extended and the following year it was announced that two new cinemas were to be built, the Royal at the junction of the High Street and Crown Quay Lane and the Argosy near Railway Terrace on the north side of the High Street. In the end it was only the cinema at the junction of the High Street and Crown Quay Lane which was built, in spite of problems with the foundations because of the ancient water course which ran there, and it was opened as the Odeon in 1937. That was the same year in which the Queen's celebrated its twenty-fifth anniversary and a history of the cinema was printed in the local paper. It referred to films, 'in the old days', arriving in paper parcels, frequently with a long trail of film hanging out of them whereas by that time, 1937, they arrived in fire-proof boxes. In the early days films had to be bargained for, and shorter ones bought outright. At that time the cinema provided seating for 700 and over the years had been at the forefront of developments, being the first cinema in the country to organise the booking of seats and to use the mirror type of arc lamp. Celebrating along with the cinema was its manager, Mr Brooks, the only cinema manager in the country to have had twenty-five years' service with one cinema. (30)

The Post-War Period: Local Politics

During the late 1940s Sir Adam Maitland resigned after seventeen years of being the Conservative M.P. for the area and Percy Wells became the town's first Labour M.P. The constituency remained Labour throughout the fifties and sixties. In the 1950s Labour Fetes held at the Sale Field in Bell Road were major summer events, over 13,000 attending in 1956, and in 1962 a new Labour Hall was built in Park Road, on the site of a house that has been demolished during a bombing raid in the Second World War. 1956 saw the appointment of the local council's first woman Chairman, Mrs Reeves, who, like Mrs Elvy the Vice-Chairman, was an Independent. (31)

It was not until the mid-1960s that the town had its first Liberal councillor, Peter Morgan. He later became Mayor (1987) and then, following a move to become a County Councillor, he was first Vice-Chairman and then Chairman of Kent County Council (1996). There was a big swing to Labour in 1971 and they gained control of the local council for the first time in seventeen years. However it was not until 1988 that Swale Council had its first Labour Mayor, Bill Vaughan. By the 1990s the political composition of the council had again changed with the Liberal Democrats having most seats, although not an overall majority. Meanwhile, in 1970 the Conservative candidate, Roger Moate, (now Sir Roger Moate) was elected to Parliament. In 1996 he is still in office. (32)

The Post-War Period: Sport
Football:
The early years after the war saw the Wednesday Football Club celebrating fifty years of mid-week football whilst Sittingbourne Football Club was experiencing the problem of football violence - a fight broke out amongst spectators during the Boxing Day match against Sheppey United in 1947. In 1950 the 'Black and Reds' were in debt, the rates they paid on the Bull Ground had been raised and they were suffering from poor attendances. However their debts were wiped out and they went on, in 1954, to win the Kent Senior Shield in front of what was a post-war record crowd of 5,000. The late 1950s was a successful time for the club, with wins in major local events, including in 1959 the treble - the Kent League, the Kent League Cup and the Thames and Medway Cup. The following year the club moved into the Southern League, but they did not do well. (33)

In 1961 the club was again in the red, the numbers attending matches and membership of the supporters' club having slumped. The crisis got worse and in 1963 the players were asked to accept a twenty-five per cent cut in wages. Even though in 1965 the club were given £1,000 compensation when the council refused their application to develop the Bull Ground their financial problems continued. In 1965 the club were without a manager and the club chairman resigned, then the following year they were forced to leave the Southern League and return to the county competition, amidst rumours that the club was closing. (34)

Problems of violence continued to affect the club. In 1966 they were threatened with the closure of the Bull Ground if there was any more crowd mis-conduct and in 1969 scores of Medway youths tried to force their way into a Social Club Dance for a revenge clash with local teenagers - there was gang warfare on the streets. The team had several wins in the Kent League during the 1970s and in 1979 the Bull Ground was improved to meet the Southern League standards. There was more violence in 1981 when a friendly against Gillingham had to be abandoned after there was a fracas, with skinheads on the pitch and fighting on the terraces. (35)

In 1982 the club celebrated its centenary but it was not to be a decade of celebration. In 1985 the club was faced with a £20,000 bill to improve ground safety when new regulations were introduced following the Bradford disaster and in 1989 the club announced plans to sell the Bull Ground and move to a site on the Eurolink Industrial Estate. Land was purchased from Blue Circle Industries and work was underway on the new Central Park site in 1990. The following year the club became Kent League Champions and were the only unbeaten senior side in Europe by the end of the season - a good way to celebrate the opening of their new ground. However by 1996 the club was in trouble again when rent arrears led the Council, who had purchased the Central Park ground, to lock them out.(36)

Smaller clubs also played football - Murston Rangers was revived in 1949 and in the 1960s the Sunday Soccer League had six divisions and included teams like Sittingbourne Social, Chilton Athletic and Fulston Manor. By 1979 indoor soccer was being played. (37)

Cricket and Other Sports:
Indoor cricket was also played at that time and there were a number of teams playing including Bowaters, Murston and Gore Court. Gore Court had their main team in the Kent League and other local teams playing in the 1960s and 1970s included Key St, Bowaters, Swale, Murston, Bapchild, Old Bordenians and Bowaters - the last two teams playing in the Evening League. Bowaters also had teams playing other sports, including bowls and table tennis. The latter sport was very popular with clubs, such as Wyvern, Kemsley, Bowaters, Crescent, Co-op, Baptist, KFI, EKP, Milton and Murston often having several teams playing in different divisions of the local league. (38)

Swimming continued to be popular and the Sittingbourne Swimming Club was reformed in 1947, it had been suspended in 1940. There was a big jump in the membership of the Swimming Club in 1958, up by 44% to 274, 223 of them juniors. They still though only had the use of the Swimming Baths during the summer months, it was used by Indoor Bowlers during the winter. There were pleas for the Baths to stay open during the winter during 1966 but it was not until 1972 that the Sittingbourne Indoor Bowlers faced eviction, after using the Baths during the winter for thirty-five years. It was not only the Sittingbourne Swimming Club who used the Baths, there was also the Sittingbourne Sub-Aqua Club and the Crescent Girls Club. In 1978 a campaign was launched for a new Swimming Pool in Sittingbourne and in 1982 plans for a new Sports Centre and Baths were announced, although no site had been decided upon. The following year it was reported that a site in Central Avenue had been chosen but it was not until 1989 that 'The Swallows' was finally opened by Princess Anne. With the advent of the new Leisure Pool came the closure of the old Swimming Baths and the building was demolished. (39)

The period saw the Sittingbourne Golf Club celebrate its 50th anniversary, in 1979, Gore Court Hockey Club celebrate its 75th Anniversary in 1983 and Milton Bowling Club celebrate its 450th anniversary in 1990. There was Speedway at the Bull Ground in the 1940s and Skateboard Championships were held at Canterbury Road School in the 1970s. Sports Centres were opened, including one at St Johns/Rowena and in 1982 Sittingbourne's first mini-marathon was held. In 1983 the snooker star Willie Thorne played at the Sittingbourne Snooker Club and in 1986 the football star, Kevin Keegan, attended the opening of a snooker club in part of Hulburds store in the High Street. Sittingbourne Rugby Club continued to play, although in 1993 their plan to build a new pitch was affected by a legal wrangle over ancient woodland at Rose Hill. (40)

Other sports for which there are local clubs or societies in the 1990s include angling, badminton, darts, netball, motor cycling, pool and numerous martial arts including Jui-Jitsu, Judo and Karate, and Greyhound Race meetings are now held in the town at the Football Club's Central Park Ground. (41)

The Post-War Period: Social Life
Improvement Societies, Fraternities and Pastimes:
The Workmen's Hall which had for so long stood next to the old Swimming Baths was demolished during this period, improvement societies with their provision of reading rooms were no longer needed. The Freemasons continued to meet, using the Masonic Hall in Albany Road and in 1945 members of St Michael's Lodge had a service at St Michael's Church at which a sermon was preached on the masonic meaning of the playing card suits. Then in 1951 members attended a Masonic Festival at Canterbury Cathedral where a Canon in his address denied, then current claims, that it was a new and heretical religion. (42)

In spite of the advent of television, it was blamed in 1957 for a decline in the number of entries to the Co-op Annual Arts and Crafts Show especially among juveniles, clubs and societies still flourished during this period. Music has continued - the Sittingbourne Orpheus Choral Society put on productions such as Handel's 'Creation', in the 1960s the combined choirs of Borden and Sittingbourne Girls Grammar schools did annual productions of Gilbert and Sullivan operettas, the Cedars Club put on Folk Nights and in the 1990s there is a local Country Music Club. In the 1990s the Orpheus and Co-op choirs continue to give performances, as do the Freeguard Singers Chamber Choir, the UK Paper Concert Band and the Wind Ensemble. There has been drama, the Holy Trinity Players performed in the 1950s and Applecarte put on performances in the 1990s at the new Avenue Theatre in the old council chamber in Central Avenue. (43)

Dance has also continued, both the Iris Thomas and the Anne Linguard Dancing Schools started in the 1950s, as did the Olde Tyme Dance Section of the Kemsley Social Club, and in 1969 the Anne Linguard Junior All Girls Latin-American Formation Team came third in a national competition. The John Kemsley School of Dancing started during the 1970s and continues to hold annual Ballroom and Latin-American examinations, there are also tap and ballet schools as well as a Scottish Country Dance Society and a new addition in the 1990s, American Line Dancing with North & South holding classes at the Swallows. As well as dance schools other dances have been held throughout the period, not always without controversy. In 1966 Saturday night 'Flower Power' dances at the Carmel Hall were banned by the Catholic Church following the publication in the local paper of 'love in' photos taken at them, even though the organisers said that there had been no drugs there. There was more trouble at the same venue in the 1980s when punks and skinheads were involved in a violent clash at a rock dance. (44)

Gardening has continued to be popular, there are still allotments in the town, and local societies such as the Chrysanthemum and Dahlia Society and the Horticultural and Floral Art Society hold annual shows. There is still a Racing Pigeon Society and a Model Aircraft Club as well as branches of county and national organisations for adults and children, newer societies such as the Sittingbourne Swallows - a troop of majorettes, and youth clubs, such as New House which celebrated its 50th anniversary in 1994. (45)

Cinemas and Night Clubs:
Both the Queen's and the Odeon had continued to operate during the war and in July 1945 the Odeon's Saturday Morning Club for children re-opened - it had 1,200 members. However by 1949 there was concern over the harmful effect of Saturday morning cinema on children. Saturday morning cinema continued though, both at the Odeon and the Queen's, known by the 1950s as 'the flea pit', and one resident remembers as a child having nightmares after watching a film with headless horsemen - so perhaps the earlier concerns had some justification! (46)

By the 1960s changes were on their way. There were plans in 1966 for the Odeon to change to be a full-time bingo hall, but the council refused to allow it and later in the year the cinema was sold to Classic Cinemas and there was talk of it becoming a gambling casino. Instead, in 1968 the Odeon was redecorated and the Vogue Bingo Hall opened there, three years later a new Classic cinema opened in part of the same building and in 1972 TV's Mr Pastry opened a second cinema there. In the same year the old Plaza cinema building (originally the Empire), in East Street, was sold to the council and two years later there were plans to turn the Queen's cinema into a Music Hall. (47)

After success for over half a century as a cinema the Queen's building was to start on a decade of disasters. In 1975 it was revamped and opened as a Variety Theatre but it lost money and in less than a year variety shows were dropped in favour of 'one-night' shows and then the building was closed, the venture having sustained losses of £100,000 in just one year. In 1979 a £40,000 project was launched to re-open the building as a top night spot with dining and cabaret but it was as a Night Club that 'Cleo's' opened in 1980, only to be closed within three months. The new owners opened it again as an American style discotheque called 'Marteens', when it opened there were brawls outside and within six months cutbacks in its licensing hours forced its closure. Shortly afterwards it was gutted in a fire and plans were announced to turn it into an up-market entertainment centre. It did re-open under new management in 1982 but by 1984 the site was for sale and the building was again ravaged by fire. In 1985 the building was sold again but plans to re-open it as 'Tootsies Night Club' came to nothing when a drinks license was refused - the owner sold the building and it was eventually demolished. (48)

The former Odeon building continued to cater for both film-goers and those who enjoy bingo through to the 1990s. It was though to be nearly ten years before the town had another Night Club, and then it had two, one in the former office space of the Bell Shopping Centre - JJ's and the other over Burtons - the Vogue. (49)

Conclusion
There have been many changes in the activities enjoyed by townsfolk over the past century and a half, with improved education and means of communication the great improvement societies of the Victorian period have given way to home entertainment. But sport, music, drama and dance all still have active supporters and television certainly hasn't destroyed the social life of the town.

Chapter Nine

The Town at War

This chapter on the town during the years of war is divided into two parts, one on the First World War (1914-1918) and the other on the Second World War (1939-1945). It is in no way a history of the wars, either military or social, rather it concentrates on the events which affected the lives of the people in the town. Each war is dealt with chronologically with subsections for each year.

THE FIRST WORLD WAR

1914

The usual round of social events was in full swing in the summer of 1914, Bronco Bill's Great Wild West Exhibition and two-ring circus had just visited the town, plans were well underway for flower shows at Milton and Borden and for the Open Tournament at Gore Court Lawn Tennis Club, when the announcement came in early August that England, France, Belgium and Russia were at war with Germany. (1)

At once there was an advertisement urging all young men who had 'served in the ranks of the Volunteer and Territorial Forces, particularly Old Members of 'E' Company to enrol at the Drill Hall, East Street'. Many young men were to join the forces and life in Sittingbourne and Milton was to change dramatically. The planned flower shows and the tennis tournament were abandoned. There was an immediate rush to buy up stocks of food which resulted in an increase in prices and the public were urged not panic as there were ample supplies of food, although there was a warning that butter, eggs and poultry, 90% of which came from Europe, might be liable to restriction. (2)

The town, like much of north Kent, became part of the War Zone. Armed sentries patrolled and civilians were warned that:

'It is dangerous to approach an armed sentry at night.

If civilians are challenged by a sentry they should stand still and explain who they are and avoid any suspicious movement, such as running away, which would render them liable to be shot.

Any attempt at rioting or unlawful assembly will be sternly suppressed.

Duck-shooters are warned that, if they shoot within the range of an armed sentry, they do so at their own risk.' (3)

Within days troops arrived to be billeted in the town, the 1st Home Counties Royal Field Artillery in Milton and the 7th and 8th Middlesex Territorials from London in Sittingbourne, houses where the latter were billeted being marked with M X. Local families were paid 9d a night for the billeting of soldiers. They were also paid 7¹/₂d if they provided breakfast of 6oz of bread, 1 pint of tea with milk and sugar and 4oz bacon. For dinner, to consist of one pound of meat, previous to being dressed, 8oz bread, 8oz potatoes or other vegetables and 1 pint of beer or mineral water and supper, of 6oz bread, 1 pint of tea with milk and sugar and 2oz cheese they were paid 1/7¹/₂ and 4¹/₂d respectively. If an officer were billeted with a family then they received 3/0 a night but he paid for his own food and the rates for stabling horses were 9d a day without forage and 2/7¹/₂ if 10lb of oats, 12lb of hay and 8lb of straw a day were provided. (4)

Relationships between local householders and their 'guests' were not always good. One local resident recalls that her mother had one soldier removed from the house when she caught him coming down at night to steal jam, the sticky finger marks on the cupboard door had given him away! She was also not impressed when on arriving at the house and being offered a cup of tea a soldier said 'Yes' with no sign of a 'Please', she discovered later that at the last house he had been he had politely replied 'If you don't mind', but the lady there had minded and he hadn't received the tea, so he wasn't taking any more chances! Sometimes those billeted on local families formed lasting friendships with them, with reciprocal visits being made for years after the war ended. Another local resident recalls an army Major and his family being billeted with them, written in chalk on the outside of the house was ' 1 Major, 1 Wife, 1 Canary'. (5)

As well as the comforts offered by individual families the YMCA provided extended reading and writing accommodation for the Territorials at the Congregational School Room, the Wesleyan Guild Room and the Holy Trinity Institute. On Thursday 20th August the Territorials had a Surprise Call. 'Just before 11.00 p.m. bugles sounded the "Alarm", whistles were shrilly blown and the whole place was alive. The whole of the Forces quartered in the town were turned out in full marching order, each Battalion parading to its own area. Bedroom windows flew up, heads popped out, ... (and) men were seen hurrying along in pyjamas to the great amusement of the onlookers.' (6)

During the first few weeks of the war the Sittingbourne National Reserve had the honour of being one of the first National Reserve troops to supply a draft to the Forces and by the end of August there was an advertisement for the New Expeditionary Force "The Buffs" for which a new battalion was being raised. Boy Scouts came forward to help the military and the police, and motor car and motor cycle scouts patrolled the London to Dover road, said to be the most important in the country. They also joined in the procession on the evening of Saturday 22nd August to a Great Patriotic Rally at Sittingbourne Football Ground to enrol recruits in Lord Kitchener's New Army. The procession started from the King's Head, Chalkwell and also included the band of the 1st

Home Counties Royal Field Artillery, the Sittingbourne and Milton Fire Brigades, St John's Ambulance Association, and local National Reservists. Lord Harris addressed a crowd of 2,000 and they sang 'It's a long way to Tipperary' and 'Rule Britannia'. By early September 108 men of the E (Sittingbourne) Company had volunteered for foreign service and others, Navy and Army Reservists, including a hundred Mill employees had been called up for service. (7)

A Milton and District War Relief Committee was formed and they organised open air concerts for Territorials, with the general public being admitted on the payment of a small sum. The first one was held on the evening of Monday 31st August at the Bull Football Ground. Over 2,000 attended and the concert was a success, although the arrival of one of the singers was delayed because of the movement of troops on the railway. Fund raising was also underway. In early September a Jumble Sale was held in aid of the Prince of Wales Fund and the newly formed Sittingbourne, Milton and District Dance Club held a dance at Holy Trinity Hall in aid of the National Relief Fund, although the Dancing Master, F Burton, was absent as he had been called to the colours. (8)

It was not long before there were reports in the paper of local men who were serving overseas. Lance-Corporal David King who had been a cornet player in the Band of the Sittingbourne Paper Mill took part in the terrible fight at Mons in Belgium. He had been a Reservist and he went to France with the British Expeditionary Force under General Sir John French. He spoke of the joyous reception given to the British troops as they made their way through France. They marched thirty-six miles at a stretch and at Mons went into action. Trenches were hastily thrown up and they held ground against a fierce German attack before, overborne by weight of numbers, they had to retire. One of King's companions popped his head over the trench and was beheaded by a shell. King crawled along the trench and assisted a comrade who had lost his foot, even though he himself had a broken leg. He lost his kit, rifle and everything before he was taken to a train filled with wounded soldiers. The train was fired on by Germans but eventually reached a port from where he was taken by boat to Southampton. Others were not so lucky, by the end of September came the news that John Richards had been killed when HMS Pathfinder was sunk by a German submarine. Even so, by early October nearly 350 men had been recruited from Sittingbourne and Milton. (9)

For those left behind the presence of thousands of Territorials billeted in the area brought considerable advantage to the town, stimulating the retail trade, and there was talk of the district becoming a permanent military centre. Weekly instrumental recitals were given at St Michael's for the troops, the Queen's and Empire Cinemas had Benefit Matinees and Football Matches were held, even though the wages of players had been reduced because of the financial situation caused by the war, over 2,500 attending the Sittingbourne versus Margate Cup Tie, the majority of them being troops. Also in October came news of how Germans viewed the war. The daughter of the Reverend Kidson, of Holy Trinity, returned from Germany and reported that they expected England to be starved within a fortnight, that the German Armies would be in London within a month and that they believed that English soldiers couldn't shoot and always ran away! (10)

During October the town was put on alert to receive Belgian refugees, Trinity Hall was commandeered, beds were secured at Gore Court RAMC Hospital and at Borden Grammar School (then a boarding school), but none arrived. News came that Private Murrel a Miltonian, had been mentioned in dispatches and that the son of Mr & Mrs Nathanial Smith, of William Street, had been killed in action. On Monday 25th October the town was honoured with a visit by His Majesty the King. The Royal train arrived from Victoria at 11.00 a.m. and the King, wearing khaki, the service dress of a Field Marshal, drove past cheering crowds lining Station Street, Park Road, Belmont Road and Albany Road before arriving at the Connaught Road entrance to the Recreation Ground. There he stopped to speak to two veterans of the Crimean War (1854-56) before reviewing the troops on parade. (11)

By the end of October the expected Belgian wounded had arrived and were doing well in the Trinity Hall Hospital. The need for hospital beds for those wounded in the war led to G H Dean of Whitehall offering to lend the house next to his own in Bell Road as a hospital, it would accommodate about thirty beds. In early November there was a change in the troops who were billeted in the town, the troops who had been reviewed by the King left for the front and were replaced by the 4th and 5th Battalions of the Royal Dublin Fusiliers who came from Queenstown where they had been under canvas for three months. (12)

They soon took part in the life of the town with their band playing concerts at the Football Ground. By the end of 1914 the life of the town had resumed a degree of normality. A Whist Drive was held at the Catholic School in aid of Red Cross Hospital Funds, the annual show of the Sittingbourne and District Cage Bird Society was held, as was the Sittingbourne Fat Stock Xmas Show. A Cinderella Dance was held at the Ufton Road School, the County School for Girls gave a Christmas entertainment, the Sittingbourne, Milton Regis and District Carol Singers, in spite of being short of members, toured the town and members of the Irish Fusiliers held a Boxing Tournament at the Drill Hall on Christmas Eve. (13)

But the war was ever present. On Christmas Day there was a German air-raid. Mr John Hinge, walking home from church, saw a German Taube machine flying over Iwade. The next minute a shell screamed past his head and buried itself in an adjoining field - the shell was a British one fired at the German plane from Sheerness. On the same day Chief Air Mechanic Budds, formerly of Sittingbourne, was flying in a British air raid on Cuxhaven, following which he received the DSM. Lance Corporal Albert Hunt, of Crown Quay

Lane, spent Christmas at the front. In a letter to his wife he spoke of travelling for a mile to the firing line through trenches waist deep in mud and water. The weather on Christmas Eve was freezing and they had to break the ice to paddle back. Two of his section died that night and he said that if someone got shot then they didn't stand much chance if they were on their own as they were sure to be drowned. He was glad to be alive and well as hundreds had died or were frost bitten. (14)

1915

The new year brought with it news of the Sittingbourne Company 4th Battalion Buffs, a card was received showing them marching into Mhow, Central India, with Captain Hoggs at their head. By the end of January it was announced that around eight hundred men from the local area had joined up since the start of the war. There also came the news of the area's first VC of the war. It was awarded to Gunner Stuart Fagg of the Royal Field Artillery who had been born at Iwade. (15)

Back in the town the new year brought with it the threat of air-raids and Milton UDC advised people not to go out into the streets if there was an air-raid, instead they should go down as low as they could into the cellars and wait for some time. The restrictions on lighting at night meant that streets were dark which was proving dangerous, however the military would not relax the restrictions. Trinity Hall Hospital continued to operate. In March the local paper received a letter from a grateful Belgian ex-patient and in the same month sixteen British soldiers, wounded in France, were taken there. The presence of the Royal Dublin Fusiliers in Sittingbourne meant that St Patrick's Day was celebrated, with an Open Air Service at the Paper Mill's Cricket Ground and a dance at the Drill Hall. (16)

Early in April news was received from local men of the 'ruinous state' of Ypres. Mr H Goatham reported that it was 'nothing but a graveyard ... all over the place there (were) little wooden crosses to mark where some poor fellow had fallen, either ours or the Germans', and Private Black, from Pembury Street, said that many of the houses had been destroyed. The war though was to come closer to home during the next few months. A local resident recalls being sent by her mother, who was busy with the Monday morning washing, to find her brother who had been sent to the doctor in East Street and had been gone too long. When she got to the junction of the High Street and Crown Quay Lane she saw what had kept him from coming home, two planes were engaged in a dog fight over the marshes and she too stayed to watch. Their mother, afraid that something serious had happened left her washing, still with sacking over her apron, and went down the High Street to find them. It was some time before she got over the disgrace of being seen out in such a state! (17)

The involvement of aeroplanes in the war was something the Government had not anticipated and so there were no restrictions on the reporting of raids made by planes although there were on those made by Zeppelin airships. In April there was a report of a raid by a German airman in a Taube monoplane over Sittingbourne. He circled over the town and descending to 600 feet dropped two bombs, one at a chalk quarry near Cryalls Farm in Borden and the other in Burley's orchard to the south of the town where there was the first casualty on local soil, or to be more precise - tree, a blackbird was killed! (18)

Unity Street Bomb Damage, First World War

The following month saw the tragedy of the Princess Irene. This ship was in the Medway when it exploded killing 78 dockyard workers who were on board at the time. The shock of the explosion was so great that it was felt in Sittingbourne. Glass in the windows of properties in the High Street and elsewhere in the town was shattered and ceilings fell down in the Town Hall and the Lion Hotel. In spite of warnings to stay indoors in the event of air-raids 'everybody with blanched faces ran out of doors and gazed up into the sky to find the supposed enemy airship. But nothing could be seen but the blue sky, and the large cloud of white smoke drifting away from the direction of Port Victoria.' When the sound of the explosion was heard, Mrs Watts of Shortlands Road exclaimed, "Oh, my George" - even though she couldn't know the cause of the sound, later she heard that her husband George had in fact died on the Princess Irene. Mr Peter Young, who had been engaged to marry Annie Smeed of West Street also died, as did the son of Mr & Mrs Clacket of Dover Street. The Princess Irene was the second ship to be destroyed in the Medway. The previous November the Bulwark had been blown up, with the loss of over 700 men. (19)

The air-raid thought to be happening when the Irene exploded, became a reality in June when Unity Street was bombed. Unlike the bombing raid in March when only a blackbird was killed no details were reported in the local paper at the time because of the restrictions on reporting Zeppelin air-raids. The only reference was an announcement from the Official Press Bureau on June 12th that 'hostile airships visited the East and South-East coasts of England. Bombs were dropped in various places, but little material damage was done. The casualties so far reported are very few.' The raid in fact took place on Friday 4th June and one resident recalls being at home in William Street and hearing noise and people calling out. Everyone rushed out into the street and watched as the Zeppelins, high up in the sky, lit by search lights and being fired on by guns at Chatham, passed over from the east to the west, dropping their bombs. Certainly in Sittingbourne 'significant' material damage was done. The Holy Trinity Boys School Log for the following week records that attendance was poor because of the raid, mothers were afraid to go to bed, many slept in fields and orchards, so children were too tired to go to school, some parents even left the town. (20)

Although the town was now actively engaged in the war, there were complaints that it was below average in the number of recruits for the Armed Forces. One writer to the newspaper referred to 'men who had given up their jobs to put on the khaki and who are indignant to find their places taken by other men of eligible age who they say ought to be taking their part in the defence of the country.' Indeed the writer said 'one need only walk down the High Street on a Saturday evening to see hundreds of fine, stalwart, young fellows, many of them with no responsibilities, apart from their work, their amusements, and their sweethearts.' When one adds to these the many lonely young men billeted in the town, far away from their own loved ones one can understand the concern expressed by the Archbishop of Canterbury that there was a danger in Kent because of the multitude of men congregated in it of 'war babies'. Certainly members of the Middlesex Territorials who had been billeted in the town in 1914 complained of the conditions in Calcutta and one officer said that the trouble was that 'at Sittingbourne they were absolutely spoilt, they lived on the fat of the land.' (21)

In May local security was increased with military passes being required to visit the Isle of Sheppey and local men carried out Night Patrols in the Park Road area of Sittingbourne, much to the comfort of women who lived there. With the advent of early summer it was time for the Royal Engineers who had been stationed in Milton, first in billets and then under canvas and the 5th Battalion Royal Dublin Fusiliers who had been stationed in Sittingbourne to leave. The latter went to the Dardenelles and in a letter a soldier described the conditions - 'the chief plague here is flies and the chief disease is diarrhoea'. Meanwhile with the first anniversary of the war came the introduction of a

National Register, one benefit of this for the Sittingbourne area was that when it was analysed those engaged in skilled agricultural occupations would be starred so that the recruiting officer wouldn't take them - there were already problems being caused by the lack of skilled agricultural workers. The price of milk locally had increased because of increases in wages and foodstuffs. The autumn saw an increase in Income Tax, duties on tea, tobacco, coffee, cocoa, chicory and dried fruits up by 50%, the duty on sugar was also raised, import duties on cars, motor cycles and parts, cinema films, clocks, watches, musical instruments, plate glass and hats were increased by a third and there was a 3d a gallon increase on motor spirit. (22)

Social events still continued to play a part of the life of the town with the annual Summer Bank Holiday Fete and Sports at the Albany Road Meadows and a Baby Show at the Town Hall. Local church groups went on summer outings and the swimming baths opened part time to the public and part time to the military. There was friendly rivalry between the locals and the military with a games contest being held between members of the Sergeants' Mess of the 4th Battalion Royal Dublin Fusiliers and the Sittingbourne Workmen's Club. (23)

Meanwhile news still came in of casualties amongst former residents including Reuben Shrubsall who was killed by a German sniper bullet when carrying water to comrades in the trenches. Others were luckier, Private Boulding of the Buffs came home on leave after being wounded at Gallipoli when a bullet went through his ear, others were captured and funds were raised through a Flag Day to help local Prisoners Of War. Towards the end of the year women became more involved in the war effort. A branch of Queen Mary's Needlework Guild was established at the Cedars and the ladies met in relays six days a week. Children also played their part with local schools providing entertainments for wounded soldiers from the hospitals in the town. Unfortunately one held at the Milton Regis Council Girls' School encountered a problem with the weather, it was so foggy that some of the men arrived late and others didn't get there at all! Soldiers from the hospital at Whitehall also visited Holy Trinity School each term, the children's mothers all provided three buns or tarts and two to three spoonfuls of tea or sugar. When the soldiers arrived those who were able to walk looked at the work on the wall and the children all sang or recited to entertain them. Christmas gifts were made up for local boys serving in Aden, each man was to receive a good shirt, a pair of socks, a towel, a khaki handkerchief, a small tin of sweets and money for Christmas cheer. Donations for these came from schools, businesses and individual townsfolk. (24)

1916
In the wake of the bombing raids during the previous year came advertisements for a Government scheme of insurance for Zeppelin raids. They should also have covered damage from air crashes. On Monday 17th

January "just before 2.30, a biplane, carrying two officers attached to the naval air station at Grain, flew over Kemsley Down, Milton, and engine trouble developed. The machine circled round and came down to about 40 feet from the ground, when it side slipped and crashed down on soft ground in Church field, wrecking the machine" and killing both occupants. (25)

Milton decided to cut off the supply of gas on nights when there were Zeppelin raids to avoid showing lights and to cut down on the risk of explosion if bombs were dropped. However, when it was cut off there was quite a panic and Sittingbourne decided that, because of this and as it would be dangerous to cut off the supply to the railway station, they would not cut off the supply to the town. In any event the black-out was working well. Government restrictions were affecting individuals and businesses. If people moved house then they were required to notify the change under the requirements of the National Registration Act and the Paper Mill was forced to shut down three machines, although they did not lay off any workers. (26)

The wounded continued to be cared for in the town. In March a matinee was held at the Queen's Cinema in aid of the Sittingbourne War Hospital and Glovers Hospital, and The Hospital of St John of Jerusalem, was re-opened after having been closed for cleaning. There was a change in the troops being billeted in the town with the arrival of the 3rd Battalion the Queens (Royal West Surrey) Regiment, a thousand attended the first public performance of the band in the Recreation Ground after Church parade. At the end of the month the troops under canvas were given temporary accommodation in barns during a blizzard which hit the town. (27)

The war was having its effect on the life of women. One young lady of a respected family was jilted by a soldier who had presented himself as well off, but had borrowed money and then went to London and didn't return. Another woman was employed as a mate on board a sailing barge when the master couldn't get a man. There were reports from Employment Bureaux and Agencies that there was a rapidly increasing demand for young educated women to take the places of men in the commercial and industrial world, although for women over forty there were few opportunities if they had never before worked for a living. Nurses in particular were in great demand and cooking was one of the best paid employments. By the summer a Milton Union Women's Agricultural Committee had been formed to encourage women to work on the land, and to persuade farmers to employ them. They may have been successful as in August there was an advertisement for a tractor being driven by a girl with the caption 'the girl on the tractor can drive the machine just as well as a man'. (28)

Events popular during the pre-war years continued to be held, although they were affected by the number of soldiers stationed in the town. The annual Easter Bank Holiday Monday Grand Fete and Sports meeting was held. Over five thousand attended and there were egg and spoon races, a musical bicycle race and a bandsmen's race with the competitors handicapped according to the size of their instrument - they had to walk and play at the same time. By that time in the year the men had left their winter billets and were in the more disciplined environment of the camp at Gore Court. They had less freedom of movement and there was on site entertainment including a picture theatre. They held military sports there and the troops also provided entertainment at the camp for the townsfolk with band concerts being held on Sundays. (29)

Gore Court Camp, First World War

During the Spring prices were rising. W Goodhew, THE Butcher, placed an ad in the paper saying that 'prices have risen and are still rising' but they promised 'good service at the lowest prices'. There was concern of the effects on public health and child welfare because of the increased price of milk, it was 5d a quart at the time. Sittingbourne Council tried to make money by separating waste paper from the rest of the rubbish - it cost them 12/- to 14/- a ton to remove it but they were able to sell it for £2 a ton, and the National Government tried to save daylight by putting the clocks forward an hour during the summer. They also decided to do away with the Whitsuntide Bank Holiday, so the annual sports were postponed and elementary schools cancelled the usual week's holiday. (30)

By the summer of 1916 weekly tribunals were being held to decide which men were fit to serve in the forces and which were unfit or in exempt occupations. In August, Lloyd applied for 111 of their men, 37 of whom they claimed to be in certified occupations, that is those whose jobs were necessary for the continuence of the business - office staff and skilled men such as machinemen and reelermen. The mill was visited and it was decided that their claim was reasonable, over 400 men having already left the mill to fight in the war. The firm of Smeed Dean had also lost over 400 employees. Of the 684 who remained 370 were over military age, 36 were aged 17 or 18 and 84 were medically unfit for military service, they applied for exemptions for skilled workers until the end of the brick making season. (31)

News continued to arrive of men from the town who were 'to be found fighting for the Empire all over the world' including South Africa and India, and the Queen's Cinema showed 'the greatest war picture yet produced - The Battle of the Somme.' Closer to home there was news of Zeppelin raids, although the closest those in Sittingbourne came was when they were able to watch the spectacle of a Zeppelin coming down in flames in Essex. An aeroplane came closer in October, dropping four bombs on Sheerness, three fell into the harbour and the fourth damaged railway carriages at the station but no casualties were reported. (32)

The end of the year saw the introduction of state food control as well as fund raising for gifts to be sent to Sittingbourne Territorials in India and Kent Prisoners of War in Germany and other parts of Europe. At home, sport helped to occupy the spare time of soldiers waiting for their turn to go abroad, and the opening match was held in the Red Cross (Whitehall) Cup competition between the Gloucestershires and the Royal Artillery. Others made use of the new recreation room opened at 40 East Street, the demand for the one at the old Post Office having become to great. (33)

1917
After two and a half years of war the country was suffering from food shortages. In March the local paper gave 'a few hints as to the prevention of food waste'. Potatoes were not to be peeled, they should be boiled or baked in their jackets, anyone who could not eat the skin could partly boil them and peel off the thin exterior coating. Peapods could be grated and sieved to make a nourishing soup, more bran could be added when making bread and tea and coffee should be reused. It was also suggested that pieces of soap should be saved, mixed with water, heated and remoulded. Soon there were to be weekly articles by a doctor on 'Food and How to Save It'. The lack of cereals meant that cakes, puddings and biscuits could no longer be sent to soldiers and it was recommended that fruit should be bottled without the addition of sugar. (34)

In the summer a controlled fruit pulping station was opened at Sittingbourne using the facilities of Lloyd's Mill and the autumn saw children collecting horse chestnuts to be used in industrial processes to replace grain. There was a need for more locally grown food and, in spite of strong opposition, by the end of the year part of the Sittingbourne Recreation Ground had been ploughed up to be used as allotments. With food shortages came rising prices, and the rates paid to those billeting troops were increased by a penny a meal. (35)

Difficulties in obtaining crews and restrictions on movements meant that there had been a serious reduction in the number of vessels using Milton Creek and there were fears for its future after the war. The armed forces were also finding it difficult to recruit men and in March a National Service campaign was inaugurated with a public meeting at Sittingbourne Town Hall. The Government were not only restricting food, they were also restricting the use of paper and the East Kent Gazette had to be ordered in advance from the newsagent, and it was not to be long before it was to be reduced in size to save paper. (36)

The year continued to bring news of military campaigns abroad, including in May a report from Private Vandepeer, whose parents lived in Shakespeare Road, of the capture of Vimy Ridge and in October a letter from Sapper Joy about the attack on Gaza. There was also news of local men who had been killed or injured whilst serving abroad, including in July the loss of Frederick Stokes, Clarence Luckhurst, William Luckhurst and John Cutter who were amongst the 800 who died when H M S Vanguard was destroyed. (37)

The war was not though always so far from home. In June there were a number of enemy bombing raids with 76 killed and 174 injured at Folkestone and 100 killed and 470 injured in London. Following these raids a siren was fixed up at the Paper Mills and people were warned to remain indoors if the siren gave the warning of an air-raid and not to use telephones during air-raids. Sittingbourne was fortunate, it did not suffer from a raid that summer, Chatham was not so lucky, 200 were killed or wounded there in September. (38)

In spite of all the difficulties the social life of the town continued, although even then the war was ever present with many of them being fund raising events for those wounded in the war. There was a Whist Drive and Dance on the night of St Valentine's Day in aid of the Red Cross and in April St George's Day was celebrated publicly for the first time in the town with fund raising efforts, including a carnival and fete, in aid of the War Hospital Supply Depot. In the summer there were Military Sports at the Football Ground and an Old English Sports and Fete on August Bank Holiday Monday, both in aid of the Sittingbourne Red Cross Hospital, and a Fete and Sports was held at Glovers Park in aid of the hospital there. Funds were again raised for the War Hospital Supply Depot in November with an American Sale and the depot received over a thousand socks, mittens and mufflers knitted by girls at local schools. (39)

1918

The start of what was to be the final year of the war was a dismal one. British supply ships were continuing to be sunk by German submarines at an alarming rate and food shortages were becoming worse. February brought the news that the queue system was to be abolished and that butter, margarine and meat were all to be rationed in the same way as sugar. Everyone over the age of ten was to have two food cards, one for meat and one for other food, which were issued for a period of twenty weeks. The cards were to be signed and taken to a registered retailer who filled in the two spaces marked 'A' and kept the detachable section 'E', the cards could not be used until registered in this way. Butcher's meat, that is fresh beef, pork and mutton had to be bought from a registered retailer, bones, offal - tripe, liver etc., could be bought elsewhere as could a meat meal from a public eating house. The local paper published a list of the authorised prices for butcher's meat in force for the Sittingbourne area for readers to cut out and keep. Meat was only in fact allowed to be eaten on two days a week and adverts appeared for macaroni as a substitute. By the autumn, beef as well as pork sausages were rationed and jam was also expected to be included in the system, however prices were continuing to rise. (40)

The war was changing life for women in particular. It was reported that their attitude towards industrial problems had changed, many being keen on joining Trade Unions. Some were engaged in heavy work such as excavation, trucking coal and helping to lay bricks as well as locally working on the land and in the Paper Mill - Lloyd employed four hundred women and girls, including some in the machine rooms. They now had the right to vote and with the possibility of a General Election that November a new Register including women voters was drawn up. They took part in sports such as Tug-of-War matches and they had stopped wearing gloves at dances as dancers no longer held each other tightly by the waist and hand for neither depended on the other - the rage for the Tango having revolutionised dancing. (41)

In January 1918 there was a United Day of Prayer of thanksgiving and intercession which brought together for the first time members of different churches in the town on neutral ground - the Drill Hall. In March reports were being received of the Buffs great stand against a colossal German attack along a fifty mile front in France. By August came the news that the German advance had been converted into the biggest defeat that the German armies had ever suffered. In October the employment of discharged soldiers was becoming a problem although Smeed Dean and Co announced that they were able to take on former employees when they returned from the war. (42)

In early November the town was in the grip of an influenza epidemic, local elementary schools, Sunday schools and the Queen's and Empire Picture Halls all closed. With Austria and Turkey out of the war Germany was isolated and alone, then came the news that on Monday November 11th an Armistice between the Allied and United States Armies on the one side and the German

Army on the other, had been signed. At Sittingbourne a siren sounded at the Paper Mills at 10.30. It was meant to have been the 'All Clear' signal but it was as near to 'Hip, Hip, Hooray' as anything could be and church bells joined in to celebrate the end of the war. (43)

1919

Although the war was over troops who had been stationed in the town still remained. The Signallers left in January 1919 and most of the 3rd Queens Regiment left in March, although a few remained to fill up the trenches and to clear up. During 1919 German Prisoners of War were encamped at Keycol Hill, Glovers Hospital, which had treated 1,600 patients was closed in February as was the Sittingbourne War Hospital Supply Depot at the Cedars. There were rival ex-Servicemen organisations, the Silver Badge Institute and the National Federation of Discharged and Demobilised Soldiers and Sailors. In March 1919 they agreed to share an Institute on the Albany Road ground, then in April the former Royal Oak Pub became their home and in May the Silver Badge Institute ceased to exist. Gradually the life of the town got back to normal, but for the wounded, bereaved and the town's 200 War orphans, life would never be the same again. (44)

THE SECOND WORLD WAR

1938

Although the war did not begin until the autumn of 1939, preparations for it began as early as the spring of 1938 when the Government appointed a Food Controller to organise a system of food control and schools were sent details of Air-Raid Precautions. Then in June members of the Air Force took part in a mock air-raid over the south east. An air-raid warning sounded from the mill - a two minute punctuated siren, Sittingbourne Town Hall became the centre of official activity and police told shoppers to take cover as a single bomber followed by three planes in a V formation roared overhead, following the line of the High Street, and a fire engine dashed through the town before the All Clear, a two minute continuous siren, was sounded. By the autumn a census had been taken of the number and sizes of respirators required and the gas masks were distributed in early October. Vehicles had to be registered and the local paper provided details of how to construct an air-raid shelter in the garden, meanwhile the council planned to dig trenches in various locations throughout the town to give cover to the inhabitants. By October the 'crisis' was over, Chamberlain having returned from Munich with his famous document signed by Hitler, thanksgiving services were held in churches that peace had been preserved. (45)

1939

However the threat of war had not gone away. In January 1939 there was an advertisement for voluntary helpers to make a survey of accommodation for the reception of evacuated children in the event of an emergency, although the council objected to the town becoming a War-time refuge. In February a Voluntary National Service Scheme was initiated to fill vacancies that existed in various branches of defence, military and civil and to safeguard essential industries and services, and there were plans for a new Air-Raid Precautions (ARP) Centre in Sittingbourne. Local industry was becoming involved in war preparations. In the First World War the firm of Wills and Packham had built coastal motor boats, flying boats and other special craft, twenty years later the Sittingbourne Shipbuilding Company continued the tradition, building two harbour service launches for the British Admiralty. (46)

In April there was an appeal for more ARP Wardens to join the scheme so that all the roads in the town would be covered, and in June all males aged between 20 and 21 had to register for Military Training. Schools were being advised as to what to do in the event of war, those in neutral areas which had suitable measures for protecting children, that is having covered trenches lined with concrete, could open, otherwise, and in evacuable areas, schools were to be closed. Teachers were given courses on elementary first aid and anti-gas measures. By the end of June preparations for war were affecting the mill, a hundred men had already been called up for service under the Conscription Act and No 14 machine making special paper was closed. At the same time came an announcement that during a time of war notices by the ARP and Police would be communicated by the Relay System, this was a special wire used as a direct method of communication between the BBC and listeners so that confidential news could be broadcast without the risk of foreign powers hearing it. There was an advertisement in the paper for the Sittingbourne Relay Service Ltd which would connect listeners to the system. (47)

Air-raid precautions were coming into effect, a Black Out being held on the night of July 8th/9th from midnight to 4 a.m. Admidst the preparations for war the usual summer activities continued, as they had done in 1914. Flower shows and fetes were held and Gore Court Cricket Club celebrated its centenary. By early September though the time of waiting came to an end. The town was prepared to receive 7,500 evacuees, residents were warned to check the gas masks issued the previous year, if normal care had been taken care of them then they would still be effective, but if the valve had been removed they would be useless and would have to be replaced. The town was divided into three sectors with several Air-Raid Wardens Patrol Posts in each. Patrol Post 8, for example, was located at Bishop's Yard, Albany Road. It covered Park Road, Albany Road, Addington Road, Unity Street, William Street and Valenciennes Road. There were six Deputy Group Wardens, H Hinton, F Bishop, F Horden, G Whitworth, W Claydon and R Maylem and each street had its own group of wardens, those for William Street being W Cole, W Whitnall, A Day and L Cole. (48)

War was declared on 3rd September 1939. Within days the first evacuees arrived. Many experienced the pleasures of hop-picking for the first time and also the pains which followed a surfeit of apples. Initially local schools all closed. By the 21st September there were sufficient trenches provided at the Borden Grammar School for the School Certificate and Higher School Certificate boys to return, using the school in the mornings only as in the afternoon it was used by the evacuated members of Rochester Junior Technical School. The younger Grammar School boys worked at home with teachers sending out weekly question papers. (49)

It was to be several months before there were trenches at Holy Trinity School and so that autumn the children worked as best they could in a number of different locations, some for half a day at the Ufton Lane School, some at the Baptist Church Clubroom, others in a converted garage at Waldene, Col & Mrs Dean's house in Park Avenue, a room at the Typewriting School in Park Road, and small groups of infants at 63 Park Road and 78 Borden Lane. Waldene was also the venue for a Sewing Party organised by Mrs Dean held every Tuesday afternoon making mufflers, helmets, mittens and handkerchiefs for the Buffs. A request was made for wool, cigarettes, chocolate and razor blades which could be sent to the troops. By early December the group had sent 620 knitted articles as well as other gifts to the Buffs and Mrs Dean was also running a series of whist drives in the Pavilion, King George's Field to raise funds. (50)

During the first few weeks of the war there were several air-raid warnings, the first being on 3rd September when shops closed, buses stopped, ARP Wardens patrolled and people went into the shelters. In preparation for any damage that might occur following air-raids the council made an agreement with fourteen local builders that they would pay for the cost of repairs at Trade Union rates for labour plus 15% profit and materials charged at net with 12$^{1}/_{2}$% profit. (51)

1940

The new year saw the introduction of meat rationing, this was on the basis of monetary value so people could get more if they bought cheaper meat. Everyone had to register by the 8th January although rationing did not start until 11th March when the adult ration was 1/10 a week and half that for a young child. In February the promised new ARP Control Room was opened on land to the rear of Sittingbourne Town Hall. One local resident recalls being a telephonist there during the war. If an air-raid warning RED came from the Maidstone HQ then the warning sirens were switched on and the various ARP posts were telephoned. There were four outside phone lines each on the bench in the cubicles on one side of the room and a switchboard with nine outside and internal lines on the other side. There was also a messenger boy with a cycle. The air-raid message WHITE was the signal for all to stand down and the All Clear signal to be sounded. The centre consisted of a large room for the Controllers, equipped with a large table and a huge wall map of the district with small coloured flags which were pinned to the map to show the location of bombs that fell and where ambulances and sitting case cars were being used. There was also a kitchen, a room with two beds for the night staff, a piano and a radio on which staff listened to the nine o'clock news each day before turning out their pockets and purses for every 'ships' halfpenny they had which went to the Merchant Navy Comforts Fund. On 31st March the ARP held a dress rehearsal with volunteers playing the part of casualties. There were to be others during the war in which the Home Guard took part including ones codenamed 'Fremlins' and 'Exercise Shepherd Neame'. (52)

During the spring that year there was a house-to-house inspection of gas masks, a fortnight's saving campaign which raised over eleven and a half thousand pounds for the war effort and a 'Growmore' campaign encouraging the growing of food on allotments. Local industry was though beginning to suffer. The war was having a disastrous effect on the brick trade as with no new building going on bricks were remaining unsold, the paper mill was also under threat as there was a shortage of raw materials following the German invasion of Norway. (53)

June saw the return of many local men of the British Expeditionary Force from Boulogne and Dunkirk. One of the last to leave was Lieut-Colonel Dean, who, with his regiment of pioneers fought his way through the streets of Boulogne when the Germans were already there, and was amongst the last of the British troops to be evacuated. Not everyone was to return, there were letters from some who had survived but had been captured, including Jack Carpenter who 'with other Sittingbourne boys was surrounded by Germans in Belgium' and was a Prisoner Of War in Germany. He said that he was being treated well and asked for food parcels to be sent to them. Children who had been evacuated to the Sittingbourne area left and there were fears that local children would themselves have to be evacuated. (54)

In an effort to counteract the effects of the severe reduction in the import of raw materials the local council imposed a compulsory household salvage scheme, all waste paper, cardboard, scrap metal and bones were to be collected. People were also advised to make temporary window repairs following air-raid damage using glass substitute, plywood or black pitch paper. The number of air-raids became more frequent, so much so that it was decided that the air-raid warning would only be sounded if an intensive air-raid was imminent. There were warnings about delayed action bombs and people were advised to clear lofts and attics of all movable objects as a precaution against fires caused by incendiary bombs. Notices were placed in the windows of the Wardens' houses where stirrup pumps were kept for use in the event of fires caused by bombs. (55)

By early August came 'the prelude to the Battle of Britain. Long processions of enemy bombers, clearly visible against the blue sky, flying in formation with, later, fighters flying high above them, weaving long white trails of vapour, which occasionally made the sign of a huge question mark or a swastika. The sky seemed full of enemy planes, the sound was of a huge threshing machine. Gradually people adapted to the conditions but below the surface of seeming normality there stewed and bubbled the consciousness of a threat.' (56)

On Sunday 18th August there was what was described as 'a tragic happening' at Kemsley involving three families as the result of which two people died. Although the local paper couldn't say so, it was the result of a German bombing raid. The number of raids, and casualties was to intensify during the next few months. In early September the funeral occurred at Murston of Mrs Hopkins and her daughter, victims of another raid and in the middle of the month an unexploded cannon shell from a German fighter smashed the plate glass window of Sam's Furniture Emporium in Sittingbourne High Street, although fortunately there were no casualties on that occasion. (57)

Bomb Damage, Second World War

It was not only British civilians who were the victims of air-raids, sometimes the German pilots did not survive, in August Sub Leuit Muller was buried at Bobbing and in September Georg Bierling and Friedrich Kurella were both buried at Borden, all were re-buried after the war in a German War Cemetery. (58)

When air-raids occurred around 124 wardens turned out during the day and 171 at night. There were three types of air-raid warning messages. YELLOW was issued by Fighter Command to all areas that raiders might pass over, PURPLE for night time raids when all exposed lighting in docks, factories, railway yards etc had to be extinguished and RED when the public were warned using the air-raid sirens. (59)

There was though no air-raid warning in operation in Sittingbourne on Sunday 29th September. One local resident remembers it as a grey overcast day. He was playing in the garden of his home in Park Road with other members of his family when they heard the sound of machine-gun fire from the east of the town and then a German bomber appeared from low cloud just above a sycamore tree in their garden and released a stick of bombs. He was fortunate, they only lost the windows, doors and some ceilings in their house, others were not so lucky. Drables the Chemist (at the bottom of Park Road) and Pullens Garage (on the north side of West Street hill) both received direct hits. The Police Station (at the corner of Park Road and West Street) was damaged and other bombs fell on Cockleshell Walk (opposite Ufton Lane) and at the rear of a cooked meat shop in West Street. The owner, Miss Alice Manuell, her seven year old nephew and Miss Nellie Gambell were all buried in the debris. Mrs Amy Clark who was walking along West Street on her way to a church meeting later died of her injuries and other casualties included Mrs Gladys Rose Crutchley and her two month old baby of Cockleshell Walk, Dennis Skinner an old Trinity Schoolboy who worked at the mill and Mrs Kate Fowley. (60)

The following week the tug 'Sirdar' was blown to bits on the Swale killing the three crew, Ronald Cole, Thomas Godman and Leslie Miller, and Kemsley was again bombed although there were no casualties. Two weeks later the village was not so lucky, the paper mill's power station was damaged, Mrs Elsie May, of The Crescent, Kemsley, was killed and several were injured. Also in October a house in Knightsfield Road Milton was destroyed by a bomb. Fortunately the only occupant at the time survived, his thirteen old daughter had watched from the window of a friend's house as the bomb fell and she reached the spot where her home had stood in time to see the head and shoulders of her father, covered in blood and dust, appearing from the ruins. He had been cooking supper at the time the bomb fell and three weeks later when the site was cleared the gas oven was unearthed still with a plate of sausages inside. The death toll, though, continued to rise that autumn. In November a bomb fell outside of a greengrocery shop in Shortlands Road killing Mrs Ruth Kennett and her nine week old baby Valerie, together with three other children, Michael Wellard aged six, and Lorna Williams and Wendy Clunn both aged four. (61)

The final tragedy of the year occurred on December 5th. A number of German planes being harried by British fighters passed over the town and dropped twelve bombs. All but one fell in open spaces. That one landed on 31 Park Road, killing Mr Robert Bennett, his wife, son-in-law Mr Frank Elliot and a young maid, Barbara Marsh. The tragedy could have been worse, the grandchildren had been taken out for a walk or they too would have been killed. The force of the explosion damaged windows in the surrounding streets. In one house in William Street a local firm put in temporary windows, of the sash type but which would not open, promising to return with permanent ones as soon as possible. The 'temporary' windows were finally replaced in the 1990s! (62)

1941

German bombing raids continued in the new year, although they became less frequent. One of the worst was in early February when the town was bombed twice. The first time bombs fell in the grounds of the hospital and on a sports field and the mortuary was destroyed. More damage was done on the second attack when the central part of the town was straddled with ten high explosive bombs. One demolished a building adjoining a brick firm's pumping station in Bell Road, four fell on a residential road damaging two houses beyond repair, four fell on the football ground and the last one on the playing field of the Girl's Grammar School. Although a lot of property was damaged fortunately the only casualty was Mrs Forster who was badly cut by flying glass. (63)

Fears at the start of the war that the Germans would use poisoned gas had proved groundless and in February a census of those in the High Street showed that only one in ten were carrying their masks. The main concern then was with the likelihood of an attack using incendiary bombs. In March instructions were given as to how to deal with them. People were warned:

'Do not rush wildly at a firebomb as soon as it drops, especially out of doors.

No harm will be done by leaving the bomb to burn for a short time when it can be more safely approached.

If you are working a stirrup pump nozzle, wriggle forward on your stomach, keeping your head as near as possible to to ground, to avoid fumes.

It is a good idea to protect your head with a dustbin lid.

Deal with the biggest fire first.

Should furniture be well alight it may be best to tackle it first, using the jet; then put the spray on the bomb.

Be particularly careful never to turn the jet on to the bomb.

Do no enter a building or a room where there is a fire unless you are prepared to deal with it at once.

If a fire bomb lodges in a gutter do not leave it there to burn where it may set fire to the rafters.

If you cannot drag it off with a rake and are unable to reach it with a ladder play a jet from your stirrup pump on to the roof above the bomb.

Use sandbags, protect your face and the upper part of your body when approaching a bomb, and dump the sandbag on the bomb.

If it is indoors drag the bomb into a metal receptacle with sand in the bottom which should then be taken outside.'

Fortunately it was to be some time before Sittingbourne residents were to need to put these instructions into practice. (64)

Fire watchers were given instructions in methods of dealing with fire bombs. Employees at firms such as Dean's Jam Factory took their turn on the 'Fire Watch' rota, usually one man and two girls at night, together with the permanent night watchman. Air-Raid Wardens were trained in the handling of stirrup pumps. Usually this was a man's job but occasionally women were also involved, one remembers taking her father's turn on duty when he was unwell, sharing the duty of patrolling Unity Street and William Street twice a week with her uncle, Mr Pepper. Women were playing an increasing part in the war effort at home. Many worked in the mill, others in reserve occupations such as being bar-maids - pubs being considered essential for morale during the war. In addition they did voluntary service, acting as telephonists for the ARP and the Fire Service. Such 'voluntary' service was for a certain number of 'compulsory' hours, in one case a telephonist worked at the Fire Station during afternoons from 2.00 p.m. to 5.00 p.m. and from 10.00 p.m. to 6.00 a.m. two or three nights a week, although on quiet nights it was possible to sleep there. When the alarm bell rang the telephonist took the call and if the fire engine needed to be called out then one of the crew would come to receive written instructions, later they would be written up in a log book. When there were air-raids then each fire station warned the next, starting from Dover, Sittingbourne usually got calls from Faversham or Teynham and in turn made calls to Newington and Gillingham. There were no barrage balloons over Sittingbourne although there were searchlight and anti-aircraft units stationed in the area, including next to Hales House in Tunstall, at Chetney Marshes, Iwade - remembered as particularly noisy, and there was a volunteer Observer Corps unit at Hearts Delight, Borden. (65)

Other women, as they had in the First World War, took strangers into their homes. At the start of the war there were the children who were evacuated to Sittingbourne from the Medway towns, but there were others throughout the war, including in the case of one home, at different times, four airmen, four soldiers and two girl evacuees. Others joined the ranks of the Land Army. In spite of initial fun being poked at them, including the poem:

'Lipstick in the stackyard,
Mirrors in the barn,
Puffs among the poultry,
Stockings that won't darn.
High-falutin breeches,
Skirts of patent weave,
And kindred affectations,
Too foolish to believe.'

By the spring of 1941 they had proved their use and there was a recruiting drive to get more. It was though at times a dangerous occupation, one Land Girl that autumn had to have her leg amputated after it became caught in a threshing machine. (66)

Girls employed in the local factories played each other in football matches, in August the Excelsior Fabric Fairies, from the collar factory, played Dean's Dainty Damsels, and they also put on entertainments for the troops stationed in the area. During the summer of 1941 the council provided more public shelters, including tunnels under the town with entrances in Bell Road and near the station. They also issued more Anderson shelters. These consisted of corrugated sheets which were assembled to give protection over a dug out in the garden. In rural areas Morrison shelters were issued which were sturdy metal tables, about 6 feet by 3 feet. Some of those living in the town were fortunate enough to have cellars to use, as did some businesses, such as Dean's Jam Factory. (67)

Another year of the war wore on. The Co-op put on its annual treat and entertainment for children, flower shows and harvest festivals came and went, and fund raising dominated the social life of the town. New ration books were issued in the summer and men born between 1881 and 1923 had to register for Civil Defence duties. As the third winter of the war began a novel paper salvage scheme was tried out in the town, people visiting the local cinemas had to take waste paper as well as the entrance fee. There was a record collection of over £500 for the Poppy Day appeal and at the beginning of December a Flag Day was held in response to an appeal for aid from Russia. (68)

1942

The campaign to save waste paper continued in the new year with a competition and prizes for the areas collecting the most paper, Sittingbourne collected 70 tons during the campaign, beating Maidstone's 67 tons. Inter-town rivalry was an important aspect of fund-raising. In March there was an appeal for more money to be deposited in the war savings scheme to pay for a new mine sweeper, £120,400 had already been raised by individuals and businesses in Sittingbourne, but another £60,000 was needed to beat Ashford. In the end Sittingbourne beat Ashford's total by over £11,000. (69)

There was a Food Production Week in February with public meetings, cookery demonstrations, a Dig for Victory display and an appearance at the Paper Mills Club House of the radio personality Freddie Grisewood, and the council promised to provide more allotments. In spite of efforts such as these food was in short supply, even with the rationing system many things were either not available or had to be queued for. The Local Food Control Committee received many complaints of people being overcharged for food. Petrol was also in short supply and in February attempts were made to cut consumption by limiting deliveries by tradesmen to only homes more than a mile from the High Street and cutting down the number of coal deliveries. In May there was an appeal to save coal by using less water, as coal was used to power the pumping process. The war was being fought not only on the battlefield, it was a war of production and raw materials. It was an offence to throw away any rag, rope or string, they could be used to make charts and maps. Kitchen waste could be used to feed pigs and poultry and old metal could be used for bombs, rifle barrels and mines. The public were urged to collect salvage as it released ships used to import raw materials for other duties. (70)

During the summer the Air Training Corps opened new headquarters over Burtons in the High Street with a March Past and a parade. The Home Guard, the Police and the Civil Defence took part in a joint invasion exercise in May and in June there was an exercise in Air-Raid Precautions during which tear gas was released and residents were warned to carry gas masks at all times. The town was fortunate in not suffering damage from bombing raids that year, other Kent towns were not so lucky. In June the Sittingbourne Fire Service was called to Canterbury when it suffered a massive attack. Many were made homeless and the Sittingbourne Co-op sent contributions of food for them, including two thousand loaves of bread. (71)

The Co-op also took part in fund-raising activities, their 'Society Follies' raised over £200 for charity and their Youth Group organised a Fun and Games Day at the Football Ground on August Bank Holiday. Later in August the Bull Ground was the venue for a Great Hospital Fete which raised over £800 for the Memorial Hospital. Fund raising continued throughout the year, in December events during Prisoner of War Week raised over £2,000, more than any other Kent town. Also in December the Army Concert Party the 'Dumbells' visited the town and the local paper had a photograph of Sgt G Gendle, 'Gloria', the leading lady. (72)

During the year there were less happy photos in the paper, those of local men held as Prisoners of War in different Stalags in Germany. News was also received of others who were missing in action or who had been killed, it is not surprising perhaps that one apparently able bodied local man received a 'white feather', the sign of cowardice, even though he had only the thumb and part of one finger left on one hand following an industrial accident and had been turned down for all forms of national service. (73)

In July 1942 the town's first 'British Restaurant' opened in the Milton Congregational Church schoolroom. The first meal to be served consisted of baked minced meat roll, boiled potatoes, cabbage and haricot beans followed by boiled fruit pudding and custard and a cup of tea, all for 11d. The winter of 1942/3 was though to be one of austerity. Local people were advised to use only one living room, to protect it from draughts, put a curtain over the door, lag pipes, eat in the kitchen to delay lighting a fire in the living room and to use fire bricks to reduce the use of coal without the loss of heat. (74)

1943

The drive for self-sufficiency continued in the new year. A hundred acres of corn was planted on marshland south of the Swale, land which had formerly only been grass. Parties were given for the children of servicemen, although some were still evacuated from the area, one women was charged with arrears in the payment due for her two evacuated children. Women's groups continued to send parcels to service men, in January it was announced that the total sent by the Kemsley Guild alone was over a thousand. News was received from abroad, both of the major events of the war and also of individuals playing their part, such as the son of a Sittingbourne couple, Staff-Sergeant John Irons who was a tail-gunner on the 'Suzy-Q', one of America's famous flying fortresses. (75)

In May there was a Book Drive, books were needed for servicemen, for libraries which had been blitzed and for salvage. The initial target of 40,000 was achieved by school children alone, in the end the town collected over 100,000, more than any other Kent town. Sittingbourne also beat its target for the Wings for Victory Appeal raising over £213,000 through gifts and investments. That summer an Agricultural Red Cross Sale raised over £2,500, the greatest amount ever raised in the town in a single day. As well as fund raising events some social events were held to boost morale, more than 10,000, over half the population, turned out for the parade, children's tea and races held on August Bank Holiday Monday that year. (76)

Overall it was a quiet year. The provision of meals for school children from a central kitchen in the grounds of the partially constructed West Central School proved to be a success, the meals were dispatched in bulk and the charge for children under 11 was 5d a day, and 6d for older children. A day nursery opened at Johnson House and the Indoor Bowling Green at the Swimming pool re-opened for the winter, it had been closed as the pool had been kept full of water in case of need during emergencies if the mains were destroyed. That autumn a trophy and certificates were presented for the best-kept allotments and gardens and there was concern that part of Keycol Sanatorium might close because of a shortage of nursing staff. (77)

1944

The opening weeks of 1944 were not to be quiet. On the night of Saturday 29th January came the air-raid that had been long feared, when hundreds of incendiary bombs fell on Sittingbourne. It was not the first town to be bombed, before it started Canterbury had been attacked and Sittingbourne Fire Station had received calls for engines to go and assist there. They were on their way there when the fires started to rage in Sittingbourne, appeals went out immediately to other towns further west to come to Sittingbourne to help. Meanwhile off-duty Service men did magnificent work and prevented many serious fires. One lady at the time said "An incendiary came into our house, but almost before we knew what had happened soldiers rushed in and put it out." Other soldiers helped nuns to put out fires that started at the Convent school and they also put out a fire that started in the ladies cloakroom of a hall where a dance was in progress. One incendiary had fallen between two saxophone players in the band, striking the drummer's cymbal, before going through the stage! (78)

Many homes were hit. In one house in William Street a mattress caught fire, but a quick-thinking resident threw it out of the window, at another house the outside toilet received a direct hit, fortunately no one was occupying it at the time. At the home of Mrs Hunt, when a bomb came through the roof and started burning in a room she helped to tackle it with a bucket of water, even though she was hampered by having her baby under one arm. Her husband had gone across the road to put a fire out and when he came back he found his own house alight. They were able to put out the fire, but Mr Armond was not so lucky, while he dealt with one bomb in an upstairs room another fell through the bathroom and cut off the water supply and the house was badly damaged. Several bombs fell into the Roman Catholic Church, but were promptly dealt with by the priest there. Another fell on the Congregational Church but it burnt itself out without setting fire to the building. The Methodist Church was not so fortunate. Children attending a meeting of the Youth Club in the adjoining schoolroom were the first to notice the fires there. Attempts were made to deal with the fires but there was a serious delay between the time fire engines from other towns arrived and action to put out the fire was taken. In a Report by the Deputy Regional Commissioner it was stated that the 13 minutes delay was 'due to the trouble experienced with the hydrant cover, a saving of time might well have been effected if another line of hose had been connected'. The result was that the Methodist Church was gutted. In addition eight shops and a number of houses were damaged. (79)

On the following Wednesday, February 2nd, General Sir Bernard Montgomery, Commander of the British invasion forces, visited Sittingbourne, although his visit had nothing to do with the air-raid. He came to review thousands of troops gathered at the Cricket Ground in Tunstall Road, who had been stationed in the town and the surrounding countryside, prior to taking part in what was being called 'the Second Front'. After walking informally through the ranks 'Monty' mounted a 'Jeep' and asked the men to close in round him. He spoke to the men and said 'I want you men to know that I never put an army into battle until I am quite certain it is going to be a good show. Never. We will not have any question of failure. If there is any question we will not start. I never move into battle until I am sure we can win and win quite easily. That is what we'll do, you and I.' A mighty cheer went up when he had finished, from not only the soldiers but the many townsfolk who had gone to see him. (80)

Air-raids continued that winter and as well as damage to property there were some fatalities, including Mr Thomas who was buried in February and Mr Pluck who died as the result of a raid in early March. Other deaths occurred as the result of the war, although not from German bombing. In February an eight year old boy was killed and his brother and two other boys were injured in an explosion in a chalk quarry used by the Army when training with explosive weapons. (81)

1944 was also the year of the V-1 flying bomb, the doodlebug. One man remembers as a child sitting on the garden wall of his home at Snipshill and looking for them. On one occasion he and his brother watched as a bomb was attacked by two Spitfires. After the engine stopped one of the Spitfires flew underneath the bomb and tipped its wing so that it turned away from the houses to which it was headed and exploded harmlessly in a nearby orchard. (82)

During the summer though came the news of the liberation of Paris and it was celebrated by the bells being rung at Milton church. The town enjoyed a Week of Music with Fred Tolhurst and the Orpheus Choir performing The Messiah, a Talent Contest and band and operatic concerts. There was also a Victory Garden Show. By the end of the year there were signs that the end of the War was in sight. Regulations requiring the total black-out of buildings that had been in force since the end of August 1939 were relaxed, allowing 'dimming' instead. There were also photos in the paper of different companies of the local Home Guard before they stood down. (83)

1945

In February the British Restaurant closed, however many restrictions still remained and in March a man was sent to prison with hard labour for transferring clothing coupons. In April the last Merchant Navy Week was held with the Crowning of the Merchant Navy Queen who attended different functions. Funds were still being raised although only £1,000, well short of the target of £1,500. By early May there were homecoming reunions with released

Prisoners of War and when Victory in Europe was announced the streets were decorated, the lights in the High Street were switched on for the first time in nearly six years, and joyous peals of bells were rung from local churches. A Thanksgiving Day Service at the Recreation Ground was attended by five thousand. (84)

Street Parties were held, and the description of one makes a fitting end to this chapter on the town at war. William Street is in the heart of the town and there would have been few houses which had not suffered damage during bombing raids. The proceedings were opened by tea in the street for the children, followed by races and games with community singing and a Punch and Judy Show. Then it was the adult's turn, more than seventy ate tea together and those residents who were unable to leave their homes had teas taken round to their houses on trays. Later the Buffs Cadets' Accordions provided dance music and the evening finished with the singing of 'Auld Lang Syne' and the National Anthem'. (85)

Chapter Ten

The Changing Face of Sittingbourne High Street and Local People

SITTINGBOURNE HIGH STREET

Introduction

In the middle of the 19th century Sittingbourne High Street was very different than it is at the end of the 20th century. All of the properties, with the exception of the inns, were private dwelling houses in some of which or from which businesses were carried on. There were no 'national' or 'chain' stores. The Co-op, which started in 1874 was located in East Street, and it was not until well into the 20th century that it opened shops in the High Street. (1)

Before the 19th century the High Street would not have been as long as it is now. All of the pre-19th century buildings, including all the main inns of the town are in the area of the hill running from Central Avenue to the Crown Quay Lane/Bell Road junction at the start of East Street. Notably most of the more impressive buildings, those of the wealthier citizens, were on the south side of the hill. Clearly, as the buildings were homes, with any business being conducted in rooms facing the road, it would have been far more pleasant to have the private rooms at the back facing south across what would have been open fields, rather than facing north and overlooking the creek, as would have been the case had they been built on the north side of the road. (2)

There is one thing though that the High Street in the late 20th century has in common with Victorian times, that is that one can actually stand back and look at the buildings. The traffic flow along the High Street has, with the new 'modernised' High Street, been much reduced and must be similar in many ways to the time of horse drawn carriages, although the speed may be even less than in the days when a servant had to hold back traffic and pedestrians who were at risk when Mr Bensted drove his horse and trap at high speed out from the driveway of The Lawns. Shopping in Sittingbourne High Street may also be far less dangerous now than it was in 1871 when Edward Hurst a Sittingbourne greengrocer was stopped by a policeman for furious driving when he nearly knocked over two women when he was 'drunk and incapable'. (3)

Certainly one has not been able to stand back and look at the buildings along the High Street for much of this century. Even in the 1930s there were problems with the amount of traffic along what was the main road from

London to the Kent coast and the Channel ports. It was always a particular problem on Bank Holidays. In August 1936 a traffic census revealed that up to 960 cars an hour were going along the High Street. By 1950 this had increased to 1,500 and by 1954 over 5,000 cars an hour were going through the town. The M2 by-pass was meant to solve the problem, but in 1963 when the decision was taken to open the stretch up to the A249 it caused major problems with eleven mile long queues waiting to get onto the motorway on the Whitsun Bank Holiday. It was not until 1973 that some relief was provided with the opening of the extended St Michael's Road route to the north. Eventually in 1980 the High Street was closed to traffic on Saturdays, and in spite of the fears of traders this proved to be successful. (4)

The following three sections consist of a 'walk' along the High Street looking at some of the shops and businesses that have been found there during the period from the mid-19th century to the end of the 20th century. It is not in any way a study of the architecture or earlier history of particular buildings as this is available elsewhere.

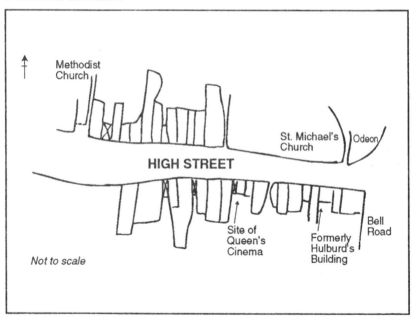

Plan of the East End of the High Street

The East End:
The 'walk' begins at the junction with East Street where, prominent on the north-west corner of the crossroads, there is the Odeon building. Before it was opened as a cinema in 1937 several smaller building had occupied the site, including a butchers shop owned by Bouldings in the 19th century and then Applebys in the 1920s. On the opposite corner stood a branch of Lloyds Bank

196

in the 1960s and before that there was a grocers shop there. This building, and the two properties to the west is now Luckhurst's furniture store. Interestingly this has been the location for selling furniture for more than a century, with Nash's in the 1960s, Sam's, the plate-glass window of which was smashed during a bombing raid in 1940, in the 1920s and Reynold's in the 1890s. Next to this was, until recent years, the town's most important department store, Hulburds. This family firm was established in the 18th century and the building underwent modernisation in the 1960s. One interesting feature of the store was the system by which customers paid for goods. Money was placed by the assistant in a cylinder which when put into a system of pipes was forced through to the cashier in a different part of the building, the change returning in the same way. (5)

Before the development of the shopping mall the next building on the south side of the High Street was occupied from the 19th century by the Tidy family. Both L and H Tidy were hairdressers and before them E Tidy was a cooper. In the 1850s W J Parrett founded the local Sittingbourne paper, the East Kent Gazette, and the business occupied several premises in this area including number 17 until moving to its current location at number 21. It was succeeded at number 17 in the 1960s by Peters' furniture store which had since the 1880s been at number 15, a building which had the family name on its gable end. Across the alley next to the East Kent Gazette Office is a building, now Cookmate, which was occupied for over a hundred years by Filmers, corn merchants and gardening stores. Next to them during the early part of this century was a shop run by Carrolls which in the 1960s sold toys and in the 1920s sold sheet music and musical instruments, it was there that a blind piano tuner worked during the years between the wars, going out to tune pianos in the days when many families, even the less well-off, had a piano. (6)

The opening between this shop and Blundells used to lead to the Sittingbourne Brewery dating from the 18th century and, from 1912, the Queen's Cinema which later became a night club. Originally the opening would have led to the stables behind the ancient White Hart Inn which is now used by Blundells Toy Shop. The 18th century brick facades of the shops in this area of the High Street mask what are older properties, and evidence has been found in them dating from Tudor and Elizabethan times. Blundells occupies a number of these premises including part of the former George Hotel, converted by the Lushington family into a family mansion in the 18th century, where they entertained Georges I and II. Before Blundells the premises were occupied in the 1920s by the firm of Crittendens, who sold clothes, and before them, in the 1890s, there were several shops, including a flower and fruit store and a hatter as well as the post office. Also at that time cremers, the bakers, had a shop there until they moved further up the High Street. The George Inn has been on its present site throughout the period from the mid 19th century, to the east of it there was a chemist's shop and to the west, in the 18th century house, occupied now by the Kent Messenger, there was a dentist's, J Roberts in the 1920s and Yerbury in the 1960s. One resident remembers going to have a tooth extracted by Mr Yerbury during the early 1960s and being asked if she was looking forward to seeing the elephants. This seemed a strange question, even when he was about to administer gas, however he was referring to the fact that later that day the circus procession was going to be passing along the High Street! (7)

The East End of Sittingbourne High Street

Before going any further up the hill it is time to look at the north side of the road. To the west of the churchyard is the modern Iceland building, the site of which was occupied from the mid 19th century through to the first part of the 20th century by the firm of Whibley, a draper and clothier. From here to the Methodist Church there are a number of small 17th and 18th century buildings. In the first of these, number 14, there was from the 1860s to the first part of this century a clothes shop run by the Willis family. A member of this family, H Willis, had by the 1890s taken over the bootmaker's shop at number 18. By the 1920s that shop was Freeman, Hardy and Willis, and the business remained there until moving to the Forum Shopping Centre after it opened in 1974. Also of interest in this group of shops is number 28 which was for many years Owens wine shop, now it is one of the many charity shops which are to be found in every town, the first one in Sittingbourne opening in 1966. (8)

The Central Area:
Returning to the south side of the road, number 47, Poppins Restaurant, was in the 1960s a centre for the local youth when it was opened as the towns only

Expresso Bar, Pelosis, before that it had been Geering's sweet shop. One of the most imposing buildings in the High Street comes next. Earlier this century it was occupied by the architect W Grant but then it was taken over by the firm of Harris and Harris, solicitors, following a move from the house which had stood on the site where Burtons is now. Numbers 59 and 61, the premises occupied by D & A Toys, were for most of this century, and in the 19th century, occupied by H Tett, ironmongers. The Bull, dating from the 14th century, was one of the most important inns in the town especially as a centre for trade. It is now much smaller than it was, as it was altered in 1972 with the shops on the west side of Roman Square being built where the original building once stood. Roman Square follows the route once taken by cattle between the station and the cattle market which was held on the Bull meadows to the south east of the Bull. To the west of the Bull is a building, number 71, which in the 18th century had been an inn and was later a workhouse. (9)

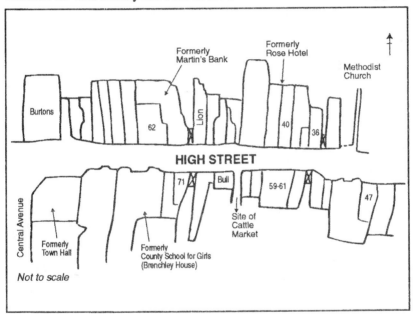

Plan of the Central Area of the High Street

Highs the opticians and Sharrocks Insurance Brokers occupy what was during the first half of this century the Sittingbourne County School for Girls. Following the opening of the new school buildings at Highsted Road in the 1950s it was for a time the Brenchley House School, earlier it had been the home of H Sutton a surgeon and an auctioneers. Barclays Bank is now larger than it once was, in the 1920s and 1960s it shared the site with a wine merchants. There had been wine merchants there from the middle of the 19th century and in the 1890s there was also an estate agent there. The modern National Westminster Bank building is on the site of what was throughout most of this century the Sittingbourne Town Hall which was built in the 1850s as a Corn Exchange.

Crossing to the north side of the road again and looking at the buildings to the west of the Methodist Church, prior to the 20th century number 36 was The Three Post Boys Inn. Next to it was a jewellers which remained there until the 1920s, Barrows and Batemans having been there since at least the 1960s. Number 40, the building currently occupied by The Halifax Building Society was originally a bank, during the 1960s and 1970s it was the Westminster Bank and in the 19th century it was a branch of the London and County Bank. One of the most important buildings in the late 18th century comes next, the Rose, its imposing facade still clear above the shop fronts below. Since the Second World War the main shop to occupy the site has been Woolworth's, earlier in the century and in the 19th century there was a grocers, Gorleys, a chemist and a drapers on the site. The Rose Inn itself, until recent years when it was converted into a Wimpey Bar, having been at number 50, to the west of its former premises.

The Central Area of Sittingbourne High Street

Close to it lies another of the town's most famous inns, The Lion, famed for its royal connections. To the west of it, where the Woolwich Building Society is now, was for many years Martins Bank which in the mid 19th century issued 'Sittingbourne' bank notes. The next property, number 62, has been since the 1890s a shoeshop, in turn Bartletts, Walters, Norvic and now Olivers.

Finally in this area of the High Street comes Burtons, built in 1937 on the site of the home of the Harris family who were solicitors. Much of the legal life of the town was conducted on their premises, even in the 1860s when they were Coal Merchants the County Court Office was situated there. The Burton building originally had ornamentation in the window openings, with along the top window panes The Chain of Merit, the links of which had the names of all the towns where there were Burtons stores. The top part of the building housed at various times a night club, a snooker hall and the town's library. (10)

The West End:
To the west of Burtons there were for much of the 20th century a number of grocers shops, amongst them David Greigs, the Maypole Dairy and Liptons. One resident recalled these shops during the early part of the century. All had Saturday boys whose job it was to take out the orders to people's homes on their bicycles. When not out on delivery they would cut up large sheets of blue paper ready for the assistant to use for wrapping dry goods. When it was needed the assistant rolled the paper into a cone shape and the end was twisted. The required product, such as tea or rice or sugar, was scooped from the tin in which it was stored into the paper cone and then the top was folded over. The storage tins were cylindrical in shape and were decorated with patterns and had the name of the product painted on them. Customers were provided with chairs to sit on, there was one inside the door to use when waiting and others at the counter when being served. Often a customer had a favourite assistant and might choose to wait to be served by him, he would know all about the customer's family and would make enquiries about the children and other relations. When buying things such as bacon the assistant would often bring several pieces for the customer to choose which one she wanted and it would then be sliced by hand to the required thickness. Jam was kept in large tubs and customers took their own two pound stone jars with them to have them filled. Butter was in huge blocks from which the required amount was cut and pressed into shape. After the First World War there were changes, no longer were chairs provided and at 'chain' stores such as Liptons and David Greigs one no longer paid the assistant, there was a cashier who sat at a special desk, the assistant called out the amount to them and the customer then went there to pay. (11)

Detouring briefly from the High Street, during the early part of the century there were often specialist meat shops, one of the most popular being the pork butchers in West Street. Queues for the Christmas rabbit could stretch down Dover Street with children holding their parent's place in the queue until they reached the shop window. Manuels, further down West Street, which was bombed with tragic results during the Second World War, was the main cooked meat shop. They sold things such as ham, corned beef, cooked pork, brawn and pease pudding and faggots, all 'home' cooked. Fish was brought round the streets on barrows. In the early 1920's one poor fishmonger made the mistake of calling out his wares 'Fresh fish, alive, alive-O' one Remembrance Day when the two minutes silence was being observed, as it was throughout the town (in those days Remembrance Day was on November 11th not on the nearest Sunday), at the Collar Factory in Ufton Lane. The young girls, standing in silence and remembering the dead found the inopportune words amusing, the manager did not and left afterwards to have words with the fishmonger. The story got home to the parents and relatives of the factory girls and people stopped buying fish from that particular man. There were also fishmongers in the High Street, Macfisheries in the 1920s and Holbrooks in the 1960s, but the main one has always been at number 112, at the end of the 19th century it was Brightmans but by the 1920s Thomsetts were running it as they do in the late 20th century. (12)

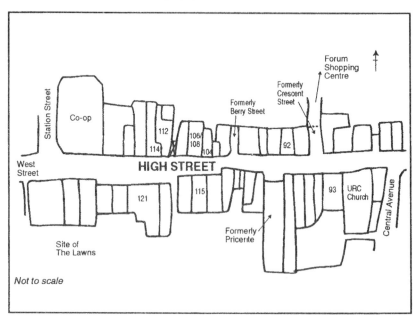

Plan of the West End of the High Street

Back now in the west end of the High Street, next to Thomsetts, at number 114, there was during the late 19th and early 20th century, Harms the bakers, the other main bakers was Cremers which was just to the east of Burtons. Bread was baked fresh on the premises, including products which are now mass produced such as 'Hovis' which was being baked and delivered by Cremers in 1900. Bakers did not only bake bread they also made sweets, the Harms family were confectioners as well as bakers, and they also baked cakes for people. In the days before gas or electric ovens cakes were often prepared at home and then taken to the bakers to be baked. One resident remembers that it was always her older brother's job to carry the cake mix in its tin to the bakers. When she felt that she was old enough she asked if she could go instead. When her brother objected their mother compromised and said that they could both take it. After leaving the house the two children argued and as a result the tin was dropped, the cake mix coming out onto the road. Unable to face their mother they scooped the mix back into the tin and took it to be baked. That weekend their mother couldn't understand why neither of the children felt like having any cake. It wasn't until the following week when a neighbour, who had seen the incident, asked how her cake had turned out and whether it had been gritty, that she discovered what had happened. (13)

Another firm which has been in the same area as Thomsetts and Harms, although not always the same building, for much of the 20th century is Boots the chemist. The large building at the north-western end of the High Street, on the corner of Station Street, was built for the Co-op in 1973. Before that there had been a Co-op Pharmacy and Grocers on the site, other specialist Co-op shops were found further down the High Street. In the mid 1960s, there was a shoe shop and hair dressers at number 55 and a TV and radio shop at number 36. Before the Co-op there had been a chemist, J French, on the corner site. The building just before it was in the 1920s Dan Eastons Stores and before that Crittenden's Clothes and Drapery Store, which later moved to numbers 33-37 where Blundells is now. Like Hulburds they had an interesting system for making payment. The money was placed by the assistant into a wooden container which was then connected to a wire, a handle was pulled and the wire pulled the container along, customers could watch their money as it travelled over their heads through the store. In the days when change might be a farthing, pins were given instead. (14)

The West End of Sittingbourne High Street

203

Turning finally to the south-west section of the High Street, the end building has been since the 1860s the Baptist Tabernacle. The driveway to the side led to The Lawns, the home of the Bensted family, local auctioneers, which was later used as the Fire Station. During the 1920s and 1960s the Cedars Club was at number 127 where QS Clothes and MacDonald's are now. Further east, at number 121 there stood, for the early part of the 20th century, the town's main Post Office which was a conversion of the home of a surgeon, F Grayling. In the early 1960s when the Post Office moved to Central Avenue the site was taken over by Victor Values, one of the town's first supermarkets. Three opened within months of each other in 1962, the first being Pricerite, where Mackays is now. The new form of shopping had an immediate effect on older style grocers including the Co-op, which suffered from reduced income. By the following year though the supermarkets themselves were in trouble and what was reported as the 'High Street Grocery War' hotted up when Pricerite was the first to introduce Green Shield Trading Stamps. Later the grocers fought back with David Greigs opening a new superstore in 1968. However the development of out of town shopping, SavaCentre off the M2 opened in the late 1970s and nearer to home Dales opened in the early 1990s, again affected the shops in the High Street, the only surviving town centre supermarkets are in the Forum and behind the south east end of the High Street. (15)

Between Victor Values and Pricerites in the 1960s were a number of small shops including, at number 115, a stationer, Ash. They also ran a private library and one resident remembers going into the room at the back of the shop stacked high with books which one paid a penny a week to borrow. The site of Pricerites had in part been occupied in the 1920s by J Easton, a manufacturer of false teeth and in the 1890s by a Servants Employment Agency. At that time there was also Gardiniers Iron Foundry in that area of the High Street and on the site of which Central Avenue now is there was a carriers and a butchers shop. To the east of the church which was built in the 1860s and has been known variously as The Free Church, The Congregational Church and most recently as The United Reform Church, there was in the 1890s, the home of a surgeon. In the 1920s there was a dentist there and for the second half of the 20th century it has been a building society. The building to the west of the church, number 93, is the last property to be 'visited' in this tour of the High Street and it typifies in many ways the experience of the High Street as a whole.

93 High Street:
The earliest records for the site refer to it as being part of a blacksmith's forge, an important trade in the days when Sittingbourne was a major national and international centre for the coaching trade. In the early 19th century the property was sold to a local builder called Sills Gibbons and he built a fashionable house in Regency style. It had five bedrooms, a box room and a dressing room upstairs and two large reception rooms and a kitchen downstairs. There was also a cellar with separate compartments for coal,

wines and meat. The first occupier of the house was a retired army surgeon, he was followed in turn by two widows and then a threshing-machine proprietor. In 1860 the house was bought by George Gouge, he was instrumental in the building of the church next to the house and his son ran a school in Crescent Street. In 1902 the house was again sold, this time to Hedley Peters Senior, a member of the local family of auctioneers and furniture sellers. He was Captain of the Sittingbourne Fire Brigade and the move from a house in Park Road meant that he was nearer to the Fire Station which at that time was in Crescent Street, where the Forum is now. (16)

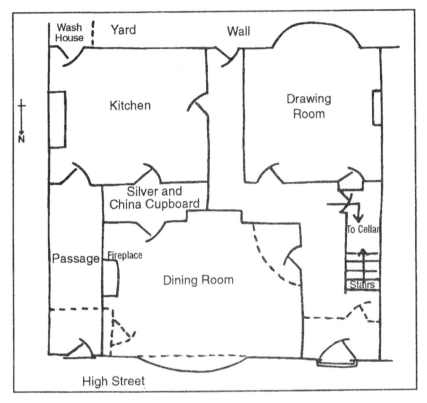

Plan of the Ground Floor of 93 High Street

For several years it remained a private house but when he left the family firm and set up in business as an 'Auctioneer, Valuer, House and Estate Agent and Agent to the Principal Steamship Companies' on his own he did so using his High Street home. Changes were made to the building with the main room and a corridor at the front being converted into two offices. There were separate entrances, as there still are, one for the business and the other to the family rooms at the rear and upstairs. When Hedley Peters Senior retired in 1937 his son, Hedley Peters Junior, and his family moved in to the property. During the

Second World War the cellars of the house were converted into an air-raid shelter with an escape tunnel leading up to the garden lawn. In 1943 the family finally moved out and the sunny lounge at the rear of the building became Mr Peters' private office. In the 1960s the family firm joined with a larger firm from Canterbury which developed into 'Ashendens', and later it became part of the Nationwide chain of estate agents. In 1969 the original bow window at the front was replaced and over the years the divisions put in when the house was first used as offices were removed and the main office area was enlarged. (17)

Changes such as these, in the change of use from private homes, to homes with offices or shops at the front and then to business use only, together with the architectural changes to the buildings both on the outside and inside and the move from independent family firms to larger national chains can be seen all along the High Street. Whilst many of the shops are modern and open-plan one only has to step back from the doorways and look up to see what are often the same buildings one would have seen over a century ago.

LOCAL PEOPLE

Just as this book as a whole has sought to provide a general rather than a detailed picture of the history of Sittingbourne, so this section does not claim to include all of those who have shaped the history of the town over the past two centuries. Certainly, as it is based largely on obituaries from the East Kent Gazette, those who are still alive get little mention. It does though include most of the more well-known names from the town's history as well as some less well-known ones and overall provides a picture of the sort of people who have been involved in the economic life of the town. As all have played their part none have pride of place, the order being strictly alphabetical.

ANDREWS George:
George Andrews was the second son of John Andrews and he went to Murston Church School before starting to work part-time in the brickfields as a barrow boy in 1873 when he was just ten years old. He then went to work in the office of Smeed Dean and he rose to the rank of Managing Director, taking over from G H Dean. He retired in 1932 having served the firm for 59 years, during this time he became involved in sailing barges, eventually owning a fleet of them and writing a column for the East Kent Gazette under the name 'Bargee'. He had a national role in business being elected President of the British Clayworkers Institute in 1903 and at one time he was Chairman of the Stock Brickmakers Association. Locally he held public office, including being Chairman of Murston Parish Council for all of its thirty-five years of existence, retiring only when it merged with the Sittingbourne and Milton Urban District Council. He then wrote a book about Murston and brickmaking, 'Memories of Murston'. He was a Justice of the Peace and

represented Sittingbourne and Milton on Kent County Council. He was for much of his life a staunch member of Sittingbourne Congregational Church and held a Young Men's Bible Class there for forty-five years. He died at his home in Tunstall in January 1934. (18)

ANDREWS John:
John Andrews, the father of George, spent his childhood on a farm near Dover. He soon became interested in the making of bricks and worked at a brickfield at Buckland becoming the first man in Dover to mould a million bricks in a season. He then moved to Sittingbourne and worked as a 'brickie' until being chosen by Mr George Smeed to be a Brickfield Foreman at Murston. Eventually, when the firm of Smeed, Dean and Co Ltd was formed in 1875 he was given a place on the Board of Directors. He was a man of very strict habits, including time keeping and it was known for people to correct their clocks in line with the time that he passed on the way to or from work! In his personal life he was an ardent member of the Methodist Church, having been converted when a young man. He was a strict teetotaller and did much to improve the moral as well as the social standards of the brickfield workers. In spite of opposition he started the first prayer meetings in Murston, supplementing them by Mission Services and finally a Christian Institute which used a building provided by Smeed Dean. He became the Constable of Murston Parish and in effect its Christian Minister, visiting the sick and dying and caring for widows and orphans. He died at his home in Park Road in December 1911. (19)

BENSTED F Austen:
Mr Bensted was born at Doddington and after attending Faversham Grammar School he studied at Blackheath. He then joined his uncle's firm studying agriculture and stock-raising. He farmed at Doddington and later at Tonge, Murston and Borden. As a young man he was a trooper in the Royal East Kent Mounted Rifles, winning the cup for being the best mounted man in the Regiment in 1885. He became well-known as a judge of stock at County and National Shows, including those of the Smithfield Club and the Royal Agricultural Society. In 1892 he raised the status of the Sittingbourne Market, which at that time was held periodically in the paddock adjoining the Bull Hotel, by introducing regular sales by auction. In 1894 he and his wife moved into The Lawn in Sittingbourne High Street. At that time he was already a manager of the Holy Trinity Day Schools and he later became more closely involved with the work of the church being a Church Warden from 1909 to 1938. He was also a Trustee of the Barrow Trust, a Governor of Borden Grammar School, a Member of the Management Committee of the Kent Friendly Society, and a Trustee for both the Spicers Homes and Holy Trinity Hall. He died in July 1941 at the age of 77. (20)

BISHOP Edward:
Edward Bishop was born at Selling and came to Sittingbourne when he was a child. His first job was as a bricklayer for George Chrisfield of Milton. He then

went to work in London for nine years during which time he worked as a foreman bricklayer for Mr Edward Lloyd. He continued to work for Mr Lloyd when he returned to Sittingbourne, building the manager's house for the paper mill as well as working for other local builders. In 1879 he started his own building firm and continued to do work for Lloyd including all of the reconstruction of the mill following the first big fire. He was also responsible for the building of the Roman Catholic Church as well as over a hundred houses in Park Road, together with many smaller repairs and improvements to houses throughout the town and surrounding area. After Edward Bishop retired his sons continued the business and the firm was responsible for the building of Kemsley mill and village as well as the Club house in Remembrance Avenue and many council houses. He died in December 1927, aged 90, at the house he had built in Albany Road. (21)

BOUCHER Reginald:
Reginald, better known as Rex, Boucher was born at Eastling. When he was seventeen he took over the running of the family farm on the death of his father. Throughout his life he thought of himself as a farmer, but it was for his business enterprises that he will be best remembered. The first of these was the purchase, in the late 1920s, of Hulburds grocery and drapery shop. Living over the business he and his wife turned it into a successful department store. In the 1970s he leased land at the back of the shop to Sainsbury's and he was instrumental in the development of the Bell Road shopping and office complex. He had the historic building, Trotts Hall, which had been on the site, removed and rebuilt in the grounds of his Milstead Manor Farm. During the Second World War he took over the running of Lowe's Dog Biscuit factory and as a result of activities at the factory during that time he started Export Packing Service, packing equipment for the Government and other businesses. In the 1950s he started a Research and Development Unit into the packing of specialised equipment, his work in this field being recognised by the award of an M.B.E. Before he handed over the business to his son he had also started two more firms, Wellwinch Engineering and Driclad. He died, aged seventy eight, at Trotts Hall in August 1885. (22)

BOWES George William:
George Bowes was born in Sittingbourne and as a young man worked as a painter at the firm of Smeed Dean. He then started his own business as a painter and house decorator. He was a good cornet player and for many years was bandmaster of the Sittingbourne Town Band. His interest in theatrical work led him to start booking travelling theatrical companies to perform at the Town Hall. He was already in a good position to do this as he had developed an advertising company that operated throughout the county. He expanded his business, booking theatrical tours all over Kent and further afield, eventually travelling with productions including a revival play entitled 'The Sign of the Cross'. He also ran his own pantomime company having two productions touring the country in 1912 and he was well known in Kent as an organiser of sporting events, the athletic sports he promoted and ran at Sittingbourne being

one of the most successful in the county. The first Bank Holiday Sports that he organised was at Gore Court Park in 1888. For many years the Sittingbourne Sports took place there and by increasing the value of the prize money Bowes was able to get some of the front rank men of the cycle and running track to compete there. After many successful years of operation he purchased the house and grounds at Glovers in Bell Road where he built a track and stand. He died in May 1913, at the age of 54, whilst on tour in South Wales with a production of Rag Time Girl. (23)

CREMER William John:
William Cremer was born in Sittingbourne, his father being a brickworker at Huggins brickfields and his grandfather carrying the mail from Sittingbourne to Sheerness. His only education was at the Church of England Sunday School and by the age of eleven he was working as a 'pug-boy' at the brickfields. At fourteen he was brick moulder but he left the brickfields to work in a grocer's shop in Faversham. He then worked in Sittingbourne for the baker and grocer George Clay as well as at Bapchild. By the age of twenty he started a business for himself, his uncle having built a shop and oven in Charlotte Street. His first day was not very successful, he sold less than half of what he baked, but he did not give up. He added the making of buns and the brewing of ginger beer to his bread-making and went round the brickfields selling directly to the workers there. It was not long before 'Cremer's Bread' had a good reputation and the business started to grow. Within ten years he was able to purchase Mr Bates' bakery business in Sittingbourne High Street and soon three horses and vans were needed to cope with the trade. The expansion of the business led to the building of a large store and four steam ovens in Crescent Street, a mineral water business was purchased from Mr Cocking and a grocery was opened in West Street. Whole-meal bread, Vienna rolls, tinned cottage bread and various new cakes, including coconut cake, were all introduced to Sittingbourne by Mr Cremer. The catering business continued to grow, sometimes supplying the needs of four thousand people a day. As well as running the business he played a part in the public life of the town being an Urban Councillor for about twelve years as well as a Guardian of the Poor. He was staunch member of the Methodist Church and a total abstainer from both alcohol and tobacco. He died in August 1923 at his home in Park Road, aged eighty-one. (24)

DANE John (Senior & Junior):
John Dane Senior and John Dane Junior were both members of the Fire Brigade as well as being involved in the Ambulance Service and working at the Paper Mill. John Dane Senior joined the Brigade in 1912 and served for 26 years. He helped to fight many fires including one at the Queenborough Chemical Works when he had to stand on boards surrounded by a lake of acid. Every few minutes, because of the fumes, he had to go into the open air to have bandages tied around his face. At a fire at Prentis Wharf he was hoisted by crane to the summit of a large pulp stock and worked for three and a half hours before being relieved by the arrival of the Gillingham Brigade. As part of his ambulance work in 1937 he handled over two hundred cases in just

seven months and was responsible for saving the life of a fellow mill worker in 1927. John Dane Senior lived for much of his life at 24 William Street and it was there that John Dane Junior was born. At one time father and son lived next door to each other as when he was married John Junior lived at 22 William Street. He joined the Fire Brigade in 1924 and like his father became involved in ambulance work, as at that time the ambulance service was operated by the Fire Brigade. One of the biggest fires he attended was at Ridham Dock in 1925 which lasted for days. When attending a fire at Tunstall Rectory he was one of the first firemen to use breathing apparatus. Perhaps the most unusual fire he attended was one at the football ground, the fire engine was already in use at the time, taking him and his bride from the church to their wedding reception but when the call went out everyone piled onto the engine to go and deal with it! (25)

Col. Donald Dean VC at Sittingbourne Recreation Ground
War Memorial (1982)

DEAN Donald John:
Donald Dean was the grandson on George Hambrook Dean and great grandson of George Smeed. In 1915 he enlisted in the Artist Rifles then in 1916 was commissioned in the Queen's Own Regiment West Kent. During the First World War he was wounded three times and in February 1919, at the age of twenty one, he received the Victoria Cross at Buckingham Palace. It was awarded for 'most conspicuous bravery, skilful command and devotion to duty during the period September 24th to 26th 1918' when withstanding, with his platoon, an enemy attack on an advance post near Lens. The post was attacked

five times, three heavily, and on each occasion the attack was driven back. Throughout the period Lieutenant Dean inspired his command with his own contempt of danger. On his return to Sittingbourne there was a public welcome and a congratulatory address was read out which was to be enclosed in a silver casket when one was available. Donald Dean said that he was overwhelmed by the reception and he was proud to belong to a Kent Regiment and to Sittingbourne.

In 1920 he left the army and was commissioned in the Territorial Army, the 4th Battalion The Buffs. When, in 1923, he married Margerie Wood at St Michael's Church he held the rank of Captain and was a Junior Director of Smeed Dean and Co. In 1930 he became a Major and then in 1936 he was given command of the 4th Buffs with the rank of Lieutenant Colonel. On the outbreak of the Second World War he was transferred to command a new Auxiliary Military Pioneer Corps composed mainly of ex-soldiers. His new unit consisted of three thousand officers, non-commissioned officers and men and they were soon sent overseas for work behind the lines. They were supposed to be non-combatant with only a quarter of them being armed with rifles for defensive purposes only. However events overtook them and when they became involved with the retreat of British forces to Boulogne in the summer of 1940 Colonel Dean, finding it necessary for his Corps to act as infantry, secured large quantities of rifles and ammunition. The Corps proved to be formidable opponents to the advancing Germans. They helped to defend the town during the British evacuation of troops, at one time dealing with a group of apparent refugees, including a pseudo French priest who proved to be Germans in disguise and started firing on Col. Dean and him men. On the last day in Boulogne the Corps fought its way down to the Harbour, only to find that the Guard's Brigade had been evacuated. A message was sent to the Naval authorities and the Corps were eventually taken off the last British troops to leave Boulogne.

In 1942 Colonel Dean again commanded a regiment of Pioneers, this time during the capture of a French naval base in Madagascar. He was then instrumental in getting seven hundred native soldiers who had been fighting against the British on the island to work for them. During the war he was made a Companion of the Order of Dannebrog by the King of Denmark for raising the 2nd Battalion, the Buffs, which in Denmark is the equivalent of a British Knighthood.

He was the last Director of Smeed Dean and after the war started his own brickmaking firm, Newington Brick. He was awarded the O.B.E. in 1961 and he also became a Deputy Lieutenant of Kent. Locally he was a J.P. and President of the Sittingbourne Branch of the British Legion, the Queens Own Buffs and the Sittingbourne Horticultural Society. He died in December 1985 and was buried at Tunstall Church where for many years he had been Churchwarden. In 1995, on the fiftieth anniversary of V.E. Day, a memorial to him, and other local VCs, was dedicated in Central Avenue. (26)

DEAN George Hambrook:

George Hambrook Dean was born at the home of his father John Dean, a tailor, in Sittingbourne High Street. He was apprenticed to the drapery business and travelled throughout the country as a representative of the firm of Copestake and Crampton of Glasgow. He returned to Sittingbourne and joined the commercial department of Mr Smeed's brickmaking firm. He was from the start interested in agriculture and soon bought his first farm, Finches, at Milsted. In association with Mr Smeed, whose daughter Mary Ann he had married, George Dean began to develop a fruit growing business becoming one of the foremost and most experienced agriculturalists in Kent. In 1875 he and George Smeed set up a company which included farming as well as brickmaking and at one time the firm owned over two thousand acres of farmland. In 1891 he built the Whitehall Preserve Works in Bell Road, at first preserving fruit in casks and them making jam. The business prospered and in 1921 on his historic visit to the town the then Duke of York visited the works and was entertained to lunch at Whitehall the home of George Dean.

As well as his farming activities George Dean was for many years Managing Director of the firm of Smeed Dean and remained Chairman of the company until his death. He was a Justice of the Peace and served on the Milton Board of Guardians and the Rural District Council. He was a founder member of the Sittingbourne Baptist Church where his son-in-law, Rev Doubleday, was Minister. He died in September 1924. (27)

DEAN Jane:

Jane Dean was the second wife of George Hambrook Dean. She was an ardent Baptist and played a prominent part in the religious and social life of the town. She was the Treasurer of the local Baptist Missionary Society, President of the Sittingbourne branch of the British Women's Temperance Association and Treasurer of the Kent Union of that organisation. Amongst her social activities was the organisation of 'The Three P's Soirees' to Police, Postmen and Porters and members of their families which were held for many years in the Town Hall. During the 1914-18 war she lent her house, Whitehall, as a war hospital and helped there as a volunteer, arranging teas and parties for the wounded soldiers and taking those unable to walk out for drives in her carriage. Together with her husband she gave a motor ambulance to the town. She died in March 1923 at the age of seventy eight. (28)

DEAN Marjorie:

Marjorie Emily Wood married Donald Dean in June 1923. She had grown up in Park Road and after her marriage lived at Waldene in Park Avenue. She founded and ran a private school and during the Second World War was actively involved in the running of a women's knitting circle as well as opening her house to evacuated school children. After the war she became President of the Buffs Ladies' Guild of Sittingbourne as well as being a Governor of Sittingbourne County School for Girls and playing a leading role in the Sittingbourne Horticultural Society. Mrs Dean died in 1988. (29)

DENCE Lewis Robert:
Lewis Dence was born at Greenstreet, the son of a master carpenter. He was apprenticed as a plumber, painter and house decorator but when he was nineteen obtained release from his indentures and set up his own business at New Road selling oils, paints and brushes. He joined the Teynham division of the St John Ambulance Brigade and then in 1903 he appealed to local young men to join him in the forming of a division at Sittingbourne. Fifteen responded and with the help of Dr Noble he trained them, becoming the new division's first officer in 1909 and superintendent two years later. The Sittingbourne Division competed in Ambulance competitions both in Kent and nationally, winning the premier national award for two years in succession and coming second twice during the four years from 1909-12. During the 1914-18 War Lewis Dence was granted the rank of Lieutenant in the Royal Army Medical Corps and was attached to the Glovers War Hospital in Sittingbourne. He was on duty at all state occasions between 1903 and 1949 and received the Order of St John of Jerusalem in recognition of his great service to St John Ambulance work. In all he served in the Brigade for sixty three years, retiring just a year before his death which occurred at his Station Street home in November 1950. (30)

DOUBLEDAY Sir Leslie:
Sir Leslie Doubleday was the grandson of G H Dean, his father being the Rev John Doubleday the Minister for many years at the Baptist Tabernacle in Sittingbourne. Sir Leslie took over the farming interests of his grandfather and became an acknowledged expert on agricultural matters, being knighted in 1957 for his services to agriculture and to Kent. He held many public offices serving as a county councillor from 1925 until 1974, and he served two terms as High Sheriff for Kent, in 1943 and 1951. He was chairman of the Sittingbourne Justices from 1946 until 1980, chairman of Bapchild Parish Council for 25 years and he became president of Kent County Cricket Club in 1971. He died in February 1975 at the age of eighty seven. (31)

GRANT William Leonard:
William Grant was born in Wiltshire in 1850 and came to Sittingbourne at the age of twenty five as an articled surveyor. He served for many years as the town's surveyor and although he resigned in 1914, when his successor, his son Leonard, went to fight in the war William resumed his job, finally retiring in 1923. William Grant was involved in the designing of many buildings in the town and surrounding area, including the Social Club in Remembrance Avenue, Keycol Hospital and Kemsley Mill and others which have since been demolished like the old Swimming Baths. He died in February 1942 at his home in the High Street, aged ninety one. (32)

LLOYD Edward:
Edward Lloyd was born near Croydon and after leaving school attended the London Mechanics' Institute where he learnt shorthand. At the age of fifteen he started on his publishing career, one of his first enterprises being Lloyd's

Weekly Miscellany a periodical depending mainly on fiction. At that time stamp duty had to be paid on news publications that came out at intervals of less than thirty days. In 1842 he published Lloyd's Weekly Newspaper which dealt mainly with books, theatricals and gossip so as to avoid the stamp duty and keep the price down. When the Stamp Duty was finally removed he reduced the price of the paper to a penny. In the 1870s, when many would have been retiring, he bought the Clerkenwell News and transformed it into an important daily paper, the Daily Chronicle. As well as the newspapers he also established a business making paper, initially for newspapers. The first mill was at Clerkenwell but then he purchased the old Sittingbourne paper mill and after using it first to store paper he developed it into one of the finest paper mills in the country. He opened up the trade in esparto as a material for paper-making, visiting Algeria and leasing over a hundred thousand acres of land for esparto production. Although he did not play an active part in public life he was made a member of the Reform Club in London in recognition for services rendered to the Liberal Party. He died at the age of seventy five in April 1890. (33)

Paper Mill Club House

LLOYD Frank:
Frank Lloyd was the eldest son of Edward Lloyd and after working at his father's paper mills in Bow came as manager to the new Sittingbourne mill. Following the death of his father in 1890 he took over the whole of the business, both newspapers and paper-making. When he came to Sittingbourne there was only one mill with three machines at Sittingbourne, over time the

business was expanded and two more mills were added, the number of machines increasing to seventeen. The business supplied not only the Lloyd newspapers but also other papers throughout the world. In 1918 the newspaper business was sold off and Frank Lloyd concentrated on the paper mills, building the Kemsley mill in the 1920s. The garden village of Kemsley was the direct result of his vision and his concern for the welfare of his employees is seen elsewhere, in the building of Trinity Hall, the Club House and Sports Ground and the provision of the Public Swimming Baths. His death in May 1927 at the age of seventy two brought to an end an association with Sittingbourne of over half a century. (34)

LOWE Frederick:
Frederick Lowe came from Devon and as a young man became involved in training field dogs. He took this up as a career, entering dogs in field trials as well in breeding and selling them and acting himself as a judge. In the 1880s he moved to Frinsted and started to manufacture Carta Carna dog biscuits there, the two words coming from the Hindustani for 'dog's food'. After fifteen years he moved to Bobbing Place and started the biscuit factory in Wellwinch Road. The Carta Carna biscuits were well known all over the country and on the continent and for many years a sign on Sittingbourne railway station proclaimed that the town was the home of Lowe's Dog Biscuits, the head of the dog featured as the firm's trade mark being that of one of the dogs which Mr Lowe had bred, Ben of Keppen. During the First World War the factory was put to a different use, manufacturing biscuits for the troops, over fifty tons a week being made there. Mr Lowe died in September 1930 at the age of eighty three. (35)

MARTIN Charles:
Charles Martin was born in Maidstone and started work at the Turkey paper mill there. After working at other paper mills, including spending two years at a mill in Cairo from the top of which he could see the pyramids, he moved to Sittingbourne in 1877 when Lloyd started to manufacture paper at the mill and he was involved in the turning out of the first reel of paper. At that time the mill boasted the largest paper making machine in the world, with a width of 125 inches and the mill employed 140 people. By the time Mr Martin retired at the end of 1925 the mill had over 2000 employees and there were two machines at Kemsley which were 230 inches wide. In 1897 Mr Martin was promoted to the post of Chief Papermaker at the mill and he held that position for 29 years. In 1904 he introduced a method of increasing the speed at which paper was produced by raising one end of the bed along which the pulp flowed. Had he patented the invention he would have become a very rich man, but he didn't do so and instead had to appear as witness in a court case when Lloyd's were sued, unsuccessfully, under a patent taken out in 1906 by another firm for the same method. He retired from the mill in 1929 after working for Lloyds for nearly forty-nine years. (36)

OPIE William:

In 1924 William Opie began to experiment with the preserving of English cherries. At that time the French dominated the glace cherry trade but William persevered and eventually he learnt to cure cherries in a way that experts judged to be as good as the French. So started the English glace cherry trade. In 1929 on the death of his father Bennett Opie who had started the firm's trade in eggs, including providing eggs to the Royal family, William became Managing Director of the firm and the 'cherry' side of the business moved to Sittingbourne at the heart of the cherry county when the factory on Chalkwell Road was opened. (37)

PARRETT William John:

William John Parrett was the eldest son of the Rev Parrett who was for many years Pastor of the Congregational Church in Milton. William was born in Lenham and moved to Sittingbourne with his family when he was eight. After leaving school he was apprenticed as a chemist and printer and in 1855 he took over Mr Read's business in the High Street Sittingbourne. Although only in his early twenties he was at one time editor, reporter, compositor and pressman. Initially the 'Sittingbourne and Faversham Gazette' was published fortnightly but by the middle of 1857 when it had become the East Kent Gazette it was being published weekly. During his fifty years in the newspaper business Mr Parrett saw many changes from the early days when single sheets produced by hand using a printing press which had changed little since the days of Caxton, through to the use of rotary machines printing from miles of paper on a reel and delivered at a rate of many thousand copies an hour of completed and folded newspapers. As well as the East Kent Gazette, William Parrett produced other local newspapers in Kent and developed a successful business as a 'printer, bookseller, stationer, binder and news agent'. He died in April 1905 at the age of seventy two. (38)

The PETERS family:

The first member of the family to live and work in Sittingbourne was Benjamin Peters (1800-1881) who operated daily horse drawn vans for passengers and goods from the 1830s. After trade was hit by the arrival of the railway he took over the Fountain and Railway Hotel in Station Street. As well as being an inn-keeper he was also a jobmaster - hiring horses, carriages, omnibuses, flys etc and in time a funeral carriage and mourning coach. His nephew John Peters junior started, in 1863, a auctioneering and furniture business in Sittingbourne High Street. After his death in 1898 the business was run jointly by his sons Frank and Hedley until 1905 when the business was divided, Frank continuing the furniture business and Hedley transferring the auctioneering business to 93 High Street.

Hedley Peters senior (1862-1943) had bought 93 High Street because of its proximity to Crescent Street, the location of the Fire Station, as he was captain of the Sittingbourne Fire Brigade. He remained the Chief Officer of the Brigade until 1931 and during that time he played a part at national level, being chairman of the National Association of Fire Brigades from 1918 to 1926, the year in which he was awarded the Order of the British Empire. Locally he was chairman of the Boy Scouts Association, President of the Sittingbourne Liberal Club and, from 1915, a JP. In the business world, as well as running a successful property and travel business, the firm arranged passage for many emigrants from Sittingbourne. He was collector of water rates for the local area.

His eldest son, Hedley junior, (1891-1959) having served with the Buffs in India during the First World War, took over both the business and and leadership of the Fire Brigade from his father, being Chief Officer from 1931 to 1941. He was for many years secretary of the Gore Court Hockey Club as well as president of the Sittingbourne and District Inter-Club Games competition. He was succeeded in the business by his son Michael Peters. (39)

SMEED George:
George Smeed was born in Sittingbourne in 1812. As his fortunes increased he moved first to the High Street, where he purchased the former Rose Hotel and converted it into private houses, and then to Gore Court Place in Tunstall. He married twice, the first time in 1834 to Eliza Jeffries and then in 1870 to Martha Greensted. According to the report of his death the rise and progress of Sittingbourne was intimately connected with Mr Smeed's success. The brickmaking enterprise which he started was at that time the largest in the country. He had also established a shipbuilding yard where the large fleet of vessels employed in his business were constructed and repaired. He was responsible for the erection of gas works which supplied the town of Sittingbourne. Together with his son-in-law G H Dean, he owned farmland and he anticipated the time of auction fruit sales by speculating largely in the purchase of growing fruit. He did much to benefit the town including contributing towards the Recreation Ground, providing the land for Keycol Hospital and allowing cricket, football, tennis, badminton and archery clubs to use the grounds of his home, as well as providing facilities there for the annual Poor People's Fete and many Sunday School Festivals. He held public office, being a member of the Burial Board and the Board of Guardians. He died in May 1881. (40)

TONGE George:
George Tonge was the youngest son of John Tonge who had a grocer's shop in Sittingbourne High Street. On his father's death in the 1830s George took over the business. In 1852 Henry Greensted joined him and on his death James Hulburd became Mr Tonge's partner. Mr Tonge was a staunch member of the Church of England. Following his retirement in 1860 he devoted much of his time to working for the church and the good of others. He played a prominent part in the expansion of the Church of England to the west of the town, first with the erection of a temporary place of worship in Pembury Street and then with the building of Holy Trinity Church in Dover Street. He was the superintendent of the Sunday School and became an active manager and

treasurer of the Holy Trinity Schools when they were built in the 1870s. He was Treasurer of the Sittingbourne Local Board, a Director of the County of Kent Friendly Society and was actively involved with the Sittingbourne Tradesmen's Benefit Society which helped widows of the town. Together with his wife he arranged annual social gatherings for the working classes. He died, aged seventy two, in January 1882. (41)

WELLS Percy:
Percy Wells left school at the age of thirteen and went to work in a cement mill, then when he was sixteen he joined the Navy. However during the First World War his involvement with the International Socialist Party, the forerunner in England of the Labour Party, brought him into conflict with the authorities and in 1916 he was sentenced to two years hard labour. He became an active Trade Unionist and for twenty five years did much to champion the cause of the underpaid, in particular agricultural workers, being their leader on the Kent Agricultural Wages Committee and later becoming a member of the Central Agricultural Wages Board. As an official of the Transport and General Workers' Union he negotiated many successful agreements in industries such as brickmaking, cement manufacture and engineering. He was a Sittingbourne and Milton Councillor and represented the town on Kent County Council. During the Second World War he was an ARP Sub-controller and after the war in the 1945 Election he came the town's first Labour M.P. He became Parliamentary Private Secretary to the then Foreign Secretary the Rt. Hon. Ernest Bevin and at one time he was a delegate to the United Nations General Assembly. He successfully defended his Faversham Constituency seat in four General Elections. After the one in 1955 he had the smallest majority of any M.P. in the country yet in spite of a strong swing against Labour in the 1959 election he increased his majority at that election. He died at his home in Park Avenue in June 1964 at the age of seventy two. (42)

WILLS George Henry:
George Wills was the eldest son of Daniel Wills who with Henry Packham started a brickmaking firm in Rainham, where George Wills was born. Wills and Packham then started brickmaking in Sittingbourne excavating brickearth from land on which the upper part of Park Road, Albany Road, Belmont Road, Connaught Road and Valenciennes Road now stand. The firm then took over land at Crown Quay and Daniel Wills lived at Garfield House in Park Road. After his marriage in 1895 George Wills also made his home in Park Road, moving to Hales House, Tunstall, in the 1920s. Although he was for many years Chairman of the Board of Wills and Packham George Wills was an accountant and was connected with the Rainham and Sheerness Water Companies as well as the Sittingbourne District Gas Company. For many years he was the honorary organist and choirmaster at Holy Trinity Church and was instrumental in having a new organ installed at that church. Later he served in the same capacity at St Mary's Church, Park Road and at Tunstall, where he was a Church Warden. He was also for many years President of the Sittingbourne Musical Society. He was acknowledged to be a great

Freemason, being a past Master of St Michael's Lodge, Sittingbourne and holding Provincial and Grand Lodge offices. When his body was laid to rest in the churchyard of Tunstall Church in August 1940 Masonic brethren dropped sprigs of acacia on the coffin. (43)

and FINALLY
William Street:
An observant reader may well have noticed that this book has not been without a certain bias, one street has certainly received more than its fair share of mentions. For this I make no apology, William Street is the street in which my mother was born, and still lives, and where I grew up, so in researching the history of Sittingbourne it is only natural that any mention of it would catch my eye, the decision to include it so often was though a deliberate one. Built of local bricks on land from which brick earth had been excavated, many of the houses on the hill having cellars, it was built at the time when the brick industry was at its height and when the paper mill was beginning to play a more important role in the economy of the town. This final section looks briefly at the history of William Street and of one family who lived there, both the street and the family can be seen as typifying the many ordinary streets and families which have, just as much as the High Street and the prominent families, played their part in the history of Sittingbourne.

The street is somewhat unusual in that it crosses over the boundary between Sittingbourne and Milton, and it was the Sittingbourne end, running south from West Street parallel to the more prestigious Park Road that was built first. By 1871 twenty nine houses had been built on the west side and twenty on the east, a significant number of them were empty and it is likely that they had only just been built. Certainly number 33, which was recorded in the census as empty, had in that year a bakery built at the back of it and in the 1881 census Hales, a master baker was living there. No new houses had been built in the Sittingbourne section of William Street by 1881 although almost all of the properties were occupied. There had been more properties built on the west side in Milton, sixteen in all compared to one in 1871, with two more recorded as being built. Building then continued on the east side as in 1891 an additional thirty houses had been built, nine in Sittingbourne and twenty-one in Milton. (44)

The occupations of those living in William Street in the late 19th century reflects the mixed nature of the town as a whole, ranging from general, agricultural, cement, brick and, in 1881, paper mill labourers through brick layers, engine fitters and drivers, coopers, tanners, cordwainers, dressmakers, tailors, carpenters, shipwrights, iron moulders and clerks to brick makers and moulders, paper makers, butchers, bakers, railway inspectors, master mariners, barge owners, town carters, coal merchants and the Manager of the Prudential Society. (45)

For much of the twentieth century there were more businesses operating in the street than there are now. The building on the north-western corner, currently a photographic shop was originally a forge and then, coming up the hill on that side, before the First World War there was the East Kent Fruit Company, managed by Edward Furminger. Between the wars there was Ballard and Sons boot factory and W J Pullen Ltd motor body building shops. In the 1960s R Baker had a garage and car hire business there and more recently there has been a cable T V company. On the opposite side of the road there was a general shop where the estate agents is now. Going up the hill on the east side there is a beauty treatment business where in the 1960s Edgar Nailor did Radio and T V repairs. Coming up the hill on the east side in the 1920s George Furminger had a fruit and greengrocery business at number 7 and next door there was Sydney Mancer, a tailor. Before the First World War John Mancer had had a hairdressers and there had been a shoemaker, Lawrence Murrey at number 7.

William Street

On the brow of the hill number 33 was in the 1870s and 1880s the home of Thomas Hales, a master baker. It had a larger upper floor than other properties as it extended over the opening to the left of the house which led to the bakehouse at the rear. In 1891 it was occupied by John Bellingham, recorded in the census as a general labourer and general shopkeeper, the business later becoming more specialised into hardware goods and the selling of oil. Much of his time was spent taking oil out to the villages around the town using a cart which he kept in the old bakery, the horse being kept in a stable in the garden of number 35. After that the house was used for many years as a general shop, Albert Long living there in the 1920s and Mr and Mrs Holness in the 1960s, then, until the 1980s when it became a private house, it was a barbers. Further up the road on the same side, at number 83, there was Eveline's Hairdressers which in the 1920s had been Thomas Denne's painting and decorating business. On the opposite side of the road to these businesses there has for many years been a builder's yard, before that it was the site of a fish and chip shop. At the top of the road on the south-east corner a taxi firm now occupies the building which was originally another general store, Petch's in the 1960s and Harvey Williams' in the 1920s. (46)

The Bellingham family:
John Bellingham who lived at number 33 William Street until just before the First World War was my great-grandfather. He had been born in Barming and before settling in Sittingbourne both he and his wife had worked both at the Barming Mental Institution and at one near Littlebourne. He had married Emma Crapnell, whose father was a policeman, at Holy Trinity, Sittingbourne in 1877 and their children were baptised there. Emma died in 1903 and John later remarried just before emigrating to the United States around 1912. He settled in Oswego, New York State where he was a member of Christ Episcopal Church. He died there in October 1926. His eldest child was christened Alice Jane, but in later life she was always known as Sis. For a time she had a confectioners shop in West Street but then married a farmer and moved to Stockbury. Her son Ted Honey though came to work at the mill in Sittingbourne and lived in Chalkwell Road. (47)

John's eldest son was George William Thomas Baker Bellingham. He worked for a time at the Sittingbourne Brewery and then got a job at the paper mill. In 1902 he married Daisy Turner at Minster Abbey and they had two children. He became a reelerman on Number 14 machine at the mill and was exempt from National Service because of his occupation during both wars. During the 1940s he contracted cancer and had to take early retirement just six months before he was due to receive his gold watch for long service at the mill. He died in July 1951. His eldest child, George, started work at the Sittingbourne mill with his father in 1918 but then transferred to Kemsley Mill when that opened. He lived with his wife in Coldharbour Lane and in 1968 was presented with £250 in Premium Bonds by Bowaters in recognition of fifty years service with the firm, having received his gold watch for forty years service in 1958. During the Second World War he served in the RAF and locally he was actively involved with Sittingbourne Football Club. He died in 1975. His sister Lilian, like her brother, was born when their parents lived at 75 William Street. The room in which she was born was at the front of the house and so was in Milton, the boundary between the then separate towns running through the middle of the property. Before the First World War their parents moved to number 35 and she was there during both of the two wars. During the Second World War she took on her father's job as Air-Raid Warden when he was on shift work as well as serving as a bar maid at the Park Tavern and working as a telephonist at the Fire Station, being on duty there on the night of the incendiary bomb attack in 1944. (48)

John's third child, Lewis, started work in the mill but then went to work as a barman and after he married a girl from Borden left to go to Snodland, another paper town, where he ran a pub. He had two girls both who died young from cancer. Albert was born next and he, along with John's seventh child, Edith, emigrated with their father. Albert eventually settled in Canada, returning to England during the Second World War when he was serving with the Canadian Forces. Edith settled in the United States. John had three other children, Arthur, who died at the age of nineteen in 1903 and two girls, Maud and Lilian. Maud married twice, first to Jim Sellen one of the early pilots of the Air Force during the First World War and then later Sid Jeffrey who was a bargeman. The couple lived for many years in Tonge Road, Murston and their son Ron went to work in the office at the Paper Mill. The youngest member of John's family. Lilian, married 'the boy across the road', Hamilton Pepper, just before her father emigrated. The couple lived for many years in Wellwinch Road and celebrated their Diamond Wedding Anniversary in the 1970s. (49)

Just an ordinary family from an ordinary street. I am proud to come from both.

NOTES AND REFERENCES

The following abbreviations are used in these references:

CKS - Centre for Kentish Studies, Archives at Maidstone. Followed by the reference number for the document used.
EKG - East Kent Gazette (available on microfilm at Sittingbourne Reference Library). Followed by the date of the paper used.
Ibid - the same publication as last referred to in the references.
Op cit - details of the publication already given in the references.
PRO - Public Record Office in London. Followed by the reference number of the document used.

INTRODUCTION

1. Everitt, Alan. Continuity and Colonization, Leicester, Leicester University Press. 1986. p 311. / See the section on settlement in Roman times. / Hussey, Arthur. Archaeologia Cantiana 1929-1935, Local Wills. / Kent Messenger January 1967

2. Even if they are reproduced in publications, such as Archaeologia Cantiana. The source, ie book, archives etc is always noted.

3. Sponges found by Mrs S. Hankin in Minterne Avenue. / Price, William (ed), Victoria County History of Kent, Volume 1, 1908, pp. 33/32. / Jessup, Frank. Kent History Illustrated, KCC, 1913. p 10-11. / Archaeologia Cantiana Vol IX, p 164. / Ibid. Vol XIII

4. Ibid. Vol IX p 164. / Ibid. 1889 p 207. / Victoria County History, Volume 3, 1932, p. 173. / Archaeologia Cantiana Vol 10. p. 47. / Ibid. Vol 16. p. 1. / Archaeologia Cantiana 1954/1955

5. EKG 20/7/1994. / Archaeologia Cantiana 1883. p. 104. / Ibid. 1978. p. 239-247. / Lecture by Rev Easton. EKG 25/10/1920.

6. Ibid. / Page, R.I. Life in Anglo-Saxon England B T Batsford, 1970. p. 83. / Archaeologia Cantiana, 1970, p. 1ff. (For a detailed description and picture see this article)

7. Victoria County History, Volume 1, p. 433. / Hasted, Edward. The History and Topographical Survey of the County of Kent Vol 6. Wakefield, E P Publishers, (Reprint) 1972 p. 165. / Ibid. p. 154. / Jessup. op cit. p. 25 / Hasted. op cit. p. 165.

8. Everitt. op cit. p. 311. / De Beayfre Apps, Chronicles of Milton, Milton

History file, Sittingbourne Library Local History section. / Everitt. op cit. p. 312. / Ibid. p. 320. / Archaeologia Cantiana 1932. p 60. / Everitt. op cit. p 315/6. / Ibid. p 317/321.

9. Morris, John, ed., Domesday Book Kent, Chichester, Phillimore, 1983. Introduction. / Archaeologia Cantiana 1965.

10. Trevelyan, G.M., A Shortened History of England, Harmondsworth, Penguin. First Published, Longman, 1942. p. 193/4. / Archaeologia Cantiana Vol 3, p71ff.

11. Ibid. 1868 p 233.

12. Ibid. Vol XI. p. 359 ff. / EKG 23/10/1920

Note: Most of the publications used throughout the book are to be found in Sittingbourne Reference Library, including The East Kent Gazette and the 19th century Census, Hasted's History of Kent and the many volumes of Archaeologia Cantiana.

Chapter One: **LOCAL AGRICULTURE**

1. Hasted, Edward, The History and Topographical Survey of the County of Kent.Vol 6. Wakefield, EP Publishers, (Reprint), 1972. / Baker, Dennis, 'The Marketing of Corn in the First Half of the Eighteenth Century; North East Kent', Agricultural History Review Vol 18, 1970, Part 2. p. 126.

2. CKS U593 A4/5. / Hasted. op cit.

3. Ibid. p. 117. / Ibid. p. 123. / CKS. TR 1411/1. / Chalklin, C.W., Seventeenth Century Kent A Social and Economic History, Rochester, John Hallewell, 1978. p. 10.

4. Hasted. op cit. p. 123. / Ibid. p. 117. / Everitt, Alan, Landscape and Community in England, London, The Hambledon Press, 1985. pp. 67/65.

5. Hasted. op cit. p. 123. / CKS. U593 A4/5. / Hasted. op cit. p. 132.

6. PRO. E190/678/1 (Coastal). / PRO. E190/646/1,8,16 (Coastal). / PRO. E190/658/3-5 (Coastal).

7. PRO. Cal State Papers Charles 1 (Domestic), May 1631. Chalklin. op cit. p. 254. / Thompson, E.P., Customs in Common, London, Merlin Press, 1991. p. 212.

8. Boys, John, General View of the Agriculture of Kent, Printed by B.

McMillan for G and W Nicol, 1805. (No place of publication given) pp. 190/193. / Hasted. op cit. p. 36. / Ibid. p. 41. / Archaeologia Cantiana 1986. p. 243/244/245

9. Hasted. op cit. p. 144/145. Canvey Island on the Essex side of the Thames estuary also suffered from agues until the marshes were drained. (Cracknell, B. E., Portrait of London River, London, Robert Hale, 1968. p. 148.)

10. Hasted. op cit. p. 113. / Everitt, Alan, Continuity and Colonization The Evolution of Kentish Settlement, Leicester, Leicester University Press, 1986. p. 314.

11. CKS. U593 A4/5. / Perks, Richard-Hugh. (Unpublished). Samuel, Raphael, ed., Village Life and Labour, London, Routledge Kegan Paul, 1975. p. 7. / Baker. op cit. p. 134. / Chalklin. op cit. p. 107

12. Hasted. op cit. p. 151. / Ibid. pp. 68/42. / CKS. U390 E24. / Chalklin. op cit. p. 91.

13. Ibid. p. 90. / CKS. U593 A4. / PRO. E190/646/16.

14. PRO. E190/678/12. / Hasted. op cit. p. 42. / Morris, Christopher, ed., The Illustrated Journey of Celia Fiennes, c1682-1712, London, Macdonald, 1984. p. 119. / Chalklin. op cit. p. 92. / CKS. U593 A5

15. Everitt. Continuity and Colonization, op cit. p. 31. / Morris, Christopher. op cit. pp. 190-193. / Malling, Elizabeth, ed., Kentish Sources, III Aspects of Agriculture and Industry, Maidstone, KCC, 1961. p. 87. /Chalklin. op cit. p. 35. / Parish Register, Sitt., 1719.

16. Hasted. op cit. p. 42. / Ibid. p. 15. / CKS. U593 A4

17. Hasted. op cit. p. 25.

18. Ibid. p. 26. / CKS. U386 E30/7. / Archaeologia Cantiana, Ashford, Invicta Press, 1932. pp. 79-81. / CKS. U386 14/3. / Hasted. op cit. pp. 26/27

19. CKS. PRC 28/5/112.428. / Chalklin. op cit. p. 96. / Ibid. p. 100. / Hasted. op cit. p. 204

20. Hasted. op cit. pp. 167-168.

21. Malling. op cit. pp. 29-31. Note: this source is used for subsequent paragraphs. CKS. PRC 27/43/150. Note: this source is used for subsequent paragraphs.

22. Archaeologia Cantiana. op cit. 1932. p. 93. / Ibid. 1932. pp. 96-97. / Ibid.

1931. pp. 50-51. / Ibid. 1932. p. 88. / Ibid. 1932. pp. 86-87

23. Ibid. 1935. pp. 183-184. / Ibid. 1934. pp. 39-40. / Chalklin. op cit. p. 92.

24. Ibid. p. 6.

25. Allison, Helen, 'The Agricultural Riots in 1830 in the Sittingbourne Area', article in Bygone Kent, Vol 3, No 4. This is used throughout the section, reference should be made to it for more details. Also Used: Copy of 'Swing' letter and Troop Memorandum, both in the 'Swing' file in Sittingbourne Library, Local History Section. Hobsbawn, E.J. and Rude, G., Captain Swing, London, Lawrence and Wishart, 1969. pp. 101-102.

26. Chalklin. op cit. p. 254. Kentish Gazette 5th June 1838 (quotes from this). / Hopker, David, Money or Blood. The 1835 riots in the Swale Villages, published privately by the author, printed by Accent, 1988.

27. Tithe Awards housed at the Cathedral Archives, Canterbury. References: B2A/ B17A/ B20A/ B27A/ H2A/ H8A/ I2A/ K3A/ M7A/ M9A/ N4A/ R6A/ SHA/ T8A/ T9A/ U2A.

28. Census Enumerators' Books Milton Hundred 1851/71/81.

29. Kelly's Directory Sittingbourne and Milton 1895. / Treble, J.H., Urban Poverty in Britain, London, Batsford, 1979. p. 167.

30. Note: the following paragraphs include data derived from Kelly's Directories for Sittingbourne and Milton of 1862 and 1895 and Census Enumerators' Books for 1851 and 1881, the relevant usage will be noted in the text.

31. The area benefited from the increased demand in the second half of the 19th century for Kentish fruit as a result of changes in national per capita levels and decreased costs for transporting fruit. The main fruit grown in the Hundred was cherries, with auctions being held to sell the fruit off the trees. It was not the only fruit growing area in Kent. The mid-Kent area around Maidstone was also well established, the main fruit there was apples, as it was in the area of the Weald which developed during the second half of the 19th century as railways linked it to London markets. The north-west Kent area which was closest to London specialised increasingly in soft fruit and on the Isle of Thanet a fruit industry developed to supply the needs of the coastal holiday resorts. (Harvey, David, 'Fruit Growing in Kent in the Nineteenth Century', in Archaeologia Cantiana Vol LXX1X, 1964. pp 95-108).

32. During the early 19th century jam had been a luxury, but following a fall in sugar prices during the 1850s and 1860s the jam trade increased, making

fruit growing more profitable as damaged fruit could be used. (Harvey, D., Ibid)

33. Willmott, F.G., Bricks and Brickies, Rainham, Meresborough Books, 1977. p. 64.

34. EKG 27/6/1857, 30/6/60, 27/10/88. / EKG 25/6/1870. / EKG 9/7/1870. / EKG 31/7/1886. / EKG 18/9/1886. / EKG 25/12/1886.

35. EKG 21/9/1878. / EKG 9/9/1876. / EKG 19/4/1879. / EKG 19/4/1873. / EKG 30/1/1869.

36. EKG 15/6/1889. / Sittingbourne Tithe Award 1840 TO/S18A Canterbury Cathedral Archives. / EKG 4/9/1858. / EKG 13/8/1892. / Courtesy of Mr Sillars. / EKG 17/12/1898, 23/3/1902. / EKG 16/4/1892.

37. Analysis by Mr Chapman, courtesy of Mr Sillars

38. EKG 29/3/1873. / EKG 21/1/1884.

39. EKG 5/1/1884.

40. EKG 26/7/1913. / Interview with Mr Goodhew.

41. EKG 18/12/1991

42. Linseed and rape were also grown increasingly in other parts of Kent. However they were also mentioned in the agricultural report in the Kentish Gazette of August 16th 1825, so they weren't exactly new!

43. This would indicate a decrease in both arable and pasture land compared to the situation when the tithe awards were made 150 years ago, and an increase in the area given over to fruit. In view of the earlier fruit growing tradition in the area it is possible that the tithe figures for the Hundred as a whole of 2% for orchards do not reflect the role of fruit growing over the whole period covered by this work and that those for Sittingbourne (11%) are more representative.

44. EKG 8/5/1996 / Information courtesy of L Ingham / EKG 13/3/1980. / Visitors Guide to Swale.

45. EKG 1/5/1961. / Courtesy of Mr Sillars. / EKG 30/9/1933.

46. EKG 5/2/1970

Chapter Two: **THE URBAN AREA IN THE PRE-INDUSTRIAL PERIOD**

1. Hussey, Arthur. Archaeologia Cantiana, Ashford, Headley Brothers, 1929. pp. 47-48. / Ibid p. 98. / There is of course the famous 'Shambles' in York, and a map of Tonbridge in the 17th century shows an area known as the shambles, although there is no indication as to whether or not it was restricted to the sale of butcher's meat. (Chalklin, C.W. 'A Seventeenth-Century Market Town: Tonbridge', in Archaeologia Cantiana Volume LXXV1, 1961. p. 155.) / Archaeologia Cantiana. op cit. 1934. pp. 39-40.

2. Ibid. 1934. p.41. / Ibid. 1932. pp. 86-87. / Ibid. 1931. p. 69. / Ibid. 1931. p. 53. / Ibid. 1932. pp. 94-95. / Ibid. 1931. p. 50.

3. Archaeologia Cantiana. op cit. 1930. pp. 39-40. / Ibid. 1933. pp. 24-25. / Ibid. 1930. p. 43. / Perks, Richard-Hugh, Guide and History of Milton Creek, Sittingbourne, AKN, 1980s. -   Ships from Sittingbourne and Milton were generally larger than those at the more important port of Hythe, as they were involved in deep-sea work. The Port Book for the Creek of Milton for the period from Easter to Michaelmas 1574 records four shipments of fish to London, these would be ling and cod, not locally caught and presumably either salted or dried.   (Dulley, A.J.F., 'Four Kent Towns at the End of the Middle Ages', in Archaeologia Cantiana Volume LXXX1, 1966. pp 104/101.)

4. Archaeologia Cantiana. op cit. 1934. pp. 46-47. / Ibid. 1931. p. 50. (See also section on the area in Roman times in the Introduction) / Ibid. 1934. p. 36. / Oyster fishing was widespread along the north Kent coast. (Dulley. op cit. p. 102) It was also common on the Essex side of the Thames at Southend. (Cracknell, Basil E., Portrait of London River, London, Robert Hale, 1968. p. 186.) / Archaeologia Cantiana. 1931. pp. 49-50.

5. PRO. State Papers Henry VIII Vol 2(8) 4348 / Ibid. Vol 5. p. 761.

6. Archaeologia Cantiana. op cit. 1931. p. 60. / Ibid. 1930. pp. 54-55. / Ibid. 1930. pp. 38-39. / Ibid. 1931. pp. 54-55. / Ibid. p. 58.

7. Ibid. 1935. p. 178. / Ibid. 1931. pp. 54-55. / Ibid. 1931. pp. 64-65. / Ibid. 1930. pp. 54-55. / Ibid. 1932. p. 100. / Ibid. 1934. p. 51. / Ibid. 1933. pp. 26-27. / Ibid. 1932. pp.96-97. (There is a windmill at the Chalkwell tannery recorded in the 1861 Census book.)

8. Ibid. 1932. p. 82. 1931. p. 69. 1932. pp. 86-87. / PRO. Letters and Papers Foreign and Domestic Henry VIII. Vol 19 (1) 610.80. / Archaeologia Cantiana. op cit. 1931. pp.58-59. / Ibid. 1932. p. 83. (See also article in the EKG 8/5/1915) / Ibid. 1833. p. 15. / Ibid. 1931. pp. 51-52. / Ibid. 1931. pp. 56-57. / Ibid. 1930. p. 45. / Ibid. 1930. p. 53. / Ibid. 1933. p. 15. (Weaving, as part of the cloth trade, as well as being a national industry, was also widespread in Kent at the time, with the main centre being in the Cranbrook

district. Milton, with 17% of known occupations in the wills relating to the textile industry was comparable with the 'industrial' villages of Smarden and Pluckley where textile workers at the time of Cade's revolution numbered 16 out of 98 in the former and 8 out of 50 in the latter. (Dulley. op cit. pp. 100/101.)) / Archaeologia Cantiana. 1934. p. 42. / Ibid. 1932. p. 84.

9. Ibid. 1932. p. 101. / Ibid. 1932. p. 101. / Ibid. 1932. p. 82. / Ibid. 1933. p. 14. (It is possible that it was cloth which had been fulled in the local mill which was stretched on them.) / Ibid. 1929. p. 53. / Ibid. 1931. p. 69. / Ibid. 1930. p. 42.

10. Ibid. 1929. p. 37. / Ibid. 1929. p. 42. / Ibid. 1930. p. 51. / Ibid. 1929. p. 50. / Ibid. 1929. p. 49. 1934. pp. 48-49/39-40. 1931. p. 67.

11. PRO. Harleian Mss. 280 594.595 / 11808.35961. / Archaeologia Cantiana. op cit. 1931. pp. 51-52.

12. Hasted, Edward, The History and Topographical Survey of the County of Kent, Volume 6, Wakefield, EP Publishers (Reprint), 1972. pp. 166-167. / CKS. Q/SB 9/32.

13. Hasted. op cit. pp. 166/167/153.

14. Parish Registers. Milton and Sittingbourne. / Post Office Directory of Kent 1845. / CKS. P253/8/4.

15. EKG 2/6/1977

16. Everitt, Alan, 'The Market Towns'. in The Early Modern Town, Clark, Peter. ed., New York, Longman, 1977. p. 174. / PRO. State Papers Domestic Edward VI-James I. Vol 1. p. 626. / Hasted. op cit. p. 153.

17. Everitt. 'The Market Towns'. op cit. p. 191. / CKS. P253/8/4.

18. CKS. Q 1SR1. / Parkes, Joan, Travel in England in the Seventeenth Century, Oxford, Oxford University Press, 1968. p.270. / CKS. U1890 M1.

19. Hasted. op cit. p. 167. (However the 1840 tithe map for Sittingbourne shows one area behind the Bull hotel used as the stock market, so it is possible that Sittingbourne did retain a specialised market role throughout the period. (Canterbury Cathedral Archives S18B) It may have been related directly to the requirements of innkeeping - in 1671 innkeepers in Tonbridge were granted the right to hold a monthly cattle market. (Chalklin. Archaeologia Cantiana, 1961. p. 158.))

20. Ogilby, John. Britannia, London, Alexander Duckham, 1939. /

Archaeologia Cantiana. op cit. 1929. p. 41. / CKS. TR2209. / PRO. Letters and Papers Foreign and Domestic. 118 Vol2(2) 433/48. / Vol 5 p. 761. / PRO. Acts Privy Council. 1591-2. pp. 252-3 and 258. / CKS. TR 2209.

21. PRO. Letter and Papers Foreign and Domestic Henry VIII. Vol 14(2) 754. / Ogilby. op cit. / CKS. TR 2209. (Tonbridge was an established coaching centre in the 17th century and the 18th century saw an increase nationally in'thoroughfare towns'. (Borsay. op cit. p. 4.)) / St James Evening Post Newspaper 1747 No 5818. / Kentish Life Newspaper January 1726. (Everitt credits Royal patronage, as well as its convenient position for making Sittingbourne one of the most important coaching centres in the south-eastern counties during the 17th and 18th centuries. (Everitt, Alan, 'The English Urban Inn 1560-1760' in Perspectives in English Urban History, Everitt, A., ed., London, McMillan, 1973. pp. 94/97.)) / Hasted. op cit. p. 152.

22. CKS. U896T. / Ibid. / CKS. Q/R Lv 4/1. / CKS. Calender Quarter Sessions 1606. / CKS. Q/M/SB 905.

23. CKS. A77/245. (The George was one of the largest provincial inns stretching for 21 bays, the Peacock Inn in another major coaching centre, Northampton, had only 11 bays. (Everitt, A., 'The English Urban Inn', op cit. p.101.)) / Parish Registers. Milton and Sittingbourne.

24. CKS. U120 P54/29. / CKS. U47/5/T5. / CKS. U47/22 T130. / CKS. U120 54/28.

25. Robinson, W. Scott, Sittingbourne and the names of lands and houses in or near it: their origin and history, Sittingbourne, W.J. Parrett, 1879. p. 28. / PRO. Calender State Papers Charles 11 Vol 6. p. 283. / PRO. PRC/11/55 1691.

26. Hasted. op cit. p. 164. / Parish Registers. Milton and Sittingbourne.

27. Hasted. op cit. p. 167. (By the end of the 18th century the income from the sale of Milton oysters varied from £3,000 to £7,000 per annum. (Goodsall, R.H., 'Oyster Fisheries on the North Kent Coast', in Archaeologia Cantiana, Volume LXXX, 1965. p. 140.)) / Hasted. op cit. p. 167. (Oyster fishing, as noted in Chapter One, was widespread along the coast including Whitstable in the east. In 1670 the fishermen there complained that others, including fishermen from Milton, were taking oysters from their grounds. (Goodsall. op cit. p. 125.)

28. Hasted. op cit. pp. 151-152 / 165-166.

29. PRO. E190/647/4 (Coastal). / Baker, Dennis, 'The marketing of Corn in the First Half of the Eighteenth Century: NE Kent', Agricultural History Review Vol 18, 1970 Part II. pp. 134-135. / Hazell, Martin, 'The Sailing Barges and the Brick and Other Industries of Milton Creek 1850-1970'.

Thesis: Department of Teaching Studies, North London Polytechnic, 1972. / Hasted. op cit. p. 166. / CKS. U120/P54/28.

30. Kentish Post Newspaper 22/11/1729. / Parish Register Milton / Perks, Richard-Hugh, Guide and History of Milton Creek. op cit.

31. Post Office Directory of Kent 1845. / Parish Registers. Sittingbourne and Milton. / W C Finch, Watermills and Windmills, Arthur Cassell, Sheerness, 1976. (First published 1933 by the G W Daniel Company) p. 279, 244, 245.

32. Hasted. op cit. p. 166. / Post Office Directory of Kent 1845. / Parish Registers Sittingbourne and Milton. / Topographical Map of the County of Kent 1769. Andrews and Durry and Herbert.

33. Bignell, Alan, Kent Lore, London, Hale, 1983. p. 130. / Parish Registers. Sittingbourne and Milton. / Perks, Richard-Hugh. (Unpublished). (In contrast 17th century Tonbridge consisted of timber framed houses and there were no bricklayers recorded in the registers of 1661-1671. (Chalklin. Archaeologia Cantiana, Volume LXXV1, op cit. p. 159.)) / Archaeologia Cantiana, 1860, p. 179.

34. Ibid. 1861, p. 236.

35. Ibid. Volume 9, p. 31.

36. Ibid. Volume 24, p. 68. / Mrs Markham, A History of England, London, John Murray, 1851, p. 410.

Chapter Three: **BRICKMAKING AND ALLIED INDUSTRIES**

1. Cordell, Alan and Williams, Leslie, The Past Gory of Milton Creek, Rainham, Meresborough Books, 1985. / Perks, Richard-Hugh, George Bargebrick Esquire The Story of George Smeed the Brick and Cement King, Rainham, Meresborough Books, 1981. / Guide and History of Milton Creek, Dolphin Sailing Barge Museum, AKN. /Sprits'l, A Portrait of Sailing Barges and Sailormen. London, Conway Maritime Press, 1975. / Sattin, D.L., Just off the Swale, The Story of the Bargebuilding Village of Conyer, Rainham, Meresborough Books, 1978. / Twist, Sydney James, Stock Bricks of the Swale, Sittingbourne, The Sittingbourne Society, 1984. / Murston Village and Parish, Sittingbourne, The Sittingbourne Society, 1981. / Willmott, F.G., Bricks and Brickies, Rainham, Meresborough Books, 1972. / Cement, Mud and Muddies, Rainham, Meresborough Books, 1977.

I am indebted to these books for some of the information on the industries described in this chapter, and to Mr Perks for information from his own records which he made available for my under-graduate research.

2. Hasted, Edward, The History and Topographical Survey of the County of Kent Vol Six, Wakefield, EP Publishers, (Reprint), 1972. / Courtesy of Mr Perks.

3. Kentish Gazette Newspaper 10/6/1825. / The tithe awards for Sittingbourne indicate that a number of parcels of ground were being used as brickfields at that time. (Canterbury Cathedral Archives. S18A.) / Census Enumerators' Books 1851/71. Evidence from the Census Enumerators' Books is used extensively throughout this chapter and the year used will be made clear in text, further references to them will not be given.

4. Smeed Dean Brochure courtesy of Mr P Morgan. / EKG 7/5/1881. / EKG 3/11/1877. / EKG 16/10/1886

5. EKG 5/12/1859. / EKG 17/6/1871

6. EKG 3/11/1877. / EKG 20/5/1911

7. Hazell, Martin, The Sailing Barges and the Brick and Other Industries of Milton Creek 1850-1970, Thesis, Department of Teaching Studies, North London Polytechnic, 1972.

8. EKG 4/8/1860

9. Smeed Dean Brochure

10. EKG 13/6/1857. / EKG 12/6/1869

11. EKG 12/9/1857

12. EKG 11/1/1862. / EKG 18/1/1862. / EKG 23/7/1864. / EKG 30/11/1878

13. EKG 22/5/1858. / EKG 14/11/1863. / EKG 20/5/1871. / EKG 19/3/1881

14. Smeed Dean Barge Yard Day Books. Courtesy of Peter Morgan

15. Hazell. op cit.

16. EKG 8th, 15th, 22nd, 29th March, 5th, 12th, 19th, 26th April and 3rd May 1890. Other quotes from this paper are detailed in the text of this section.

17. Kelly's Directory 1895 & 1862

18. EKG 21/7/1900

19. EKG 9/2/1901

20. EKG 4/4/1914. / EKG 23/1/1969. / EKG 24/8/1972

21. EKG 12/11/1970. / EKG30/12/1971

22. EKG 19/8/1911

23. EKG 13/10/1950. / EKG 26/2/1960. / EKG 23/10/1969. / EKG 5/1/1962. / EKG 12/3/1981. / Interview with former employee.

Chapter Four: **THE PAPER INDUSTRY & THE 20th CENTURY ECONOMY**

1. Sittingbourne Parish Registers: P338-1-2: 14/4/1703, 16/10/1705, 20/10/1714 and 28/8/1719. / CKS: 11/81/66. / Victoria County History, Volume 3, 1932, p.417. / The Kentish Post January 29 1752. / Census Enumerators' Books, 1841/1851. (Smith was also recorded in the Tithe Awards and the mill was on the Tithe Map. (Canterbury Cathedral Archives. S18A/B)) / Roach, Donovan John, 'The History and Development of Bowater's Mills at Sittingbourne and Kemsley'. Published in East Kent Gazette Newspaper, 11/18 April 1952. Note: Unless specified otherwise details of the development of papermaking have come from this source. / Census Enumerators' Books 1841/1851

2. EKG 17/4/1858. / EKG 11/7/1857

3. EKG 11/4/1863. / EKG 8/6/1867. / Census Enumerators' Books, 1871.

4. Ibid 1881.

5. EKG 14/10/1876. / EKG 8/9/1877. / EKG 21/9/1861. / Perks, Richard Hugh, George Bargebrick Esquire, Rainham, Meresborough Books, 1981.

6. EKG 11/10/1884. / EKG 8/8/1888. / Dane, John. Interview. 28/10/1991. I am indebted to Mr Dane for the information in this chapter on the papermaking process. / EKG 20/4/1889. / EKG 29/9/1884. / Census Enumerator's Books, 1891.

7. EKG 8/2/1890. / EKG 13/2/1892.

8. EKG 11/4/1952

9. EKG 11/4/1952

10. EKG 25/9/1902. / EKG 22/8/1908. / EKG 1/10/1910. / EKG 18/3/1911. / EKG 6/5/1911.

11. EKG 7/3/1914. / EKG 4/4/1914

12. My thanks to Mrs J Potts for this information. / Reader, W.J., Bowater A History, Cambridge, Cambridge University Press, 1981. p108.

13. EKG 8/5/1920. / EKG 31/7/1920. / EKG 6/1/1923. / EKG 18/10/1924

14. Brochure.

15. Reader. op cit. p. 30. / EKG 4/1/1933. Reader. op cit. p. 118. / EKG 18/7/1936

16. Reader. op cit. p. 165/ 169

17. EKG 18/6/1948. / Reader. op cit. pp. 187-188. / EKG 5/3/1954 and 30/12/1955. / Reader. op cit. p. 296.

18. EKG 28/3/1878. / EKG 2/7/1892. / EKG 5/10/1895. / EKG 9/5/1952

19. EKG 14/10/1965. / Bailey, P.M., Pollution in Milton Creek, National Environmental Competition Winner, 1974.

20. EKG 14/8/1991. / EKG 25/5/1994

21. EKG 1/3/1963. / EKG 2/3/1967. / EKG 9/3/1967. / EKG 11/10/1973. / EKG 15/9/1977. / EKG 12/2/1980

22. EKG 14/8/1991. / EKG 1992. / EKG 10/8/1994

23. EKG 5/1/1951. / EKG 3/4/1915. / EKG 5/1/1951. / EKG 19/12/1859. / EKG 9/7/1864

24. Directory 1862. / The Past Glory of Milton Creek, op cit. / Directory 1862. / The Past Glory of Milton Creek, op cit. / EKG 8/12/1877

25. EKG 2/3/1872. / EKG 31/5/1873. / EKG 8/12/1877 / EKG 21/5/1881. / EKG 18/3/1882. / Directory 1887 & 1895

26. EKG 12/3/1859. / EKG 14/1/1871, / EKG 25/2/1905. / EKG 20/1/1900

27. EKG 20/4/1867. / EKG 17/8/1867. / EKG 2/4/1932. / EKG 27/4/1935

28. EKG 5/6/1915. / EKG 11/8/1977. / EKG 26/6/1915. / EKG 1/6/1967. / EKG 29/10/1881

29. EKG 25/5/1867. / EKG 4/1/1879. / EKG 1/9/1961

30. EKG 12/10/1912. / EKG 17/12/1961. / EKG 6/6/1974. / EKG 22/10/1954. / EKG 3/6/1982

31. EKG 20/4/1972. / EKG 20/6/1963. / EKG 6/1/1972. / EKG 16/5/1973

32. Kelly's Directory 1887. / See Chapter Two. / PRO. Letter and Papers Foreign and Domestic Henry VIII. Volume 19 (1) 610.80. / Hasted op cit. p. 151/2 & 166.

33. 1861 Census. / Tithe Records Milton

34. Kentish Gazette Newspaper 27/3/1838. / EKG 9/11/1861

35. The Sittingbourne Society are engaged in reconstructing Periwinkle Mill.

Chapter Five: **THE URBAN POOR & IMPORTANT EVENTS**

1. I am indebted to Mr Allen for allowing me to make use of his original research into the poor. These and following records come from Parish Registers. / Nov. 1676. / 1671/2. / 1674/5

2. 22/5/1676. / April-June 1676. / May-Oct 1680

3. Ibid. / 1668. / 10/2/1703

4. 14/8/1722. / 10/10/1724-17/4/1725. / 17/4/1755-29/10/1725. / 4/5/1726-22/10/1726

5. 1766. / 25/6/1797. / 3/10/1773. / 1786. / 14/5/1777. / 27/12/1788. / 7/4/1774-10/10/1774

6. 14/12/1817. / 7/2/1820. / 4/9/1822

7. 15/10/1823. / 4/9/1833. / 1/12/1830. / 26/1/1831. / 30/2/1829. / 30/7/1841

8. Allinson, Helen, 'Bygone Kent' Volume 4, No 1, p30

9. Kentish Post 18/12/1838, 31/3/1840. / 1841 Census (Following information also from censuses)

10. EKG 9/1/1869. / EKG 8/12/1900

11. EKG 19/6/1858. / Parish Records 1/7/1858. / EKG 23/11/1867. / EKG 18/5/1889. / Plaque on wall of Spicer Homes. / EKG 9/12/1870

12. Interview with Fred Hughes. / EKG 28/8/1909. / EKG 2/1/1909. / EKG 29/3/1990. / EKG 11/2/1939

13. I am indebted to Mr and Mrs Foster for providing information about their relatives.

14. EKG 29/1/1870. / EKG 18/3/1871. / EKG 25/3/1882

15. EKG 15/4/1882. / EKG 7/10/1885. / EKG 28/1/1888. / EKG 21/8/1897. / 12/3/1904

16. EKG 4/2/1911. / EKG 22/4/1911

17. EKG 20/11/1926. / EKG 26/8/1949. / EKG 15/2/1913

18. EKG 26/1/1867. / EKG 26/2/1870. / EKG 14/1/1871. / EKG 7/1/1871. / EKG 29/1/1881. / EKG 27/3/1909

19. EKG 23/7/1859

20. EKG 4/8/1860

21. EKG 20/7/1861. / EKG 27/8/1864

22. EKG 29/6/1867. / EKG 4/8/1877. / EKG 16/7/1881. / EKG 13/2/1897

23. EKG 7/11/1857. / EKG 29/12/1860   Sometimes masqueraders came from Sheerness on Boxing Day. EKG 28/12/1861

24. EKG 14/3/1863. / EKG 14/5/1887

25. EKG 25/11/1893

26. EKG 7/11/1896

27. EKG 26/6/1897. / EKG 2/12/1899. / EKG 26/5/1900

28. EKG 28/7/1900. / EKG 4/7/1908. / EKG 20/6/1914. / EKG 16/8/1902. / The celebration in London was even greater and Lloyds made table cloths, 70 miles long, for the 'King's Dinner'. EKG 12/7/1902. / EKG 24/10/1903. / EKG 25/6/1904. / EKG 29/10/1910

29. EKG 9/6/1900. / EKG 5/7/1890. / EKG 11/4, 18/7 & 8/8/1903

30. EKG 31/10/1857. / EKG 31/8/1858. / EKG 6/8/1864. / EKG 17/7/1858. / EKG 24/7/1858. / EKG 25/6/1859. / EKG 28/8/1875. / EKG 6/7/1889. / EKG

15/6/1861. / EKG 16/11/1872. / EKG 11/1/1873. / EKG 4/3/1882. / EKG 14/6/1884. / EKG 7/4/1883. / EKG 1/3/1884

31. EKG 28/7/1860. / EKG 25/5/1872. / EKG 12/10/1872. / EKG 4/5/1872. / EKG 4/6/1881

32. EKG 26/7/1919

33. EKG 30/8/1919. / EKG 17/7/1920, / EKG 21/5/1921. / EKG 31/7/1920. / EKG 24/12/1921

34. EKG 28/10/1922. The newspaper owned by Lloyd.

35. EKG 7/7/1923. / EKG 28/6/1924. / EKG 21/7/1934. / EKG 11/5/1935. / EKG 26/6/1937

36. EKG 5/6/1953. / EKG 9/6/1977. / EKG 31/7/1981. / EKG 4/2/1982. / EKG 2/9/1961. / EKG 3/9/1964. / EKG 3/6/1971. / EKG 12/12/1968. / EKG 9/7/1970. / EKG 5/7/1957. / EKG 16/7/1964. / EKG 14/7/196

37. Courtesy of Miss D Harris. / Dr P Bellingham

38. EKG 16/7/1921

39. EKG 16/3/1972

40. EKG 2/10/1937. / EKG 28/8/1953. / EKG 5/10/1962. / EKG 9/11/1967. / EKG 22/5/1986. / EKG 30/11/1989. / Kent Messenger Extra 29/11/1991.

41. EKG 3/10/1908. / EKG 5/12/1908. / EKG 13/1/1950. / EKG 9/10/1959. / EKG 8/5/1964. / EKG 12/1/1976

42. EKG 11/12/1873. / EKG 21/1/1881. / EKG 3/2/1883. / EKG 6/12/1902. / EKG 31/12/1892. / EKG 11/1/1908

43. EKG 12/8/1911. / EKG 9/3/1912. / EKG 20/4/1912

44. EKG 23/12/1922. / EKG 30/12/1922. / EKG 25/7/1925. / EKG 8/5/1926

45. EKG 19/2/1938. / EKG 28/1/1939

46. EKG 1/2/1947. / EKG 6/2/1953. / EKG 27/2/1953. / EKG 12/2/1954

47. EKG 19/9/1968. / EKG 13/2/1969. / EKG 27/9/1973. / EKG 19/1/1978. / EKG 4/1/1979. / EKG 19/5/1983. / EKG 17/1/1985

48. EKG 15/1/1987. / EKG 21/1/1987. / EKG 2/4/1987. / EKG 22/10/1987

49. Courtesy of L Ingham

Chapter Six: **URBAN GROWTH**

1. EKG 30/1/1858. / EKG6/2/1858

2. EKG 3/3/1860. / EKG 17/6/1865. / EKG 27/3/1869. / EKG 25/8/1866. / EKG 9/11/1861

3. EKG 26/12/1863. / EKG 18/2/1860. / EKG 20/2/1846. / EKG 7/5/1864. / EKG 3/4/1869. / EKG 24/7/1869

4. EKG 26/6/1869. / EKG 27/11/1858

5. EKG 2/1/1864

6. EKG 14/11/1857. / EKG 23/1/1858. / EKG 19/6/1859

7. EKG 3/3/1860. / EKG 3/11/1860. / EKG 6/4/1861. / EKG 21/12/1861. / EKG 5/1/1861

8. EKG 26/12/1857. / EKG 22/5/1858. / EKG 8/1/1859. / EKG 15/1/1859

9. EKG 15/1/1859. / EKG 30/6/1860. / EKG 28/5/1859. / EKG 30/5/1857. / EKG 12/11/1870. / EKG 22/8/1859

10. EKG 3/9/1859. / EKG 8/10/1859. / EKG 15/10/1859. / EKG 26/11/1859. / EKG 11/2/1860. / EKG 25/2/1860. / EKG 12/5/1860. / EKG 13/10/1860

11. EKG 15/5/1858. / EKG 16/2/1861. / Census data. / EKG 7/5/1864. / EKG 8/10/1864. / EKG 30/12/1864

12. EKG 30/1/1858. / R-H Perks George Bargebrick Esquire p 12. / EKG 14/1/1860. / EKG 31/1/1863. / EKG 20/11/1869

13. EKG 13/3/1870. / EKG 30/4/1870. / EKG 20/4/1871. / EKG 27/9/1871

14. EKG 30/7/1870. / EKG 2/1/1869. / EKG 21/12/1895. / EKG 30/7/1870. / EKG 5/7/1879

15. EKG 30/7/1870. / EKG 18/10/1879. / EKG 27/12/1879. / EKG 13/6/1896. / EKG 27/5/1899

16. Archaeologia Cantiana 1967 p179ff: Quarter Sessions 24/7/1599. / Ibid. July 1607. / CKS P253 5/5/1736-4/10/1736. / CKS P253/8/2 31/3/1832. / EKG 9/9/1882

17. EKG 8/3/1973. / EKG 18/2/1871

18. EKG 25/3/1871. / EKG 19/3/1881

19. EKG 31/8/1889. / EKG 3/5/1884. / EKG 6/6/1885. / EKG 2/5/1891

20. EKG 2/8/1879. / EKG 15/11/1879. / EKG 17/7/1880. / EKG 29/1/1881

21. EKG 20/11/1875. / EKG 1/3/1873

22. EKG 12/8/1871. / EKG 24/5/1873. / EKG 7/9/1878. / EKG 12/10/1878

23. EKG 22/7/1899. / Kellys Directory 1895 p545. / P O Directory 1876 p1651

24. EKG 12/11/1870. / EKG 19/11/1870. / EKG 29/11/1879. / EKG 30/7/1886. / EKG 14/6/1873

25. EKG 26/5/1894

26. EKG 16/10/1875. / EKG 20/4/1889. / EKG 9/9/1882. / EKG 31/12/1898. / EKG 24/12/1872. / EKG 16/11/1889. / EKG 4/9/1879. / EKG 9/4/1898. / EKG 11/6/1898. / EKG 23/9/1899

27. EKG 5/2/1870. / EKG 19/4/1879. / EKG 23/5/1885. / EKG 10/9/1892

28. EKG 1/7/1899. / EKG 17/6/1899. / EKG 9/9/1899. / EKG 12/11/1887. / EKG 15/12/1888. / EKG 3/4/1897

29. EKG 18/6/1904. / EKG 10/3/1906. / EKG 22/4/1905. / EKG 1/10/1932. / EKG 16/4/1938. / EKG 14/4/1934

30. EKG 1/3/1913. / EKG 21/1/1911. / EKG 27/9/1930. / EKG 4/2/1928. / EKG 15/5/1915

31. EKG 6/12/1919. / EKG 6/6/1925. / EKG 11/7/1925. / EKG 3/12/1927

32. EKG 18/1/1930. / EKG 15/1/1954

33. EKG 6/2/1932. / EKG 1/4/1933. / EKG 15/1/1954. / EKG 9/9/1933. / EKG 13/7/1935. / EKG 12/1/1935

34. EKG 25/8/1945. / EKG 27/5/1960. / EKG 25/5/1946. / EKG 30/1/1948. / EKG 20/8/1948

35. EKG 9/4/1938

36. EKG 7/5/1927. / I am indebted to Mr Faulkner, Deputy Clerk S&MUDC 1948-1973 for making a copy of the Milton UDC Minutes available to me.

37. EKG 2/10/1926. / EKG 26/2/1927. / EKG 29/1/1927. / EKG 7/5/1927

38. EKG 23/11/1929. / EKG 30/3/1935. / EKG 21/8/1937. / EKG 9/7/1948

39. EKG 4/1/1930. / EKG 5/9/1931. / EKG 7/11/1931. / EKG 27/2/1932. / EKG 20/4/1935

40. EKG 2/3/1901. / EKG 1/9/1928. / EKG 3/12/1921. / EKG 22/2/1902. / EKG 9/6/1906. / EKG 22/10/1938. / EKG 12/7/1924. / EKG 8/10/1932

41. EKG 17/11/1900. / EKG 9/1/1926. / EKG 9/2/1929. / EKG 6/1/1934. / EKG 13/7/1929. / EKG 18/1/1930. / EKG 23/4/1932

42. EKG 13/5/1911. / EKG 4/11/1911. / EKG 20/8/1921. / My thanks to Mr High for this information

43. EKG 26/10/1901. / EKG 16/5/1903. / EKG 18/2/1911. / EKG 18/1/1930. / EKG 21/3/1931. / EKG 4/4/1931. / EKG 18/1/1931. / EKG 24/6/1939. / EKG 3/2/1934. / EKG 14/1/1949

44. EKG 18/7/1931

45. EKG 11/3/1935

46. EKG 8/2/1963. / EKG 24/4/1972. / See Chapter Four. / EKG 7/1/1988. / EKG 17/6/1976. / EKG 13/9/1979. / EKG 1/3/1984. / EKG 7/2/1985. / EKG 7/7/1988. / EKG 9/10/1991. / EKG 1/10/1981. / EKG 24/1/1985

47. EKG 28/7/1950. / EKG 14/3/1952. / EKG 25/11/1953. / EKG 11/1/1957. / EKG 28/2/1958. / EKG 6/2/1959

48. EKG 11/3/1960. / EKG 9/2/1967. / EKG 9/12/1965. / EKG 8/6/1967. / EKG 26/10/1973. / EKG 13/8/1881. / EKG 28/3/1885. / EKG 24/3/1881

49. EKG 11/1/1957. / EKG 21/8/1959. / EKG 5/5/1961. / EKG 11/3/1965. / EKG 8/5/1969. / EKG 20/3/1969

50. EKG 12/2/1970. / EKG 3/4/1970. / EKG 12/10/1973. / EKG 19/9/1974. / EKG 13/4/1972. / EKG 6/9/1973. / EKG 10/8/1978

51. EKG 25/8/1883. / EKG 26/9/1985. / EKG 22/2/1991. / EKG 13/3/1991

52. EKG 21/3/1953. / EKG 24/6/1955. / EKG 28/10/1960. / EKG 2/3/1962. / EKG 22/2/1963. / EKG 22/6/1967. / EKG 12/10/1967

53. EKG 5/11/1970. / EKG 14/3/1974. / EKG 16/6/1982. / EKG 5/10/1973. / EKG 4/9/1969

54. EKG 28/7/1966. / EKG 11/11/1970. / EKG 4/12/1980. / EKG 12/9/1985

55. EKG 29/8/1958. / EKG 22/3/1963. / EKG 16/5/1963. / EKG 16/1/1964. / EKG 6/2/1964. / EKG 27/2/1964. / EKG 2/6/1966. / EKG 9/6/1966. / EKG 15/6/1967

56. EKG 18/3/1976. / EKG 2/10/1980. / EKG 16/9/1982. / EKG 15/7/1982. / EKG 22/7/1982. / EKG 19/1/1984. / EKG 19/7/1984. / EKG 19/3/1987. / EKG 15/12/1988. / EKG 12/5/1988. / Dairy Site, Mill Road-personal observation

57. EKG 30/9/1955. / EKG 19/12/1958. / EKG 23/2/1962. / EKG 14/3/1960

58. EKG 16/12/1960. / EKG 11/11/1965. / EKG 6/10/1960. / Information from Mrs Lewis. / EKG 8/1/1973. / EKG 29/12/1977. / EKG 19/1/1994. / EKG 24/10/1958. / Milton Regis Trail, The Sittingbourne Society, 1984

59. EKG 9/7/1954. / EKG 23/11/1951. / EKG 9/10/1953. / EKG 23/7/1954. / EKG 1/4/1955

60. EKG 5/12/1958. / EKG 29/4/1971. / EKG 20/1/1961. / EKG 1/5/1959. / EKG 30/5/1958. / EKG 1/9/1966

61. Information from Sittingbourne Police Station. / EKG 20/6/1963. / EKG 20/2/1964. / EKG 10/12/1981

62. EKG 27/9/1957. / EKG 4/11/1971

Chapter Seven: **RELIGION and EDUCATION**

1. Milton Legend - see file in Sittingbourne Library Local History section. / Details about the church, unless noted otherwise, come from the Church History.

2. Archaeologia Cantiana 1932 p. 101, p. 83. / EKG 9/4/1859

3. Details about the church, unless noted otherwise, come from the Church History. / Archaeologia Cantiana Wills: John Dylott, 1929; Thomas Garrard, 1930; John Kypping, 1930; Thomas Mayhew, 1930; William Springett, 1931; Richard Weyman, 1931; Thomas Thomas, 1931; William Cayme, 1929. / EKG 30/11/1962.

4. EKG 6/10/1923. / EKG 24/2/1883

5. EKG 8/10/1860. / Other details, unless noted otherwise, come from the Church History. / EKG. 14/10/1865. / EKG 6/10/1866. / EKG 20/5/1871

6. EKG 17/12/1873. / EKG 23/8/1879. / EKG 12/11/1898. / EKG 27/9/1902

7. EKG 23/7/1872. / EKG 17/10/1925. / EKG 10/4/1926

8. EKG 16/4/1859. / EKG 18/4/1863. / EKG 19/9/1863. / EKG 19/9/1863

9. EKG 30/4/1898. / EKG 23/3/1901. / EKG 25/1/1902. / EKG 12/9/1925

10. Milton Holy Trinity Parish History. / Other information, unless noted otherwise, from the history of the Roman Catholic Church.

11. EKG 5/11/1892. / EKG 27/7/1893

12. EKG 29/6/1901. / EKG 30/8/1902. / EKG 12/11/1910. / EKG 8/6/1929. / EKG 28/5/1932. / EKG 29/4/1933. / EKG 27/8/1938

13. EKG 2/2/1907. / EKG 21/3/1863. / EKG 3/10/1863. / EKG 4/9/1875. / EKG 27/5/1899. / EKG 25/3/1852. / EKG 22/8/1903

14. EKG 21/1/1859. / EKG 22/3/1879. / EKG 29/10/1887. / EKG 29/10/1889. / EKG 14/2/1920

15. EKG 10/6/1871. / EKG 23/6/1883

16. EKG 28/3/1860. / EKG 18/8/1863. / EKG 23/8/1863. / EKG 26/5/1877. / EKG 1/12/1877. / EKG 28/2/1885

17. EKG 19/11/1898. / EKG 12/5/1961. / EKG 12/10/1951

18. History of Paradise Chapel (Sittingbourne Library) p. 3/5, 32-37. / EKG 14/4/1860. / EKG 18/2/1860. / EKG 4/4/1863. / History of Paradise Chapel. 74, 27. / EKG 27/2/1975. / EKG 2/9/1992

19. EKG 21/3/1863. / EKG 31/8/1878. / EKG 3/12/1892. / The Latimer Chapel was later used as the Working Men's Club. / EKG 16/10/1920. / EKG 24/12/1928. / EKG 19/1/1929

20. EKG 28/4/1866. / EKG 11/8/1866. / EKG 4/5/1867

21. EKG 5/2/1881. / EKG 8/3/1884. / EKG 4/9/1886. / EKG 5/4/1890. / EKG 16/1/1897. / EKG 23/3/1901

22. EKG 13/2/1909. / Local knowledge

23. EKG 7/6/1884. / EKG 2/8/1884. / EKG 23/8/1884. / EKG 28/2/1914. / 1920s Directory

24. EKG 31/5/1984. / Information courtesy of L Ingham. / EKG 31/5/1984. / EKG 6/6/1857. / EKG 5/6/1858. / EKG 27/11/1858. / EKG 1/1/1880. / EKG 5/3/1887. / EKG 22/6/1895

25. EKG 13/2/1897. / EKG 30/6/1928. / EKG 17/8/1929. / EKG 19/11/1970

26. EKG 25/11/1899. / Local Directory

27. EKG 25/6/1821. / EKG 18/1/1957. / EKG 8/7/1933. / EKG 18/4/1974

28. EKG 29/7/1955

29. EKG 30/7/1859. / EKG 5/9/1857. / EKG 14/8/1858. / EKG 28/5/1859

30. Cirlis, S.J. History of the Education of Great Britain, 7th Edition, University Tutorial Press, 1968, p. 276. / EKG 29/10/1870

31. EKG 31/5/1873. / EKG 10/1/1874. / EKG 4/5/1872. / EKG 8/3/1873. / EKG 12/7/1873. / EKG 3/6/1871. / EKG 6/10/1875. / EKG 12/4/1879

32. EKG 1/12/1877. / EKG 2/2/1877

33. EKG 4/1/1879. / EKG 18/8/1894. / EKG 3/8/1889. / EKG 15/9/1894. / EKG 4/7/1896. / EKG 2/5/1896

34. EKG 1/9/1894. / EKG 30/1/1897. / EKG 30/1/1897. / EKG 30/10/1897. / EKG 30/4/1898. / EKG 2/6/1900

35. The Log Book of St Michael's - see the file in Sittingbourne Library (Local History section) and the Log Book of Holy Trinity (CKS, Maidstone, QES 338.)   St Michael's - 2, 12, 14, 23/10/1863. Holy Trinity - 11-15 May 1873, 15/8/1873

36. Ibid. Holy Trinity - 23/10/1863, 14/5/1873, 23/6/1873, 18/8/1873, 23/6/1873, 28/5/1905

37. Ibid. Holy Trinity May 1903. St Michael's 2nd, 20th & 30th October 1863

38. Ibid. St Michael's 7, 14, 21/10/1863

39. EKG 9/9/1893. / EKG 6/1/1894. / EKG 19/11/1898. / EKG 19/11/1898

40. Borden School History (in Sittingbourne Library Local History file) used for this section unless noted otherwise. / EKG 7/5/1892

41. EKG 5/9/1857. / EKG 26/5/1866. / EKG 2/10/1869. / See also St Michael's School Log. op cit. / EKG 8/8/1885. / EKG 15/10/1892. / EKG 18/5/1895. / EKG 8/6/1895. / EKG 21/9/1895. / EKG 23/5/1896. / EKG 3/1/1896. / EKG 15/10/1898. / EKG 19/8/1899

42. EKG 18/7/1903. / EKG 18/7/1903. / EKG 21/11/1903

43. Highsted and Borden School Histories in Sittingbourne Library Local History file.

44. EKG 29/4/1905. / EKG 2/2/1907. / EKG 2/7/1909. / EKG 29/7/1955. / EKG 6/3/1920

45. EKG 2/2/1921. / EKG 8/9/1965. / EKG 28/8/1978

46. EKG 15/10/1904. EKG 16/8/1919. / Highsted School History op cit. / EKG 10/9/1938

47. EKG 10/1/1958. / EKG 11/9/1969. / EKG 23/2/1946. / EKG 3/5/1957. / EKG 30/8/1984

48. EKG 11/9/1969. / EKG 8/6/1978. / EKG 1/4/1992

49. EKG 19/7/1947. / EKG 12/9/1952. / EKG 28/9/1956. / EKG 1/6/1962. / EKG 14/1/1965. / EKG 28/8/1969. / EKG 21/5/1970. / EKG 19/6/1975. / EKG 4/6/1981

50. EKG 1/3/1973. / EKG 13/6/1985. / Information about St Michael's from CKS Maidstone. / EKG 12/5/1993

51. EKG 18/8/1993

Chapter Eight: **LOCAL POLITICS, SPORT and SOCIAL LIFE**

1. EKG 11/4/1868. / EKG 18/4/1868. / EKG 2/5/1868. / EKG 9/5/1868. / EKG 9/7/1881. / EKG 15/11/1884. / Trevelyan, G.M., A Shortened History of England, 1970, Penguin, Harmondsworth. / EKG 13/6/1885 (First meeting Liberal League 20/2/1869)

2. EKG 3/4/1869. / EKG 2/8/1879. / EKG 15/11/1879. / EKG 22/1/1881. / EKG 12/11/1881. / EKG 24/2/1883 (First reported match 26/3/1881). / EKG 14/1/1982 (formed 1882). / EKG 23/1/1886. / EKG 9/10/1886. / EKG 17/9/1887

3. EKG 27/6/1857. / EKG 4/7/1857. / EKG 15/7/1939. / EKG 7/4/1860. / EKG

4/5/1861. / EKG 20/6/1863. / EKG 19/4/1879. / EKG 5/5/1883. / EKG 6/7/1889. / EKG 2/3/1889

4. Information from Milton Regis Bowling Club 1540-1990, compiled by Don Kent, p.20. / EKG 25/9/1875. / EKG 10/9/1887. / EKG 21/5/1879. / EKG 21/12/1867. / EKG 4/1/1862. / EKG 19/4/1879. / EKG 25/6/1881 (Sittingbourne Cycling Club dissolved 1885). / EKG 4/9/1886. / EKG 1/1/1881. / EKG 12/7/1884. / EKG 5/4/1876

5. EKG 9/5/1857. / EKG 22/8/1857. / EKG 12/12/1857. / EKG 19/2/1859. / EKG 26/2/1869. / EKG 20/4/1861. / EKG 28/2/1863. / EKG 28/3/1863. / EKG 11/4/1863. / EKG 27/1/1866. / EKG 27/6/1863

6. EKG 16/11/1872. / EKG 12/7/1873. / EKG 25/9/1875. / EKG 21/10/1876. / EKG 17/2/1877. / EKG 19/1/1878. / EKG 3/2/1877. / EKG 10/11/1877. / EKG 19/1/1878. / EKG 8/2/1879. / EKG 14/2/1880. / EKG 8/1/1881. / EKG 23/7/1881. / EKG 26/2/1887. / EKG 6/12/1884. / EKG 24/1/1885. / EKG 21/2/1885

7. EKG 22/8/1857. / EKG 11/7/1857. / EKG 30/10/1858. / EKG 10/12/1859. / EKG 16/6/1860. / EKG 30/8/1862. / EKG 25/3/1882. / EKG 28/4/1883. / EKG 12/1/1861. / EKG 17/8/1861. / EKG 23/8/1873. / EKG 13/2/1886. / EKG 9/3/1889. / EKG 16/11/1889

8. EKG 21/9/1869. / EKG 2/10/1869. / EKG 21/9/1878. / EKG 20/9/1879. / EKG 24/3/1883. / EKG 30/6/1888. / EKG 30/6/1888. / EKG 29/6/1889

9. EKG 12/6/1858. / EKG 24/2/1872 (First society to refer directly to having women members). / EKG 17/4/1886. / EKG 8/12/1860. / EKG 16/12/1882. / EKG 13/5/1882. / EKG 21/12/1861. / EKG 18/12/1875. / EKG 25/12/1880. / EKG 4/4/1885. / EKG 7/11/1868. / EKG 7/3/1885. / EKG 2/12/1871. / EKG 26/3/1887. / EKG 30/5/1874. / EKG 21/1/1888. / EKG 9/1/1886

10. EKG 17/2/1872

11. EKG 10/2/1894. / EKG 27/1/1906. / EKG 7/9/1907. / EKG 29/1/1910. / EKG 26/2/1910

12. Sittingbourne Wednesday Club were playing games in 1896. EKG 22/8/1896. / EKG 20/5/1899. / EKG 14/1/1982. / EKG 31/10/1908. / EKG 14/11/1908. / EKG 14/5/1910. / EKG 4/1/1905. / EKG 2/1/1909

13. EKG 3/7/1909. / EKG 16/4/1892. / EKG 21/11/1908

14. EKG 18/8/1894. / EKG 26/1/1895. / EKG 11/5/1895. / EKG 4/1/1905. / EKG 1/8/1896. / EKG 15/8/1896. / EKG 12/9/1896. / EKG 28/8/1897. / EKG

21/11/1896. / EKG 2/1/1897. / EKG 14/9/1901. / EKG 31/5/1902. / EKG 26/8/1905. / EKG 12/2/1910. / EKG 5/11/1910

15. EKG 22/9/1983. / EKG 2/6/1900. / EKG 8/5/1909. / EKG 25/8/1906

16. EKG 12/9/1896. / EKG 5/6/1909. / EKG 28/3/1903. / EKG 29/4/1905. / EKG 17/6/1905. / EKG 16/6/1905. / EKG 11/8/1906

17. EKG 24/3/1894. / EKG 13/8/1898. / EKG 8/10/1898

18. EKG 2/8/1890. / EKG 22/5/1909. / EKG 14/5/1910. / EKG 28/5/1892. / In 1898 50 years of Forestry in Milton was celebrated. / EKG 24/9/1898. / EKG 16/6/1894. / EKG 5/1/1895. / EKG 30/3/1895. / EKG 28/8/1897. / EKG 25/10/1913

19. EKG 25/10/1890. / EKG 9/7/1892. / EKG 9/11/1895. / EKG 13/2/1897. / EKG 13/4/1901. / EKG 5/11/1898. / EKG 28/1/1905. / EKG 26/10/1907. / EKG 29/10/1910. / EKG 20/1/1900. / EKG 20/10/1900. / EKG 1/11/1890. / EKG 25/9/1897. / EKG 11/2/1898. / EKG 1/2/1902. / EKG 25/3/1905. / EKG 15/4/1905. / EKG 20/3/1909. / EKG 10/9/1910

20. EKG 13/2/1904. / EKG 6/5/1905. / EKG 24/11/1906. / EKG 2/4/1910. / EKG 9/7/1910. / EKG 30/7/1910. / EKG 24/2/1912. / EKG 4/10/1913. / EKG 24/1/1914

21. EKG 19/7/1919. / EKG 21/10/1922. / EKG 3/4/1920. / EKG 9/4/1921. / EKG 24/11/1923. / EKG 15/12/1923. / EKG 1/11/1924. / EKG 14/1/1928. / EKG 28/4/1934. / EKG 29/4/1939. / EKG 13/5/1939

22. EKG 12/4/1919. / EKG 9/8/1919. / EKG 14/1/1982. / 14/5/1927. / EKG 24/11/1928. / EKG 14/1/1982. / EKG 5/9/1931. / EKG 8/6/1935. / EKG 18/7/1937

23. EKG 5/1/1929. / EKG 7/1/1939

24. EKG 15/2/1919. / EKG 15/7/1939. / EKG 21/8/1929. / EKG 6/7/1929. / EKG 1/7/1939. / EKG 15/7/1939

25. EKG 17/5/1919. / EKG 29/10/1921. / EKG 4/2/1922. / EKG 6/5/1939. / EKG 20/3/1926. / EKG 24/11/1928. / EKG 6/6/1931. / EKG 3/10/1931. / EKG 28/5/1938. / EKG 5/1/1929. / EKG 22/9/1938. / EKG 29/4/1922. / EKG 26/8/1922. / EKG 3/2/1934. / EKG 4/1/1936. / EKG 1/7/1939. / EKG 5/1/1929

26. EKG 30/8/1930. / EKG 5/1/1929. / EKG 10/11/1934. / EKG 22/9/1983. / EKG 4/4/1931. / EKG 7/12/1935. / EKG 9/10/1937

27. EKG 23/1/1926. / EKG 3/2/1934. / EKG 7/1/1939

28. EKG 17/4/1920. / EKG 24/4/1920. / EKG 17/4/1920. / EKG 8/10/1921. / EKG 2/2/1924

29. EKG 15/3/1919. / EKG 8/11/1919. / EKG 14/2/1920. / EKG 6/9/1919. / EKG 29/1/1921. / EKG 11/12/1921. / EKG 26/8/1922. / EKG 20/5/1922. / EKG 26/2/1938. / EKG 14/5/1938. / EKG 25/2/1939. / EKG 3/12/1932. / EKG 1/12/1923. / EKG 21/1/1939

30. EKG 31/5/1919. / EKG 5/4/1930. / EKG 28/4/1934. / EKG 30/3/1935 - the latter in the area where the Forum was built. / EKG 9/1/1937. / EKG 13/2/1937

31. EKG 28/7/1945. / EKG 20/2/1948. / EKG 31/8/1956. / EKG 26/1/1962. / EKG 25/5/1956

32. EKG 19/5/1966. / EKG 21/5/1987. / Swale had had a mayor since 1978, EKG 29/12/1977. / EKG 20/5/1971. / EKG 19/5/1988. / EKG 5/6/1970. / EKG 18/6/1987

33. EKG 11/6/1948. / EKG 2/1/1948. / EKG 17/2/1950. / EKG 3/3/1950. / EKG 14/1/1982. / EKG 14/1/1982

34. EKG 7/7/1961. / EKG 7/11/1963. / EKG 13/5/1965. / EKG 23/12/1965. / EKG 14/1/1982. / EKG 6/1/1966

35. EKG 9/11/1966. / EKG 15/5/1969. / EKG 14/1/1982. / EKG 31/5/1979. / EKG 13/8/1981

36. EKG 14/1/1982. / EKG 22/8/1985. / EKG 15/6/1989. / EKG 15/3/1990. / EKG 22/8/1985 / EKG 31/7/1996

37. EKG 1/7/1949. / EKG 2/1/1969. / EKG 4/1/1979

38. EKG 11/1/1979. / EKG 5/7/1979. / EKG 15/5/1969. / EKG 5/7/1979. / EKG 3/7/1969. / EKG 4/1/1979. / EKG 2/1/1959. / EKG 4/1/1979

39. EKG 31/5/1947. / EKG 7/2/1958. / EKG 20/2/1959. / EKG 29/9/1966. / EKG 29/3/1972. / EKG 22/5/1978. / EKG 28/1/1982. / EKG 31/8/1978. / EKG 11/2/1982. / EKG 17/11/1983. / EKG 23/11/1989

40. EKG 2/8/1979. / EKG 22/9/1983. / Club History - Sittingbourne Library. / EKG 19/8/1949. / EKG 20/4/1978. / EKG 21/11/1974. / EKG 11/2/1982. / EKG 25/8/1983. / EKG 26/3/1986. / EKG 1/9/1993

41. List of Clubs and Societies - Sittingbourne Library.

42. EKG 6/10/1945. / EKG 27/7/1951

43. EKG 10/5/1957. / EKG 30/4/1948. / EKG 20/9/1965. / EKG 20/6/1968. / List of Clubs & Societies. / EKG 1/2/1952. / EKG 9/11/1989

44. EKG 21/10/1965. / EKG 13/10/1983. / EKG 20/3/1959. / EKG 2/10/1969. / List of Clubs and Societies. / EKG 10/8/1966. / EKG 29/10/1981

45. List of Clubs and Societies. / EKG 20/4/1994

46. EKG 14/7/1945. / EKG 7/1/1949. / Personal memories

47. EKG 21/7/1966. / EKG 20/10/1966. / EKG 2/11/1966. / EKG 2/11/1966. / EKG 15/7/1971. / EKG 6/4/1972. / EKG 2/11/1972. / EKG 16/5/1974

48. EKG 17/4/1975. / EKG 19/6/1975. / EKG 17/1/1976. / EKG 18/3/1976. / EKG 5/4/1979. / EKG 14/2/1980. / EKG 24/4/1980. / EKG 24/4/1980. / EKG 3/7/1980. / EKG 26/2/1981. / EKG 24/9/1981. / EKG 8/10/1981. / EKG 27/5/1982. / EKG9/2/1984. / EKG 2/8/1984. / EKG 18/7/1985. / EKG 9/1/1986

49. EKG 8/1/1992. / EKG 6/10/1993. / EKG 28/10/1993. / EKG 21/4/1993

Chapter Nine: **THE TOWN AT WAR**

First World War

1. EKG 25/7/1914. / EKG 8/8/1914

2. EKG 8/8/1914. / EKG 15/8/1914

3. EKG 29/7/1916. / EKG 15/8/1914

4. EKG 8/8/1914. / EKG 22/8/1914. / EKG 22/8/1914

5. Courtesy of L Ingham & Miss D Harris

6. EKG 22/8/1914. / EKG 22/8/1914

7. EKG 22/8/1914. / EKG 29/8/1914. / EKG 5/9/1914

8. EKG 5/9/1914. / EKG 12/9/1914

9. EKG 12/9/1914. / EKG 26/9/1914. / EKG 3/10/1914

10. EKG 26/9/1914. / EKG 3/10/1914. / EKG 17/10/1914. / EKG 10/10/1914

11. EKG 17/10/1914. / EKG 24/10/1914. / EKG 31/10/1914

12. EKG 31/10/1914. / EKG 7/11/1914

13. EKG 5, 12, 19, 26 /12/1914

14. EKG 2/1/1915. / EKG 9/1/1915. / EKG 16/1/1915

15. EKG 9/1/1915. / EKG 23/1/1915

16. EKG 6/2/1915. / EKG 27/2/1915. / EKG 6/3/1915. / EKG 20/3/1915

17. EKG 10/4/1915. / Courtesy of L Ingham

18. EKG 17/4/1915

19. EKG 29/5/1915

20. EKG 23/11/1918. / EKG 12/6/1915. / Courtesy of L Ingham. / Holy Trinity Log Book 9/6/15 & 11/6/15. / Postcard

21. EKG 8/5/1915. / EKG 12/6/1915. / EKG 22/5/1915

22. EKG 28/8/1915. / EKG 21/8/1915. / EKG 19/6/1915. / EKG 17/7/1915. / EKG 25/9/1915

23. EKG 31/7/1915. / EKG 19/6/1915. / EKG 26/6/1915. / EKG 2/10/1915

24. EKG 4/9/1915. / EKG 18/9/1915. / EKG 7/8/1915. / EKG 13/11/1915. / EKG 4/12/1915. / Courtesy of L Ingham. / EKG 27/11/1915

25. EKG 8/1/1916. / EKG 22/1/1916

26. EKG 12/2/1916. / EKG 26/2/1916.

27. EKG 11/3/1916. / EKG 18/3/1916. / EKG 1/4/1916

28. EKG 29/1/1916. / EKG 1/4/1916. / EKG 15/4/1916. / EKG 17/6/1916. / EKG 19/8/1916

29. EKG 22/4/1916. / EKG 15/4/1916. / EKG 20/5/1916. / EKG 6/5/1916

30. EKG 6/5/1916. / EKG 6/5/1916. / EKG 20/5/1916. / EKG 3/6/1916. / EKG 10/6/1916

31. EKG 26/4/1916. / EKG 5/8/1916

32. EKG 26/8/1916. / EKG 9/9/1916. / EKG 30/9/1916. / EKG 28/10/1916

33. EKG 18/11/1916. / EKG 16/12/1916

34. EKG 24/3/1917. / EKG 5/5/1917. / EKG 12/5/1917. / EKG 16/6/1917

35. EKG 18/8/1917. / EKG 6/10/1917. / EKG 25/8/1917. / EKG 24/11/1917. / EKG 31/3/1917

36. EKG 12/5/1917. / EKG 31/3/1917. / EKG 17/11/1917. / EKG 9/2/1918

37. EKG 26/5/1917. / EKG 20/10/1917. / EKG 21/7/1917

38. EKG 2/6/1917. / EKG 16/6/1917. / EKG 27/10/1917. / EKG 8/9/1917

39. EKG 17/2/1917. / EKG 21/4/1917. / EKG 2/6/1917. / EKG 11/8/1917. / EKG 7/7/1917. / EKG 10/11/1917. / EKG 22/12/1917

40. EKG 5/1/1918. / EKG 2/2/1918. / EKG 9/2/1918. / EKG 23/2/1918. / EKG 14/9/1918. / EKG 7/9/1918

41. EKG 5/1/1918. / EKG 23/2/1918. / EKG 20/7/1918. / EKG 10/8/1918. / EKG 9/3/1918

42. EKG 12/1/1918. / EKG 23/3/1918. / EKG 17/8/1918. / EKG 5/10/1918. / EKG 16/11/1918

43. EKG 2/11/1918. / EKG 9/11/1918. / EKG 16/11/1918

44. EKG 4/1/1919. / EKG 1/3/1919. / EKG 24/5/1919. / EKG 8/2/1919. / EKG 24/2/1919. / EKG 8/3/1919. / EKG 19/4/1919. / EKG 10/4/1920

Second World War

45. EKG 7/5/1938. / EKG 30/4/1938. / EKG 4/6/1938. / EKG 1/10/1938. / EKG 24/9/1938. / EKG 8/10/1938

46. EKG 14/1/1939. / EKG 21/1/1939. / EKG 4/2/1939. / EKG 25/2/1939. / EKG 26/4/1919. / EKG 25/3/1939

47. EKG 8/4/1939. / EKG 3/6/1939. / EKG 10/6/1939. / EKG 1/7/1939

48. EKG 8/7/1939. / EKG 29/7/1939. / EKG 15/7/1939. / EKG 2/9/1939

49. EKG 9/9/1939. / EKG 16/9/1939. / EKG 23/9/1939

50. CKS: QES 338/8/3. / EKG 21/10/1939. / EKG 9/12/1939

51. EKG 11/10/1941. / EKG 25/11/1939

52. EKG 6/1/1940. / EKG 9/3/1940. / EKG 24/2/1940. / Courtesy of J Walker. / EKG 16/3/1940.

53. EKG 16/3/1940. / EKG 6/4/1940. / EKG 13/4/1940. / EKG 23/3/1940. / EKG 20/4/1940

54. EKG 8/4/1940. / EKG 20/6/1942. / EKG 22/6/1940. / EKG 8/6/1940. / Some children of paper mill families went to Canada in 1941, EKG 28/12/1941

55. EKG 29/6/1940. / EKG 27/7/1940. / EKG 6/7/1940. / EKG 3/8/1940. / EKG 24/8/1940

56. EKG 11/10/1941

57. EKG 31/8/1940. / EKG 14/9/1940. / EKG 21/9/1940

58. High's funeral records

59. EKG 21/9/1940

60. Courtesy of Mr Bedelle. / EKG 5/10/1940

61. EKG 12,19/10/1940. / High's Records. / Peter Payne EKG 24/5/1995. / EKG 9/11/1940

62. EKG 14/12/1940. / Courtesy of Mrs Dolding. / Courtesy of L Ingham

63. EKG 8/2/1941

64. EKG 1/3/1941. / EKG 15/3/1941

65. EKG 19/4/1941. / Courtesy of B Spice. / Courtesy of L Ingham

66. Mrs Phipps EKG 24/5/1995. / EKG 29/3/1941. / EKG 25/10/1941

67. EKG 16/8/1941. / EKG 12/4/1941. / EKG 21/6/1941. / Courtesy of L Ingham. / Courtesy of B Spice.

68. EKG 20/9/1941. / EKG 27/9/1941. / EKG 4/10/1941. / EKG 5/7/1941. / EKG 23/8/1941. / EKG 12/7/1941. / EKG 6/9/1941. / EKG 15/11/1941. / EKG 29/11/1941. / EKG 6/12/1941

69. EKG 7/2/1942. / EKG 31/1/1942. / EKG 7/3/1942. / EKG 14/3/1942

70. EKG 7/2/1942. / EKG 14/2/1942. / EKG 10/1/1942. / Courtesy of L Ingham. / EKG 28/2/1942. / EKG 9/5/1942. / EKG 25/7/1942

71. EKG 30/5/1942. / EKG 9/5/1942. / EKG 20/6/1942. / EKG 6/6/1942

72. EKG 6/6/1942. / EKG 8/8/1942. / EKG 22/8/1942. / EKG 19/12/1942

73. EKG 28/3/1942. / EKG 8/3/1942. / EKG 14/11/1942

74. EKG 25/7/1942. / EKG 29/8/1942

75. EKG 13/2/1943. / EKG 6/2/1943. / EKG 30/1/1943. / EKG 24/4/1943

76. EKG 8/5/1943. / EKG 29/5/1943. / EKG 3/7/1943. / EKG 4/9/1943. / EKG 7/8/1943

77. EKG 7/8/1943. / EKG 9/10/1943. / EKG 30/10/1943. / EKG 4/12/1943. / EKG 18/12/1943

78. Courtesy of L Ingham. / EKG 5/2/1944

79. Courtesy of L Ingham. / EKG 5/2/1944. / EKG 26/2/1944

80. EKG 5/2/1944

81. EKG 12/2/1944. / EKG 11/3/1944. / EKG 4/3/1944. / EKG 19/2/1944

82. Mr Horton from Buzz Bomb Diary by David Collyer in EKG 17/8/1994

83. EKG 26/8/1944. / EKG 2/9/1944. / EKG 23/9/1944

84. EKG 24/2/1945. / EKG 17/3/1945. / EKG 21/4/1945. / EKG 28/4/1945. / EKG 5/5/1945. / EKG 12/5/1945. / EKG 19/5/1945

85. EKG 2/6/1945

Chapter Ten: **THE CHANGING FACE OF SITTINGBOURNE HIGH STREET AND LOCAL PEOPLE**

Sittingbourne High Street

1. EKG 10/2/1877

2. Architectural information from Sittingbourne Town Trail, Tony Buckingham, Published by the Sittingbourne Society. 1990.

3. Courtesy of Mr Sillars. / EKG 24/6/1871

4. See the Sittingbourne Town Trail / EKG 22/8/1936. / EKG 22/6/1950. / EKG 23/4/1954. / EKG 23/5/1963. / EKG 7/6/1973. / EKG 7/8/1980

5. Sources used for all of this section on the location of High Street businesses unless stated otherwise come from: 1861 Census, 1895 Kelly's Directory, 1926 Sittingbourne Directory, 1965 Sittingbourne Directory, 1990s Goad Plan, all at Local Studies section of Sittingbourne Library. / EKG 21/9/1940. / EKG 12/9/1963 & personal memory

6. Sittingbourne Trail. / 90 Years at 93, Michael Peters. / Courtesy of L Ingham

7. Sittingbourne Trail. / EKG 19/10/1989. / Personal Memory.

8. EKG 3/10/1974. / EKG 12/5/1966

9. EKG 2/4/1954. / Sittingbourne Trail. / EKG 16/3/1972

10. EKG 8/5/1937 / Information on Sittingbourne bank note courtesy of P Litchfield.

11. Courtesy of L Ingham

12. Courtesy of L Ingham

13. EKG 20/1/1900. / Courtesy of L Ingham

14. EKG 9/8/1973. / Courtesy of L Ingham

15. EKG 4/5/1962. / EKG 23/11/62. / EKG 17/10/63. / EKG 24/10/1968. / EKG 5/10/1978

16. Personal memory

17. 90 Years at 93, Michael Peters.

18. EKG 27/1/1934

19. EKG 9/12/1911

20. EKG 12/7/1941

21. EKG 17/12/1927

22. EKG 8/8/1885

23. EKG 10/5/1913

24. EKG 25/8/1923

25. EKG 21/5/1938. / EKG 20/10/1991

26. EKG 22/2/1919. / EKG 9/6/1923. / EKG 29/2/1936. / EKG 15/6/1941. / EKG 20/6/1942. / EKG 16/6/1961. / EKG 12/12/1985. / EKG 1/6/1994

27. EKG 6/9/1924
28. EKG 3/2/1923

29. EKG 15/6/1989

30. EKG 10/11/1950

31. EKG 20/2/1975   .

32. EKG 28/2/1942

33. EKG 12/4/1890

34. EKG 28/5/1927

35. EKG 13/9/1930

36. EKG 23/1/1926

37. History of Bennett Opie Ltd 1880-1955, pp 16/17, Sittingbourne Library.

38. EKG 22/4/1905

39. Courtesy of Michael Peters. / EKG 6/2/1943

40. EKG 7/5/1881

41. EKG 14/1/1882

42. EKG 9/6/1964.

43. EKG 3/8/1940

44. EKG 11/3/1871. / 1871, 1881 & 1891 Censuses

45. 1871, 1881 & 1891 Censuses

46. Courtesy of L Ingham. / 1891 Census. / Sittingbourne Directories: 1908/9, 1926, 1965/6

47. Information from Holy Trinity Parish Records courtesy of J Kemsley. / Family details courtesy of L Ingham

48. EKG 7/3/1968. / Courtesy of L Ingham

49. Courtesy of L Ingham

ACKNOWLEDGEMENTS

My greatest thanks are to my mother, Lilian Ingham. If it had not been for her help during the research for my PhD Thesis this book would never have been written. I am also indebted to her and others who have shared with me their memories of the town and those who have loaned me photographs.

I would also like to thank the following: Alison Long for helping to proof read the book; all of those who have given me their support, especially Christine Rayner, editor of EKG, Michael Peters, Peter Morgan and Jon Hawke; the staff of Sittingbourne Reference Library, in particular Carole, Sue and Margaret for their help during the years of research; and Allison Wainman for her invaluable help through the publishing process.

Finally, this book is dedicated with love, to my mother, who has been involved in so much of the history recorded in it, to my grandchildren who will with their lives help to shape the history of the future and to all those for whom the present is enriched by knowledge of the past.